D1216148

# elevate science

**SAVVAS**
LEARNING COMPANY

# You are an author!

This is your book to keep. Write and draw in it! Record your data and discoveries in it! You are an author of this book!

Print your name, school, town, and state below.

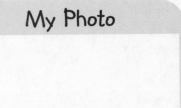
My Photo

**Name**

**School**

**Town, State**

Copyright © 2019 by Savvas Learning Company LLC. All Rights Reserved. Printed in the United States of America.

This publication is protected by copyright, and permission should be obtained from the publisher prior to any prohibited reproduction, storage in a retrieval system, or transmission in any form or by any means, electronic, mechanical, photocopying, recording, or otherwise. For information regarding permissions, request forms, and the appropriate contacts within the Savvas Learning Company Rights Management group, please send your query to the address below.

Savvas Learning Company LLC, 15 East Midland Avenue, Paramus, NJ 07652

Cover: The cover photo shows a high-speed train. FCVR: Scanrail/iStock/Getty Images; BCVR: Marinello/DigitalVision Vectors/Getty Images.

Attributions of third party content appear on pages EM35–EM37, which constitute an extension of this copyright page.

Next Generation Science Standards is a registered trademark of WestEd. Neither WestEd nor the lead states and partners that developed the Next Generation Science Standards were involved in the production of this product, and do not endorse it. NGSS Lead States. 2013. Next Generation Science Standards: For States, By States. Washington, DC: The National Academies Press.

**Savvas™** and **Savvas Learning Company®** are the exclusive trademarks of Savvas Learning Company LLC in the U.S. and other countries.

**Savvas Learning Company** publishes through its famous imprints **Prentice Hall®** and **Scott Foresman®** which are exclusive registered trademarks owned by Savvas Learning Company LLC in the U.S. and/or other countries.

**Savvas Realize™** is the exclusive trademark of Savvas Learning Company LLC in the U.S. and/or other countries.

littleBits, littleBits logo and Bits are trademarks of littleBits Electronics, Inc. All rights reserved.

Unless otherwise indicated herein, any third party trademarks that may appear in this work are the property of their respective owners, and any references to third party trademarks, logos, or other trade dress are for demonstrative or descriptive purposes only. Such references are not intended to imply any sponsorship, endorsement, authorization, or promotion of Savvas Learning Company products by the owners of such marks, or any relationship between the owner and Savvas Learning Company LLC or its authors, licensees, or distributors.

ISBN-13:    978-0-328-94876-5
ISBN-10:    0-328-94876-4
11   21

# Program Authors

**ZIPPORAH MILLER, EdD**
*Coordinator for K-12 Science Programs, Anne Arundel County Public Schools*
Zipporah Miller currently serves as the Senior Manager for Organizational Learning with the Anne Arundel County Public School System. Prior to that she served as the K-12 Coordinator for science in Anne Arundel County. She conducts national training to science stakeholders on the Next Generation Science Standards. Dr. Miller also served as the Associate Executive Director for Professional Development Programs and conferences at the National Science Teachers Association (NSTA) and served as a reviewer during the development of Next Generation Science Standards. Dr. Miller holds a doctoral degree from University of Maryland College Park, a master's degree in school administration and supervision from Bowie State University, and a bachelor's degree from Chadron State College.

**MICHAEL J. PADILLA, PhD**
*Professor Emeritus, Eugene P. Moore School of Education, Clemson University, Clemson, South Carolina*
Michael J. Padilla taught science in middle and secondary schools, has more than 30 years of experience educating middle grades science teachers, and served as one of the writers of the 1996 U.S. National Science Education Standards. In recent years Mike has focused on teaching science to English Language Learners. His extensive leadership experience, serving as Principal Investigator on numerous National Science Foundation and U.S. Department of Education grants, resulted in more than $35 million in funding to improve science education. He served as president of the National Science Teachers Association, the world's largest science teaching organization, in 2005–2006.

**MICHAEL E. WYSESSION, PhD**
*Professor of Earth and Planetary Sciences, Washington University, St. Louis, Missouri*
An author on more than 100 science and science education publications, Dr. Wysession was awarded the prestigious National Science Foundation Presidential Faculty Fellowship and Packard Foundation Fellowship for his research in geophysics, primarily focused on using seismic tomography to determine the forces driving plate tectonics. Dr. Wysession is also a leader in geoscience literacy and education, including being chair of the *Earth Science Literacy Principles*, author of several popular geology *Great Courses* video lecture series, and a lead writer of the *Next Generation Science Standards\**.

---

\*Next Generation Science Standards is a registered trademark of WestEd. Neither WestEd nor the lead states and partners that developed the Next Generation Science Standards were involved in the production of this product, and do not endorse it. NGSS Lead States. 2013. Next Generation Science Standards: For States, By States. Washington, DC: The National Academies Press.

## Program Consultants

### Carol Baker
**Science Curriculum**

Dr. Carol K. Baker is superintendent for Lyons Elementary K-8 School District in Lyons, Illinois. Prior to that, she was Director of Curriculum for Science and Music in Oak Lawn, Illinois. Before that she taught Physics and Earth Science for 18 years. In the recent past, Dr. Baker also wrote assessment questions for ACT (EXPLORE and PLAN), was elected president of the Illinois Science Teachers Association from 2011-2013 and served as a member of the Museum of Science and Industry advisory boards in Chicago. Dr. Baker received her BS in Physics and a science teaching certification. She is a writer of the Next Generation Science Standards. She completed her Master of Educational Administration (K-12) and earned her doctorate in Educational Leadership.

### Jim Cummins
**ELL**

Dr. Cummins's research focuses on literacy development in multilingual schools and the role technology plays in learning across the curriculum. *Elevate Science* incorporates research-based principles for integrating language with the teaching of academic content based on Dr. Cummins's work.

### Elfrieda Hiebert
**Literacy**

Dr. Hiebert is the President and CEO of TextProject, a nonprofit aimed at providing open-access resources for instruction of beginning and struggling readers, and a former primary school teacher. She is also a research associate at the University of California Santa Cruz. Her research addresses how fluency, vocabulary, and knowledge can be fostered through appropriate texts, and her contributions have been recognized through awards, such as the Oscar Causey Award for Outstanding Contributions to Reading Research (Literacy Research Association, 2015), Research to Practice Award (American Educational Research Association, 2013), William S. Gray Citation of Merit Award for Outstanding Contributions to Reading Research (International Reading Association, 2008).

## Content Reviewers

**Alex Blom, Ph.D.**
Associate Professor
Department Of Physical Sciences
Alverno College
Milwaukee, Wisconsin

**Joy Branlund, Ph.D.**
Department of Physical Science
Southwestern Illinois College
Granite City, Illinois

**Judy Calhoun**
Associate Professor
Physical Sciences
Alverno College
Milwaukee, Wisconsin

**Stefan Debbert**
Associate Professor of Chemistry
Lawrence University
Appleton, Wisconsin

**Diane Doser**
Professor
Department of Geological Sciences
University of Texas at El Paso
El Paso, Texas

**Rick Duhrkopf, Ph. D.**
Department of Biology
Baylor University
Waco, Texas

**Jennifer Liang**
University Of Minnesota Duluth
Duluth, Minnesota

**Heather Mernitz, Ph.D.**
Associate Professor of Physical Sciences
Alverno College
Milwaukee, Wisconsin

**Joseph McCullough, Ph.D.**
Cabrillo College
Aptos, California

**Katie M. Nemeth, Ph.D.**
Assistant Professor
College of Science and Engineering
University of Minnesota Duluth
Duluth, Minnesota

**Maik Pertermann**
Department of Geology
Western Wyoming Community College
Rock Springs, Wyoming

**Scott Rochette**
Department of the Earth Sciences
The College at Brockport
 State University of New York
Brockport, New York

**David Schuster**
Washington University in St Louis
St. Louis, Missouri

**Shannon Stevenson**
Department of Biology
University of Minnesota Duluth
Duluth, Minnesota

**Paul Stoddard, Ph.D.**
Department of Geology and
 Environmental Geosciences
Northern Illinois University
DeKalb, Illinois

**Nancy Taylor**
American Public University
Charles Town, West Virginia

## Safety Reviewers

**Douglas Mandt, M.S.**
Science Education Consultant
Edgewood, Washington

**Juliana Textley, Ph.D.**
Author, NSTA books on school
 science safety
Adjunct Professor
Lesley University
Cambridge, Massachusetts

## Teacher Reviewers

Jennifer Bennett, M.A.
Memorial Middle School
Tampa, Florida

Sonia Blackstone
Lake County Schools
Howey In the Hills, Florida

Teresa Bode
Roosevelt Elementary
Tampa, Florida

Tyler C. Britt, Ed.S.
Curriculum & Instructional
 Practice Coordinator
Raytown Quality Schools
Raytown, Missouri

A. Colleen Campos
Grandview High School
Aurora, Colorado

Ronald Davis
Riverview Elementary
Riverview, Florida

Coleen Doulk
Challenger School
Spring Hill, Florida

Mary D. Dube
Burnett Middle School
Seffner, Florida

Sandra Galpin
Adams Middle School
Tampa, Florida

Margaret Henry
Lebanon Junior High School
Lebanon, Ohio

Christina Hill
Beth Shields Middle School
Ruskin, Florida

Judy Johnis
Gorden Burnett Middle School
Seffner, Florida

Karen Y. Johnson
Beth Shields Middle School
Ruskin, Florida

Jane Kemp
Lockhart Elementary School
Tampa, Florida

Denise Kuhling
Adams Middle School
Tampa, Florida

Esther Leonard M.Ed. and L.M.T.
Gifted and Talented Implementation Specialist
San Antonio Independent School District
San Antonio, Texas

Kelly Maharaj
Science Department Chairperson
Challenger K8 School of Science and
 Mathematics
Elgin, Florida

Kevin J. Maser, Ed.D.
H. Frank Carey Jr/Sr High School
Franklin Square, New York

Angie L. Matamoros, Ph.D.
ALM Science Consultant
Weston, Florida

Corey Mayle
Brogden Middle School
Durham, North Carolina

Keith McCarthy
George Washington Middle School
Wayne, New Jersey

Yolanda O. Peña
John F. Kennedy Junior High School
West Valley City, Utah

Kathleen M. Poe
Jacksonville Beach Elementary School
Jacksonville Beach, Florida

Wendy Rauld
Monroe Middle School
Tampa, Florida

Bryna Selig
Gaithersburg Middle School
Gaithersburg, Maryland

Pat (Patricia) Shane, Ph.D.
STEM & ELA Education Consultant
Chapel Hill, North Carolina

Diana Shelton
Burnett Middle School
Seffner, Florida

Nakia Sturrup
Jennings Middle School
Seffner, Florida

Melissa Triebwasser
Walden Lake Elementary
Plant City, Florida

Michele Bubley Wiehagen
Science Coach
Miles Elementary School
Tampa, Florida

Pauline Wilcox
Instructional Science Coach
Fox Chapel Middle School
Spring Hill, Florida

# Energy and Motion

4-PS3-1, 4-PS3-2, 4-PS3-3

## Quest

In this Quest activity, you meet a vehicle safety engineer who presents you with a design challenge. You must design a safety feature for a new car.

Like a vehicle safety engineer, you complete activities and labs to gather information about how speed and energy are related to collisions and how energy changes and transfers during a collision. You use what you learn in the lessons to design a new safety feature for a car.

Find your Quest activities on pages 2–3, 13, 22–23, 32, 4–41, 42

Career Connection Vehicle Safety Engineer page 43

### The Essential Question

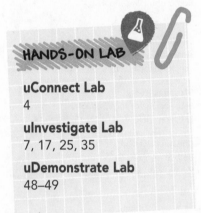

### HANDS-ON LAB

# Topic 2

# Human Uses of Energy

## *Quest*

In this Quest activity, you meet an electrical engineer who presents you with a design challenge. You must design a mechanical device that provides electric power.

Like a vehicle safety engineer, you complete activities to design and build your device. You will demonstrate how your device works and think about ways to improve it.

Find your Quest activities on pages 52–53, 63, 72–73, 91, 92

Career Connection Electrical Engineer page 93

- ▶ **VIDEO**
- 📖 **eTEXT**
- 👆 **INTERACTIVITY**
- 🧪 **VIRTUAL LAB**
- 🎮 **GAME**
- 📄 **DOCUMENT**
- ☑ **ASSESSMENT**

## The Essential Question

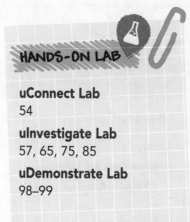

## HANDS-ON LAB

# Waves and Information

 **VIDEO**

 **eTEXT**

 **INTERACTIVITY**

 **VIRTUAL LAB**

 **GAME**

 **DOCUMENT**

 **ASSESSMENT**

## Quest

In this Quest activity, you meet an intelligence analyst who presents you with a communication code challenge. You must develop a code that spies can use.

Like an intelligence analyst, you complete activities and labs to design a code that secret agents can use to catch a jewel thief in a new movie. You use what you learn in the lessons to write a code that the actors can use in a dimly lit, noisy museum.

Find your Quest activities on pages 102–103, 113, 123, 132–133, 140, 142

Career Connection Intelligence Analyst page 143

**HANDS-ON LAB**

# Earth's Features

## Quest

In this Quest activity, you meet a geologist who shares a map. It provides clues to hidden treasures that are buried deep within three land areas. You need to identify clues that will help you find the treasures.

Like a geologist, you complete activities and labs to gather information about how landforms may change. You use what you learn in the lessons to search for the treasure and present your findings.

Find your Quest activities on pages 152–153, 163, 173, 182–183, 192, 194

Career Connection Geologist page 195

 VIDEO

 eTEXT

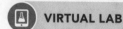 INTERACTIVITY

 VIRTUAL LAB

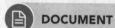 GAME

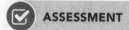 DOCUMENT

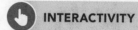 ASSESSMENT

## The Essential Question

## HANDS-ON LAB

# Topic 5

# Earth's Natural Hazards

## Quest

In this Quest activity, you meet a volcanologist who would like your help with advising a city about the impacts of natural hazards. You will find ways to reduce the impacts of a volcanic eruption.

Like a volcanologist, you complete activities and labs to learn about how volcanoes can affect the environment. You use what you learn in the lessons to write a letter to the city officials advising them of actions they can take.

Find your Quest activities on pages 204–205, 215, 224, 232–233, 234

Career Connection Volcanologist page 235

**VIDEO**

**eTEXT**

**INTERACTIVITY**

**VIRTUAL LAB**

**GAME**

**DOCUMENT**

**ASSESSMENT**

## HANDS-ON LAB

# The History of Planet Earth

VIDEO

eTEXT

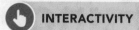
INTERACTIVITY

VIRTUAL LAB

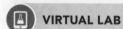
GAME

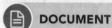
DOCUMENT

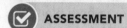
ASSESSMENT

## Quest

In this Quest activity, you meet a museum fact checker who presents you with a fossil challenge. You need to determine whether a newly found fossil matches an already identified animal fossil.

Like a museum fact checker, you complete activities and labs to study rock layers where both fossils were found. You use what you learn in the lesson to provide evidence for your decision about the fossils.

Find your Quest activities on pages 244–245, 254, 266–267, 268

Career Connection Museum Fact Checker page 269

## The Essential Question

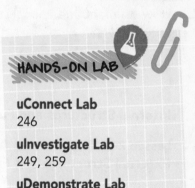

**HANDS-ON LAB**

# Topic 7

# Structures and Functions

## Quest

In this Quest activity, you meet a nature photographer who challenges you to solve a human problem. Like a nature photographer, you observe how plant and animal structures help them do different tasks. You use what you learn to choose a feature that could help solve a human problem.

Find your Quest activities on pages 278–279, 290–291, 299, 307, 314, 323, 326

Career Nature Photographer page 327

 VIDEO

 eTEXT

 INTERACTIVITY

 VIRTUAL LAB

 GAME

 DOCUMENT

ASSESSMENT

## The Essential Question

**HANDS-ON LAB**

# Topic 8

# Human Body Systems

## Quest

In this Quest activity, you meet a medical imaging technician who presents you with design challenge. You need to develop camera that can be used in a human body imaging procedure.

Like a medical imaging technician, you complete activities and labs to gather information about the human body. You use what you learn in the lessons to help develop an remote-controlled camera that can take pictures inside the body.

Find your Quest activities on pages 336–337, 347, 357, 364–365, 374, 376

Career Connection Medical Imaging Technician page 377

 **VIDEO**

 **eTEXT**

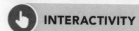 **INTERACTIVITY**

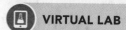 **VIRTUAL LAB**

 **GAME**

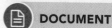 **DOCUMENT**

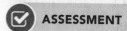 **ASSESSMENT**

## The Essential Question

## HANDS-ON LAB

# Elevate your thinking!

*Elevate Science* takes science to a whole new level and lets you take ownership of your learning. Explore science in the world around you. Investigate how things work. Think critically and solve problems! *Elevate Science* helps you think like a scientist, so you're ready for a world of discoveries.

## Explore Your World

Explore real-life scenarios with engaging Quests that dig into science topics around the world. You can:

- Solve real-world problems
- Apply skills and knowledge
- Communicate solutions

## Make Connections

*Elevate Science* connects science to other subjects and shows you how to better understand the world through:

- Mathematics
- Reading and Writing
- Literacy

**Quest Kickoff**

**STEM** Find the Right Mix— and Step on It!

*How can we mix ingredients to make a model stepping stone?*

Hi, I'm Alicia Gomez, a materials scientist! Suppose a school is setting up a prairie habitat. In this problem-based learning activity, you will build a model stepping stone so that students can observe the habitat without damaging the plants.

Like a materials scientist, you will evaluate your design and learn how different combinations of materials can make your design solution more useful. And you can decorate your model stepping stones, too!

Follow the path to learn how you will complete the Quest. The Quest activities in the lessons will help you complete the Quest! Check off your progress on the path when you com

**Visual Literacy Connection**

**What is the matter?**

All matter is made up of smaller particles. How can you observe the magnification of matter?

If you were to look at a solid object, such as cotton shirt closely, describe what you might observe with your unaided eye?

Sample answers: I might be able to see strands of threads.

Properties of Matter

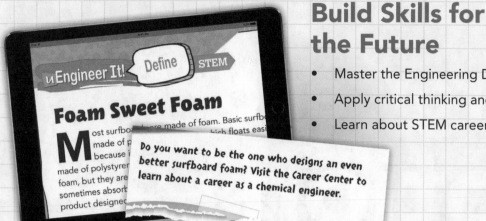

## Build Skills for the Future

- Master the Engineering Design Process
- Apply critical thinking and analytical skills
- Learn about STEM careers

## Focus on Reading Skills

*Elevate Science* creates ongoing reading connections to help you develop the reading skills you need to succeed. Features include:

- Leveled Readers
- Literacy Connection Features
- Reading Checks

**Literacy ▸ Toolbox**

**Use Evidence from Text**
Water is formed by the combination of atoms of two different elements— hydrogen and c... smallest particl... atom or a mole... you think so?

**READING CHECK Use Evidence from Text** Why do you think aerogels could be used to clean up oil spills in your community? Underline the important facts from the text that support your claim with evidence.

## Enter the Lab

Hands-on experiments and virtual labs help you test ideas and show what you know in performance-based assessments. Scaffolded labs include:

- STEM Labs
- Design Your Own
- Open-ended Labs

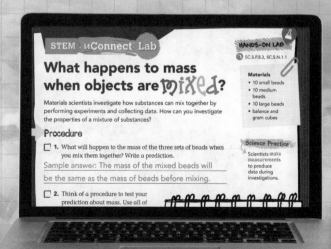

# Energy and Motion

**Next Generation Science Standards**

**4-PS3-1** Use evidence to construct an explanation relating the speed of an object to the energy of that object.

**4-PS3-2** Make observations to provide evidence that energy can be transferred from place to place by sound, light, heat, and electric currents.

**4-PS3-3** Ask questions and predict outcomes about the changes in energy that occur when objects collide.

Go online to access your digital course.

▶ VIDEO

📖 eTEXT

👆 INTERACTIVITY

🖥 VIRTUAL LAB

🎮 GAME

☑ ASSESSMENT

## The Essential Question

*What is energy, and how is it related to motion?*

### Show What You Know

The race cars are moving around the track. In what ways do you think energy is important for car racing?

_____

_____

_____

# Quest Kickoff

# Energy Changes in Collisions

*How can you design a safe car?*

**Phenomenon** Hi, my name is Anna Alomar, and I am a vehicle safety engineer. I study what happens to cars and trucks involved in accidents. In this problem-based learning activity, you will design a new safety feature for a car. The most important criterion for your design is the safety of your passengers. You will consider how speed and energy affect auto collisions. Then you will find out how energy changes and transfers during a collision. You will use what you learn about energy to design a new safety feature.

Follow the path to learn how you will complete your Quest. The Quest activities in the lessons will help you complete the Quest. Check off your progress every time you complete an activity with a QUEST CHECK ✓ OFF. Go online for more Quest activities.

## Quest Check-In 1

**Lesson 1**
Learn how energy affects the speed and direction of moving vehicles.

**Next Generation Science Standards**
**4-PS3-1** Use evidence to construct an explanation relating the speed of an object to the energy of that object.

**▶ VIDEO**

Watch a video about a vehicle safety engineer

## Quest Check-In 3

### Lesson 3

Look at evidence from crash tests to find out how energy was transformed during a collision.

## Quest Check-In Lab 4

### Lesson 4

Learn about electric circuits, and design an alert system to prevent car crashes.

## Quest Check-In Lab 2

### Lesson 2

Review some data from crash tests, and use a model to study the motion of cars before, during, and after a collision.

## Quest Findings

Use everything you have learned to design a safe vehicle.

## uConnect Lab

# How can you compare the energy of objects?

Scientists measure the amount of energy that is transferred during events. How can you compare the amount of energy of two objects with different sizes?

**Materials**
- golf balls
- large marbles
- ruler
- balance and gram cubes
- pan
- fine sand
- safety goggles

 Wear safety goggles.

## Procedure

☐ **1.** Predict which object will have more energy: a larger or smaller object.

_____

_____

☐ **2. SEP Plan an Investigation** Use all the materials to plan an investigation that tests your prediction.

☐ **3.** Show your plan to your teacher before you begin. Record your observations.

**Science Practice**

Scientists collect data to use as evidence.

## Analyze and Interpret Data

**4. SEP Interpret** Did your results support your prediction? Explain.

_____

_____

_____

**5. SEP Explain** What evidence did you use to compare the amount of energy of each object?

_____

_____

_____

_____

_____

## Observations

# Cause and Effect

Cause-and-effect relationships can explain how two events are related. A cause is the reason something happens. An effect is what happens. Use these strategies to help you identify causes and effects when reading informational texts.

- Ask yourself questions such as *What happens?* or *How did it change?* to identify an effect.

- Ask yourself *why* to identify the cause.

- Look for clue words such as *because* and *so*. They can signal cause and effect.

 **GAME**

Practice what you learn with the Mini Games.

### Just One Tiny Push

Have you ever seen a long line of falling dominoes? Dominoes have to be carefully set up to ensure that energy can move from domino to domino. With a tiny push, the dominoes fall because energy is transferred from one to the next. If enough energy moves from domino to domino, they will keep falling. Sometimes, all the dominoes fall. Other times, the dominoes stop falling, and some dominoes are left standing.

☑ **READING CHECK** **Cause and Effect** Circle words that identify a cause. Underline words that identify an effect.

# Energy, Speed, and Moving Objects

## I can...

Explain what energy is and describe some forms of energy. Explain how a moving object's speed and energy are related.
**4-PS3-1**

**Literacy Skill**
Cause and Effect

**Vocabulary**
energy
potential energy
kinetic energy
speed

**Academic Vocabulary**
transfer
transform

▶ **VIDEO**

Watch a video about moving objects.

## ENGINEERING ▶ Connection

Have you ever noticed how many cars have a similar shape? Most cars are curved in the front. They have a gentle slope over the hood, windshield, and roof. The side mirrors are curved as well. The gentle curves and slopes of the car's design allow air to pass easily over the car.

Air is matter, so energy is needed to move it. Cars that come in contact with less air lose less energy, which means the cars can go faster and use less fuel. Engineers study how air can affect objects so that they can design cars that are faster and more fuel efficient.

📓 **Write About It** How would you design a new car? List criteria you may consider when developing your design.

# How does starting height affect an object's energy?

When doing work involving vehicle safety, engineers consider factors that affect the speed and direction of a vehicle. How can you study the energy of a moving object?

**Materials**
- toy ball
- meterstick
- stopwatch
- masking tape
- several books
- smooth, flat board

## Procedure

☐ **1.** Predict how the height of a ramp will affect how fast an object travels down it.

_____

_____

_____

**Science Practice**

Scientists **construct explanations** based on evidence.

☐ **2.** **SEP Plan an Investigation** Use the materials to make a plan to test your prediction. Show your procedure to your teacher before you begin.

☐ **3.** Conduct your test. Record your observations.

## Analyze and Interpret Data

**4.** **SEP Explain** How does the starting height of an object traveling downward affect how fast it moves? Support your answer with evidence from this lab.

Observations

_____

_____

_____

_____

_____

_____

## Literacy ▸ Toolbox

**Cause and Effect** A cause can result in more than one effect. Find a cause in the photo that has two effects.

## Energy

**Energy** is the ability to do work or to cause change. Energy is involved when anything moves or changes. Energy cannot be made nor destroyed, but it can change form and be transferred. When energy is **transferred**, it moves from one object to another.

**Infer** Some forms of energy are more easily observed than others. Suppose you were riding this roller coaster. What forms of energy do you think you would observe?

_____

_____

_____

## Quest Connection

How can energy be transferred in a car?

_____

_____

## Energy at Rest

When these dominoes are first set up, they have stored energy. Stored energy in an object at rest is called **potential energy**. The potential energy of the dominoes comes from how they are positioned. As soon as each domino starts to fall, its potential energy changes into energy of motion. The amount of potential energy an object has depends on its shape or position.

## Energy in Motion

The energy of a moving object is called **kinetic energy**. The kinetic energy of an object depends on its mass and how fast it is moving. We see the effects of kinetic energy when something moves from place to place. Falling dominoes have kinetic energy. Some kinetic energy is transferred from one domino to the next when they collide. When energy is **transformed**, it is changed from one kind of energy to another kind. When the dominoes fall, some energy is transformed into sound energy. That is why you hear the dominoes click. Heat, light, and electricity are some other forms of kinetic energy.

☑ READING CHECK **Cause and Effect** How would kinetic energy of the dominoes be affected if the first domino did not hit the second one?

_____

_____

_____

_____

_____

INTERACTIVITY

Complete an activity on kinetic and potential energy.

# How does energy affect particles of matter?

Just like larger objects, the smallest particles of matter have energy, too.

## Potential Energy

Potential energy is involved when objects are bent, stretched, or compressed.

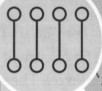

normal pillow

compressed pillow

cold water

hot water

## Thermal Energy

Thermal energy is energy that an object has because of the movement of its particles.

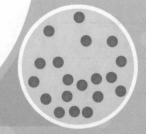

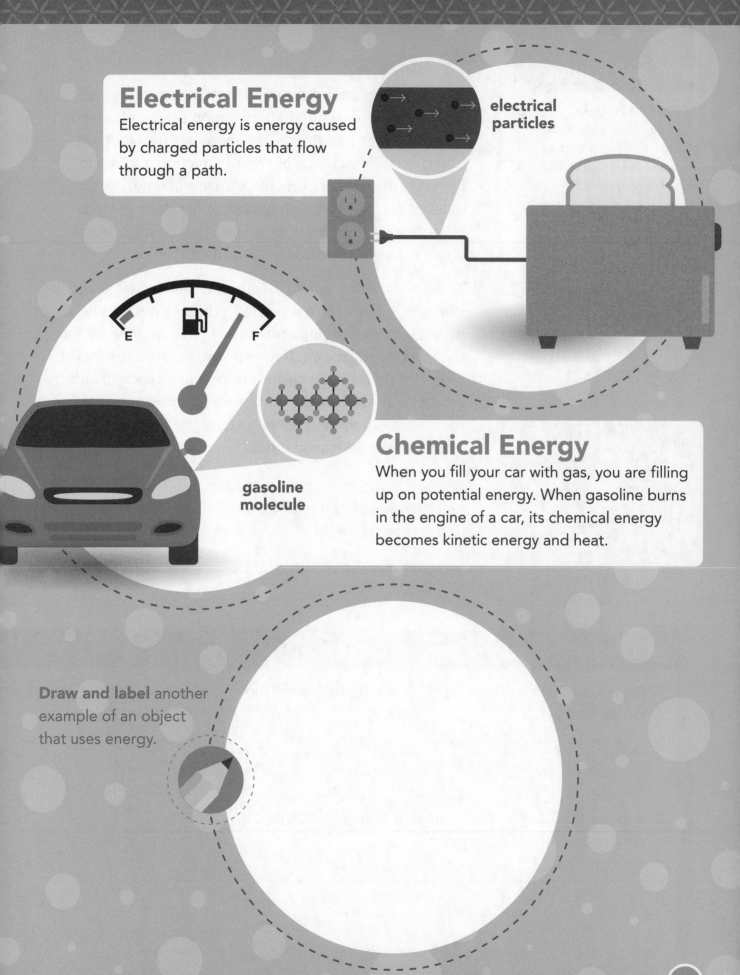

# Electrical Energy

Electrical energy is energy caused by charged particles that flow through a path.

**electrical particles**

# Chemical Energy

When you fill your car with gas, you are filling up on potential energy. When gasoline burns in the engine of a car, its chemical energy becomes kinetic energy and heat.

**gasoline molecule**

**Draw and label** another example of an object that uses energy.

## Force and Speed

Find a ball that you can easily roll. With an adult, measure how far the ball travels if you give it a small push. Then measure how far it goes with a big push. How are the force and distance traveled related?

## Motion and Energy

Motion is a characteristic of all matter, including the particles that make up matter. Motion can be observed, described, and measured. Two characteristics that are often used to describe motion are direction and speed. **Speed** is the distance an object travels in a particular amount of time, such as a minute or an hour. Speed is often described as *fast* or *slow*. Direction is which way an object is moving, such as north or south.

The speed or direction of an object is affected by forces. For example, a large force is needed to launch a rocket because the rocket's weight pulls downward on it. An upward force is applied to the rocket. If the upward force on the rocket is greater than the downward force, the rocket will launch upward. The greater the force pushing upward, the faster the rocket will move. That is because the faster an object moves, the more energy it has.

**Apply** A ball slowly starts to roll downhill, but its speed increases as it rolls. How are the ball's speed and energy related?

_____

_____

## ✓ Lesson 1 Check

**1. Draw Conclusions** What causes an object that is not moving to gain kinetic energy?

_____

_____

**2. Explain** How do you know that a falling domino that causes another domino to move has energy?

_____

_____

_____

# Energy, Speed, and Motion

How are energy, speed, and motion related? Vehicle safety engineers use test crashes to investigate how energy, speed, and motion interact. The results from the investigations can help design safer cars.

**1.** Draw an arrow that shows the direction you think the cars were moving in each crash.

**2.** Why do you think vehicle safety engineers test vehicles at different speeds and directions in the test crash investigations?

_____

_____

_____

_____

_____

_____

_____

_____

# uEngineer It! Design STEM

 **VIDEO**

Watch a video about how toys are designed.

# Toys on the Move

**Phenomenon** Almost anywhere you look, you are likely to see a machine that can move. Each kind of machine is designed to do a certain job. For example, a car is designed to move forward. A helicopter is designed to move both forward and straight upward. Some machines are toys. Guiding a remote-controlled toy car around a sidewalk can be a lot of fun. People love to watch toy helicopters do aerial stunts. In order for people to enjoy playing with a toy that moves, an engineer first had to build it. Engineers consider what the toy needs to do. Then they use their science knowledge and problem-solving skills to get the job done. If you could build any kind of moving toy, what would you build?

# Design It

You have been asked by a toy company to build a moving toy that will race against other moving toys. Your toy must travel a distance of at least 1 meter (3.3 feet) in 10 seconds or less. There is no one way to build your machine. Figuring out how to do it will be up to you!

☐ Identify what form your toy will take.

☐ Describe how the parts of your toy will have to work together.

☐ Decide on which materials you will use to build your machine.

☐ Draw the design for your toy. Label each part. Include a sentence or two that tells how the parts work together.

## Lesson 2

# Collisions

**I can...**

Predict changes in energy that occur when objects collide.

4-PS3-3

**Literacy Skill**
Cause and Effect

**Vocabulary**
collision

**Academic Vocabulary**
simulate

▶ **VIDEO**

Watch a video about collisions.

**SPORTS** ⟩ **Connection**

SLAM! A stick hits a hockey puck. The motion requires an energy transfer from the hockey stick to the hockey puck. Hockey players use the force from their bodies to hit the puck. The harder the puck is hit, the farther the puck will travel. Hockey players are not the only athletes to use energy transfer to their advantage. Tennis, baseball, and cricket are sports where players also use transfer of energy to their advantage.

**Identify** What are two other sports that involve energy transfers between objects? Where do the transfers happen?

_____

_____

_____

_____

# How does energy *transfer* between objects?

Vehicle safety engineers investigate the factors affecting collisions. What happens to the energy of objects when they bump into each other?

**Materials**
- marbles of different sizes and masses
- small ramp or chute

## Procedure

**Science Practice**

Scientists *design investigations* to answer a scientific question.

☐ **1.** Choose a variable that you want to investigate about two objects that bump into each other. Choose between different masses, different speeds, moving or not moving, or starting from different heights. Make a prediction about what will happen to the objects when they collide.

_____

_____

_____

_____

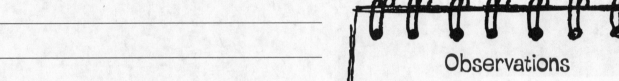

Observations

☐ **2.** Use the materials to make a plan to test your prediction. Show your plan to your teacher before you begin.

☐ **3.** Conduct your investigation and record the data.

## Analyze and Interpret Data

**4. SEP Explain** What energy transfer occurred in your investigation? How do you know?

_____

_____

_____

_____

# Energy Changes IN A COLLISION

When one object bumps into another object, the action is called a **collision**. During a collision, energy is transferred. Observe what happens when a basketball strikes the floor of the basketball court.

Energy is transformed as the ball moves downward.

Objects slightly compress when they collide. The ball becomes compressed as if it were made of springs.

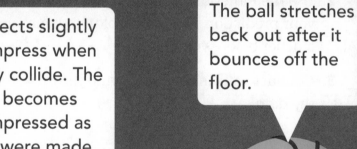

The ball stretches back out after it bounces off the floor.

**!** **What changes in energy occur when the bowling ball strikes the pins?**

_____

_____

_____

_____

_____

_____

_____

## Other Energy Changes

When a bowling ball strikes the pins, a loud sound is heard. The sound is evidence of an energy change. Some of the bowling ball's kinetic energy is changed into sound energy. Collisions can also result in a change of kinetic energy to light energy, thermal energy, or other types of energy.

**Model It!** Draw a picture of two objects that are colliding and transferring kinetic energy into another type of energy. Label the energy changes that are happening.

### Engineering Practice ▸ Toolbox

**Design a Solution** A company wants to improve its bowling ball so that it rolls in a straighter line. Define one problem that engineers would have to solve when improving the design of the ball.

**Quest Connection**

Why would the collision between two cars both traveling at a fast speed most likely cause more damage than a collision between two slow-moving cars?

_____

_____

_____

_____

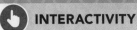

**INTERACTIVITY**

Complete an activity
on kinetic energy.

### uBe a Scientist

**Construct a Cradle**
With an adult, find some
objects around your home
that you can use to make your
own version of a Newton's
cradle. How do the energy
transfers of different objects
compare? What properties
do you think make objects
better for this purpose?

The device in the picture is a Newton's cradle. It shows how
energy can move between objects in a collision. When you
lift one of the spheres and drop it, the first sphere's energy is
transferred to the other spheres. This causes the sphere on the
opposite side to fly upward. Then the second sphere comes
down, and the first sphere you dropped pops back up. The
spheres in the middle barely move. Much of the kinetic energy
is transferred through them.

## ✓ Lesson 2 Check

1. **✓ READING CHECK Cause and Effect** In Newton's cradle, why do
   the spheres in the center barely move?

   _____

   _____

2. **Predict** Suppose you went bowling without a bowling ball and had only
   a softball and a large plastic ball to hit the pins. How would the speed
   and motion of these objects be different from when you use a heavy
   bowling ball?

   _____

   _____

   _____

# How does modeling help you understand a **collision?**

**Materials**
- toy cars
- colored pencils or markers
- paper

Vehicle safety engineers use models to understand what happens in a collision. By studying the effects of the collision, engineers can use the data to develop designs that improve the safety of the car. How can a model help you understand what happened in the collision shown in the picture?

**Engineering Practice**

Scientists use models to help identify cause and effect relationships.

## Procedure

☐ **1.** Identify any evidence that helps explain the causes and effects of the car crash. What chain of events do you think led to the collision? Write the information on the Accident Report.

☐ **2.** Use the toy cars and other materials to model the collision. Re-create the crash. Draw pictures on the Accident Report to show the scene before, during, and after the collision.

## Accident Report

_____
_____
_____
_____
_____
_____
_____
_____

## Evaluate Your Model

3. **Evaluate** Does your model provide enough information to determine what caused the crash? How could you improve the model to make it more useful?

_____
_____
_____

4. **CCC Cause and Effect** Based on your data, what do you think caused the crash?

_____
_____
_____

5. **SEP Use Models** What can you infer from your model about the energy changes that occurred in the crash?

_____
_____
_____

# Energy Transfer

**I can...**

Give examples
of energy being
transferred from place
to place.
Explain that heat flows
from hot objects to
cold ones.
Demonstrate that some
materials are good
conductors of heat and
others are not.
**4-PS3-2, 4-PS3-3**

**Literacy Skill**
Cause and Effect

**Vocabulary**
heat
radiation
light
sound
wave

**Academic Vocabulary**
generate

## STEM Connection

Many animals, such as bats and owls, are active only at night. Scientists want to know how animals behave in their natural habitat. However, a normal camera needs visible light to make an image, so it would not work well at night. How can we see animals at night?

To help capture images in the dark, scientists use thermal cameras, or cameras that sense the warmth of an animal's body rather than the visible light that common cameras use. The images that thermal cameras produce do not show the same images you see with your eyes. Instead, the images look like the one shown here, which show differences in temperature. In a thermal photo of an animal in its habitat, the red areas show the warmest parts of an animal and its surroundings, and the blue areas show the coolest parts. Plants are also detected by using thermal imaging.

📓 **Write About It** In your science notebook, tell how you would use thermal imaging to analyze an animal in its habitat.

# uInvestigate Lab

# How does *heat* move?

Scientists study how easily heat can move through different materials. How can you identify materials that allow heat to move easily?

## Procedure

☐ 1. Look at the suggested materials. Make a hypothesis about which materials will allow heat to move easily through them and which ones will not.

_____

_____

☐ 2. **SEP Plan an Investigation** Make a plan to test your hypothesis. Show your plan to your teacher before you begin. Record your observations.

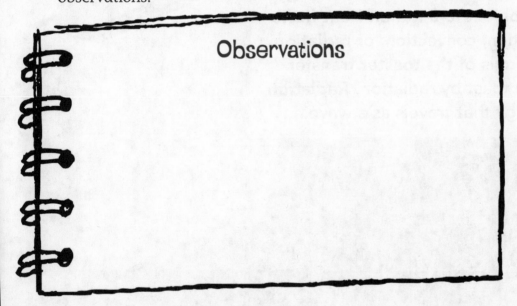

### Observations

**Materials**
- ice bath
- hot water
- thermometer
- graduated cylinder

**Suggested Materials**
- plastic cups
- foam cups
- paper cups
- metal cups
- glass cups
- ceramic cups

 Be careful handling hot water.

 Be careful using glassware.

**Science Practice**

Scientists *collect evidence* by performing experiments.

## Analyze and Interpret Data

3. **SEP Analyze** What did the results of your experiment show? Did they support your hypothesis?

_____

_____

_____

# How is ENERGY transferred?

Energy can be transferred through heat, sound, light, and electricity.

**Heat** is the transfer of thermal energy from one object to another. Heat flows by conduction, convection, or radiation. The hot coils of the toaster transfer heat to the toast by radiation. **Radiation** is energy that travels as a wave.

**Infer** Circle examples of where you think energy is being transferred.

## Energy and Particle Motion

All matter, including your body, is made of moving particles. These moving particles have kinetic energy. When you use a thermometer to find the temperature of a substance, you are finding the average kinetic energy of its particles. The energy is carried away from the matter by radiation.

**Compare** Look at the particles in the two diagrams. What difference do you see?

_____

_____

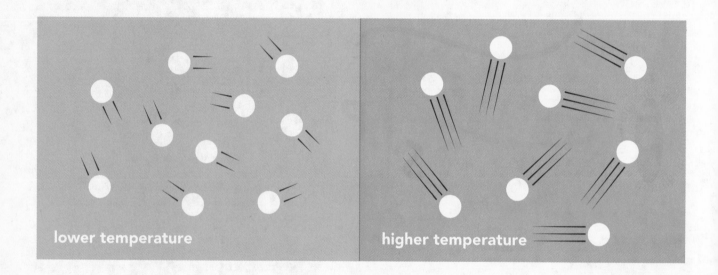

lower temperature

higher temperature

When heat is transferred to an object, the object's particles move faster. That is why the temperature of the object increases. When radiation carries energy from the sun to your skin, you feel hotter. The sun's radiation is making the particles of your skin move faster.

✓ READING CHECK **Cause and Effect** What do you think happens to the particles of matter of the object that is transferring the heat to another object? How will this affect its temperature?

_____

_____

## Light Energy

Any object that is a source of light has light energy. **Light** is a form of energy that we can see. Some of the energy that is radiated to Earth from the sun can be seen as light. The same kind of radiation is given off by other stars, which is why we can see them in a dark sky. You can also see light produced when lightning streaks across the sky. Some animals, such as these jellyfish, **generate**, or produce, their own light. Many of these animals live deep in the ocean where the sun's energy does not reach. The light these animals produce are examples of natural sources of light energy. Scientists have also developed ways to generate other sources of light energy, such as light bulbs, flashlights, and lasers.

**Question It!**

What are some other forms of light energy that you can identify? How do you use different forms of light energy every day?

_____

_____

_____

_____

_____

_____

_____

_____

## Sound Energy

When you strike a bell, you hear a sound—the bell's ring. To ring the bell, the kinetic energy of your hand is transferred to the bell, causing it to vibrate. **Sound** is energy in the particles that vibrate as they pass through matter. As the vibrating particles bump into each other, they form a pattern similar to the one in the picture. Sound can travel through solids, liquids, or gases. Sound is often described in terms of pitch, or how fast or slow the particles vibrate as they pass through matter. A sound with a high pitch has particles that vibrate faster than a sound with a low pitch.

**☑ READING CHECK Compare and Contrast**
Which sound has more energy—the croak of a frog or the squeal of a pig? _____

## Quest Connection

Each time an air particle interacts with another air particle, some, but not all, kinetic energy is transferred. What do you think ultimately happens to the energy of the sound as it moves through the air?

_____

_____

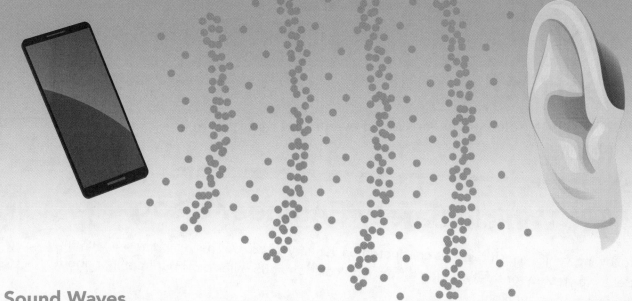

## Sound Waves

Sound energy travels outward as a wave from the source of the sound, such as a cell phone. A **wave** is a form of the transfer of energy. When a wave moves through matter, the matter does not move with the wave. A sound wave moves in all directions from the source of the sound.

Think again about the ringing bell. You may not be able to see it vibrate, but you can feel it. The metal of the bell moves back and forth as it vibrates. Each time it moves forward in a vibration, it pushes against air particles, and the air particles move outward and closer together. When the metal moves backward in a vibration, the air particles spread out again. That is what causes the pattern.

## ☑ Lesson 3 Check

1. **Explain** What happens to the particles of matter as they are heated?

_____

_____

2. **Draw Conclusions** A hot pot is placed on a cool table. Which way will heat flow between the pot and the table? Why?

_____

_____

_____

# Crash It!

Read the vehicle safety engineer's log of events and report from a crash test.

 ## Vehicle Safety Engineer's Log

The following vehicle crash test was conducted on January 20, 2017. The vehicle was a passenger vehicle. It was tested for safety during a front-end collision at 35 miles per hour (mph), or about 56 kilometers per hour (kph).

1:00 P.M. – Vehicle placed on test track with crash-test dummies inside. Electric tow cable attached.

1:10 P.M. – Pretest safety check conducted. All safety engineers in position to safely monitor the test.

1:12 P.M. – Crash sequence started. Electric tow cable began pulling the vehicle.

1:13 P.M. – Vehicle impacted concrete barrier at 35 mph.

1:15 P.M. – Final safety check completed. Vehicle crash test completed.

**Crash Test Results**

A loud boom sounded at the time of impact. The front end of the vehicle was compressed by 30%. The frame of the car was also bent. The vehicle's windshield was cracked over 90% of its surface. All other windows were completely shattered. The vehicle's restraints (seat belts) and airbags worked correctly. Crash-test dummies showed only minor signs of damage.

1. What are three pieces of evidence from this investigation that show energy was transferred?

_____

_____

2. What are two ways that energy was transformed in the test?

_____

_____

# Relative Distance

The pitcher stands on the mound 60 feet away from home plate. She looks over her shoulder to see the runner on first base. She winds up and throws the ball to the catcher. The ball takes exactly 1 second to get to the catcher's glove. How fast was the ball going?

As you have learned, speed is how fast an object goes. The pitcher threw the ball 60 feet in 1 second. Usually, the speed of a pitch is measured in miles per hour (mph). But a baseball never actually goes a mile. The distance from the pitcher to home plate is about 60 feet. One mile is the same as 5,280 feet! How many pitches fit inside a mile? Complete this equation to find out.

[feet in a mile] / [feet between pitcher and catcher] = _____

If the ball went 60 feet per second, what was the ball's speed in mph? To answer this question, first find out how long it would take the ball to travel 1 mile. How many seconds would it take the ball to travel 1 mile?

_____

There are 3,600 seconds in an hour. How many miles could the baseball go in 1 hour if its speed did not change? Round your answer to the nearest whole number.

3,600 / _____ = ~ _____

Convert your answer to kilometers. _____

1 mile = 1.6 kilometers

# Electric Circuits

## I can...

Use models to describe how electric currents flow in circuits.

**4-PS3-2**

**Literacy Skill**
Cause and Effect

**Vocabulary**
electric charge
electric current
conductor
insulator
resistor

**Academic Vocabulary**
source

▶ **VIDEO**

Watch a video about electric currents.

## CURRICULUM ▸ Connection

The tubes of neon signs are filled with certain gases that produce light when they absorb energy. Each kind of gas produces a particular color of light. For example, neon produces red light, and argon gas produces blue light. The gases can be mixed to make many different colors of light. If you mix argon gas with a gas that gives off yellow light, the light that fills the tube will be green. The source of energy to make these different colors of light is electricity.

📓 **Describe** What kind of energy change does electricity cause in the sign's tube?

_____

_____

# uInvestigate Lab

# How does *electric energy* flow in circuits?

Engineers use models to design products that use electrical energy in newer and safer ways. How can you use a model to describe how electrical energy flows?

**Materials**
- 2 pieces of wire
- bulb and holder
- battery and holder

**Science Practice**

Scientists **use models** to describe phenomena.

## Procedure

☐ 1. **SEP Plan an Investigation** Look at the materials. How can you connect them to make the bulb light? Draw a picture.

☐ 2. **SEP Carry Out an Investigation** Show your plan to your teacher before you begin. Test your idea. If the bulb does not light, revise your plan. Keep testing until you have put the materials together in a way that makes the bulb light.

## Analyze and Interpret Data

3. **CCC Systems** How does energy move in this system? Draw arrows on your drawing to show the path.

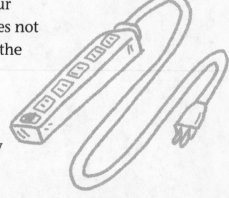

# Electric Charge

When you turn on a light, electrical energy moves. The flow of electrical energy happens because the particles that make up matter move. These particles have an electric charge. **Electric charge** is a property that causes matter to have a force, called electric force, when it is placed near other charged matter. Electric charges can be positive (+) or negative (–). Two particles that have the same charge will repel, or push away, each other. If their charges are opposite, they will attract, or pull toward, each other.

**Infer** Do you think the balloon and the towel have opposite charges? Explain your answer.

_____

_____

## Model It!

The circles in the diagram represent particles with electric charges. Draw arrows to show whether each pair of particles will attract or repel each other.

| ( + ) | ( + ) |
| ( + ) | ( – ) |
| ( – ) | ( – ) |

## Moving Electric Charges

Particles with electric charge can move from place to place. The flow of charged particles in the same direction is called **electric current**.

Some materials allow electric current to easily flow through them. A material that allows electric current to flow through it is called a **conductor**. Metal is a good conductor of electricity. For that reason, copper is a metal that is used to make electrical wires.

Other materials do not allow current to flow. A material that does not allow electrical current to flow through it is called an **insulator**. Plastic is an insulating material.

**Infer** Why do you think that the inside and the outside of electrical wires are made from different materials?

_____

_____

_____

_____

## Quest Connection

How can you use what you know about conductors and insulators to improve the safety design of your vehicle?

_____

_____

_____

_____

## Electric Circuits

In a conducting material, such as a wire, the electric current needs a **source**, or starting point, of energy to keep it moving. The electric current must flow in a complete path. This path is called an electric circuit. The picture shows the path of an electric circuit.

☑ READING CHECK **Cause and Effect** How do you think the switch can stop the electric current from flowing in this electric circuit?

_____

_____

_____

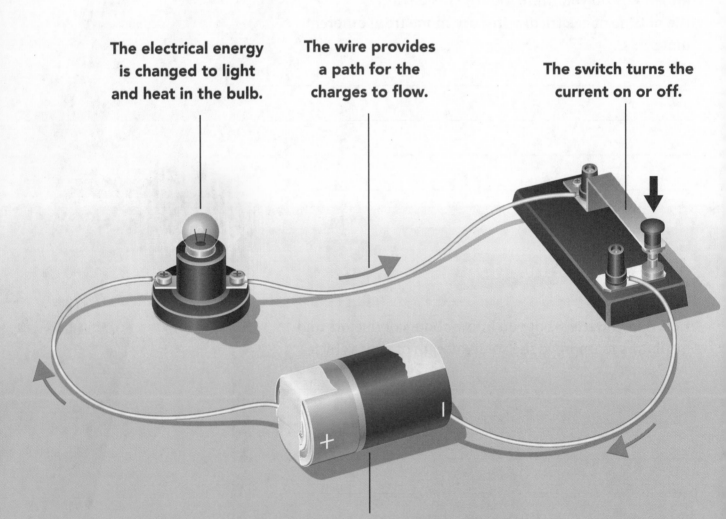

**The electrical energy is changed to light and heat in the bulb.**

**The wire provides a path for the charges to flow.**

**The switch turns the current on or off.**

**The battery is the power source.**

## Resistance

In the circuit, current flows through both the wire and the bulb. The bulb glows, but the wire does not. The difference is that the light bulb has a wire made of a material that does not allow electric current to flow easily. The wire is a **resistor**, which is a device to control the flow of electricity. When current is pushed through a resistor, often the electrical energy is changed into another form of energy, such as light or heat. The wire that carries the current to and from the light bulb is made of a conductor.

**Make Meaning** Do a survey of your home to see how many objects make heat or light. Which of these do you think result from electric current flowing through a resistor?

resistor

---

### ☑ Lesson 4 Check

**1. Cause and Effect** What causes a light bulb to glow in an electric circuit?

_____

_____

_____

**2. Explain** Describe how electric currents flow in circuits.

_____

_____

_____

_____

_____

# How can an electric circuit help prevent collisions?

The red-signal traffic lights that are common almost everywhere in the United States were designed by engineers to control traffic and prevent accidents. But they cannot control all accidents, such as the collision you learned about in the earlier Quest Check-Ins. How can you use an electric circuit to design an alert system to prevent rear-end collisions?

**Materials**
- electric buzzer
- battery with holder
- insulated wire
- scissors

**Suggested Materials**
- light with holder
- cardboard
- aluminum foil

## Plan and Build

☐ **1.** List two ideas for using an electric circuit to develop an alert system.

_____

_____

_____

_____

⚠ Be careful using scissors.

**Engineering Practice**

Engineers **provide and receive critiques** about models and procedures.

☐ **2.** Choose one idea and write or draw a plan to make a model of it. Include the materials you will use and how you will test your model. Use all the materials and any of the suggested materials.

My Model

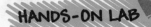
☐ **3.** Share your plan with another classmate. What suggestions does the classmate have for a design improvement?

_____

_____

_____

☐ **4.** Incorporate any useful suggestions into your plan. Show your final plan to your teacher before you begin.

☐ **5.** Build your model, and test it. Record your observations.

### Observations

## Evaluate Your Design

**6.** Did your model work the way you thought it would? Based on your observations, do you think your new safety feature would help prevent collisions?

_____

_____

_____

_____

**INTERACTIVITY**

Get support to design your safe car.

STEM

# Energy Changes in Collisions

## How can you design a safe car?

### Design a Solution

**Phenomenon** Throughout the Quest, you learned about energy and how forms of energy change. You designed a safety device for a car. Now you will make a model drawing of a car that shows where the device will be located. You will also show how energy will turn on the device.

My Model

### Communicate Your Solution

Present the design of your vehicle to your classmates. Explain how your design will keep passengers safe.

QUEST CHECK ✓ OFF

# Vehicle Safety Engineer

Do you like cars or trucks? Do you want to make the world a safer place? Vehicle safety engineers use their knowledge of energy, forces, and materials to design safer vehicles. They use data from the real world, computer simulations, and crash-test experiments to develop their designs.

Vehicle safety engineers can work in government labs or for private companies. They are an essential part of the teams that design new cars and trucks. If you want to be a vehicle safety engineer, you will need a degree in engineering. Vehicle safety engineers can help make the world a safer place!

**Reflect** In your science notebook, write about some other parts of the career you want to know more about.

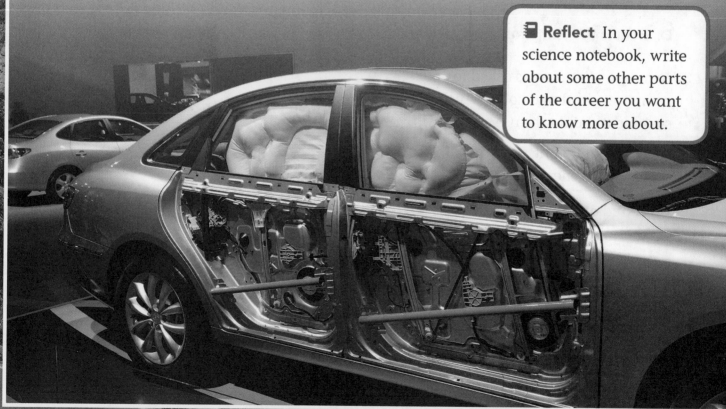

1. **Vocabulary**  Lamar plugs a lamp into a wall. Electricity goes from the outlet, through the cord, and to the light bulb. Which choice best describes the cord?

   **A.** conductor

   **B.** current

   **C.** insulator

   **D.** resistor

2. **Describe**  Which statement best describes heat?

   **A.** Heat moves from hot objects to cold ones.

   **B.** Heat only moves by conduction.

   **C.** Heat increases as objects become colder.

   **D.** Heat is the temperature of an object.

3. **Compare**  A student is asked to compare sound and light. Which statement should she use?

   **A.** Sound and light are forms of electrical energy.

   **B.** Sound and light are forms of thermal energy.

   **C.** Sound and light are forms of potential energy.

   **D.** Sound and light are forms of energy.

4. **Identify**  Which of the following would you expect to be a thermal conductor?

   **A.** plastic

   **B.** paper

   **C.** metal

   **D.** wood

5. **Explain**  What causes sound energy?

   **A.** heated objects

   **B.** charged particles

   **C.** light energy

   **D.** vibrating objects

6. **Compute**  Which vehicle was moving at the fastest speed?

   **A.** a car that traveled 96 kilometers in 2 hours

   **B.** a bus that traveled 160 kilometers in 5 hours

   **C.** a bike that traveled 64 kilometers in 4 hours

   **D.** a truck that traveled 320 kilometers in 5 hours

7. **Explain** What determines the pitch of a sound?

   **A.** the speed of charged particles

   **B.** the size of the sound source

   **C.** the speed of vibrating particles

   **D.** the temperature of the source

8. Four different-colored bowling balls with the same mass are rolling down the bowling lane. Use the data in the table. Which one has the most kinetic energy?

| Ball color | Average speed (m/sec) |
|---|---|
| | 7.15 |
| | 6.26 |
| | 8.94 |
| | 6.71 |

   **A.** blue ball

   **B.** red ball

   **C.** green ball

   **D.** black ball

9. **Vocabulary** Which is the ability to cause motion or create change?

   **A.** conduction

   **B.** energy

   **C.** speed

   **D.** temperature

## The Essential Question

*What is energy, and how is it related to motion?*

## Show What You Know

What energy transformations take place in a race car during a race?

_____

_____

_____

_____

_____

_____

_____

_____

_____

_____

_____

_____

A scientist was watching a baseball game and became curious about what was happening as the ball was hit. He collected data about what happened when balls were hit. Use the data in the table to answer the questions.

| Swing | Bat Speed | Ball Velocity |
|-------|-----------|---------------|
| 1 | 9 m/s | 24 m/s |
| 2 | 12 m/s | 30 m/s |
| 3 | 15 m/s | 34 m/s |
| 4 | 18 m/s | 37 m/s |
| 5 | 21 m/s | 40 m/s |
| 6 | 24 m/s | 20 m/s |

**1.** Write a question that could possibly be answered using the data in the table.

_____

_____

**2.** During swing 6, the player's bat broke. Which of these conclusions do the data from the table about swing number 6 support?

**A.** Energy from the swing was lost to inertia.

**B.** Energy from the swing was absorbed by the bat.

**C.** Energy from the swing was transformed to heat.

**D.** Energy from the swing was transferred to the player.

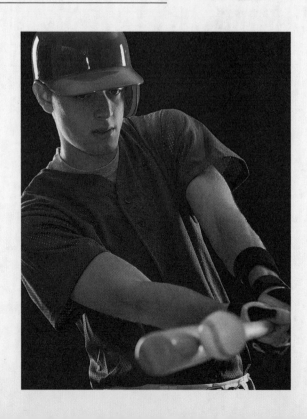

**3.** Given the same swing speed, what would be likely to happen if the bat used was heavier?

    **A.** The baseball would travel more slowly.

    **B.** More kinetic energy would be transferred.

    **C.** Less kinetic energy would change to sound energy.

    **D.** More energy would be changed to potential energy.

**4.** Which swing made the loudest sound when hitting the ball?

    **A.** Swing 1

    **B.** Swing 2

    **C.** Swing 3

    **D.** Swing 4

**5.** What are two variables that could affect how fast the ball travels after being hit?

    **A.** height of the player and length of the bat

    **B.** size of the stadium and speed of the wind

    **C.** speed of the pitch and elevation of the stadium

    **D.** weight of the bat and the amount of light energy

**6.** Write an explanation of how the speed and energy of an object are related. Use evidence from the table to support your explanation.

_____

_____

_____

_____

_____

# uDemonstrate Lab

# What affects energy transfer?

**Phenomenon** Vehicle safety engineers use what they know about different materials to make new and safer vehicles. How does speed affect how much energy is transferred during a collision?

## Procedure

☐ **1.** Predict how the height from which an object is dropped affects the amount of energy it transfers.

_____

_____

_____

_____

☐ **2. SEP Plan an Investigation** Use all the materials. Make a plan to test your prediction. Show your plan to your teacher before you begin.

_____

_____

_____

_____

_____

_____

_____

**Materials**
- rubber ball, 1-inch
- meterstick
- safety goggles
- paper bowl
- sand

 Wear safety goggles.

**Science Practice**

Scientists **collect data** to use as evidence.

**3.** Record your data.

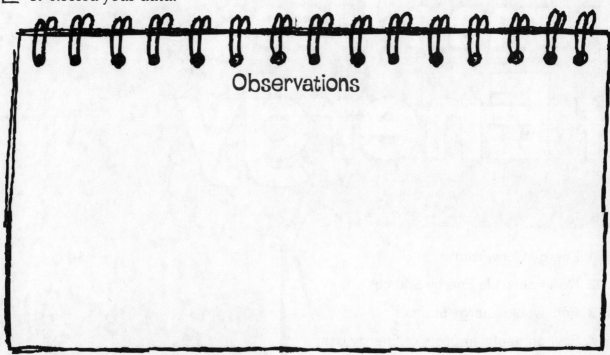

Observations

## Analyze and Interpret Data

**4. Use Evidence** Do the data you collected support your prediction? Use evidence to support your answer.

_____

_____

_____

_____

_____

_____

**5. Explain** How does the speed of an object relate to its energy?

_____

_____

# Human Uses of Energy

**Next Generation Science Standards**

**4-ESS3-1** Obtain and combine information to describe that energy and fuels are derived from natural resources and their uses affect the environment.

**4-PS3-4** Apply scientific ideas to design, test, and refine a device that converts energy from one form to another.

**3-5-ETS1-1** Define a simple design problem reflecting a need or a want that includes specified criteria for success and constraints on materials, time, or cost.

Go online to access
your digital course.

▶ VIDEO

📖 eTEXT

👆 INTERACTIVITY

📱 VIRTUAL LAB

🎮 GAME

☑ ASSESSMENT

## The Essential Question

*How do we convert energy to meet our needs?*

### Show What You Know

People use a lot of electrical energy in homes, schools, and businesses. What are some ways to produce electrical energy from other kinds of energy?

_____

_____

_____

### STEM ▸ Power from the People

*How can a device convert energy from one form to another?*

**Phenomenon** Hi, I'm Barry Arnold, an electrical engineer. I work for a company that designs exercise equipment. That might sound like an unusual job for an electrical engineer, but it isn't. Right now, my big project is designing an exercise bike that provides power to your home as you work out. A one-hour ride on your bike can provide enough power to keep your laptop computer working for ten hours.

I need your help to design a mechanical device that provides electric power. Maybe it could charge your cell phone. To test the device, you will use it to run a small electric motor. Then you will demonstrate how your device works and think about ways to improve it.

Follow the path to learn how you will complete the Quest. The Quest activities in the lessons will help you complete the Quest! Check off your progress on the path when you complete an activity with a **QUEST CHECK ✓ OFF**. Go online for more Quest activities.

## Quest Check-In 1

**Lesson 1**
Identify some criteria and constraints of your energy device.

**Next Generation Science Standards**

**4-PS3-4** Apply scientific ideas to design, test, and refine a device that converts energy from one form to another.

**3-5-ETS1-1** Define a simple design problem reflecting a need or a want that includes specified criteria for success and constraints on materials, time, or cost.

▶ VIDEO

Watch a video about an electrical engineer.

## Quest Check-In Lab 3

### Lesson 3

Convert your charging device from a battery-operated device to a solar-powered one.

ON

OFF

## Quest Check-In 4

### Lesson 4

Evaluate the environmental impact of your device.

## Quest Check-In Lab 2

### Lesson 2

Build a device that uses a battery to create motion.

## Quest Findings

Build your final exercise device that charges the cell phone.

# How are *energy* resources used?

**Materials**
• 160 tokens
• number cubes

Scientists consider the availability of an energy source. How can you show the effect of use on renewable and nonrenewable energy sources?

## Procedure

**Science Practice**

Scientists obtain and combine information to explain phenomena.

☐ **1.** Decide who will be the 2 energy suppliers and the 2 energy users in this lab. Energy supplier A and energy supplier B each have 45 units (tokens) of energy to start. Each supplier has one user.

☐ **2.** Users take turns rolling a number cube. At each turn, the user gets the number of tokens that shows on the number cube. On each turn, supplier B gets 10 additional tokens. Supplier A gets 0 additional tokens. Write the amounts in the table.

☐ **3.** Repeat rolling the cubes until each user has had 5 turns.

| Turn | Supplier A | | | Supplier B | | |
|------|-------|------|-------|-------|------|-------|
|      | Added | Used | Total | Added | Used | Total |
| 0    | 45    | 0    | 45    | 45    | 0    | 45    |
| 1    | 0     |      |       | 10    |      |       |
| 2    | 0     |      |       | 10    |      |       |
| 3    | 0     |      |       | 10    |      |       |
| 4    | 0     |      |       | 10    |      |       |
| 5    | 0     |      |       | 10    |      |       |

## Analyze and Interpret Data

**4. SEP Explain** Which supplier will be able to provide units longer? Construct an explanation.

_____

_____

# Use Text Features

Text features help organize the information given to you in the text. They help you better understand the text's overall meaning. Some common types of text features are images, captions, headings, and highlighted words.

Read the following text about wind turbines. Pay attention to text features.

**GAME**

Practice what you learn with the Mini Games.

### Energy of the Future

Finding and using energy sources other than fossil fuels is an important goal of scientists and people around the world. Here are two newer alternatives.

### Wave Energy

The energy of moving water can be used to turn the blades of a turbine. The turbines change this moving energy into electricity. Wave energy can be captured on or below the ocean surface, near or far from the shore. Like wind energy, it is a safe and clean source.

### Solar Energy

Many homes now use solar panels to collect solar energy that can be changed to electricity for their homes. Scientists are currently developing window glass that acts as a solar collector. The glass will capture the energy in sunlight that we cannot see while letting regular visible light pass through.

☑ **READING CHECK** **Use Text Features** Circle the text features that helped you understand what you read.

# Energy Conversions

**I can...**

Describe how natural resources are converted to energy and fuel.

**4-ESS3-1, 4-PS3-4**

**Literacy Skill**
Use Text Features

**Vocabulary**
fuel
combustion
turbine
generator
battery

**Academic Vocabulary**
device
primary

## STEM Connection

The world has more than a billion cars! Almost all of them use a gasoline engine for power. Some new kinds of cars are very different, though. Many people now drive hybrid cars. These cars use both gasoline and electricity to run. Other cars use only electricity. These cars have electric motors connected to large batteries and use only electricity. They get their batteries recharged instead of gas tanks filled. Electric cars are much more efficient than cars that use gas—they use less total energy.

What if the batteries did not need to be recharged? Some research engineers have built solar cars. Solar panels charge the batteries whenever enough light is available, so you do not have to plug the car into an electric station. These new cars are experiments, so you cannot buy one yet. Someday, though, you might travel in a car that needs no fuel other than sunlight.

📖 **Make Meaning** In your science notebook, explain why a solar car might have trouble traveling at night. Write a plan to solve this problem.

# How can a potato provide energy to a light bulb?

Engineers design devices that use natural resources as an energy source. How can a potato provide the energy to light a bulb?

**Materials**
- copper strips
- zinc strips
- LED light bulb
- fresh potatoes
- safety goggles
- alligator clips

## Build and Improve

☐ 1. Insert a piece of copper into the potato. Then insert a piece of zinc into the potato. Connect one end of an alligator clip to the copper. Connect the other end of the alligator clip to the zinc. Connect the LED wires to the two metal strips, and observe what happens. Record your observations.

☐ 2. Improve your circuit by designing one that produces more electrical energy. Show your design to your teacher before you begin. Record your observations.

⚠ Wear safety goggles!

⚠ Do not taste lab items.

**Engineering Practice**

Engineers apply scientific ideas to solve design problems.

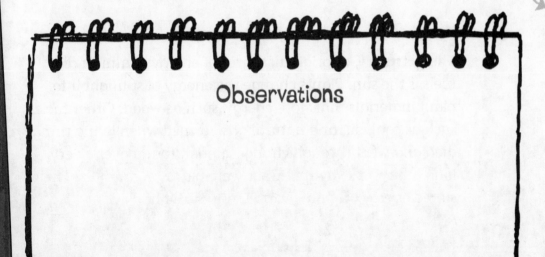

Observations

## Evaluate Your Design

3. **SEP Use Evidence** How do you know whether a change in energy occurred in the electric circuit?

_____

_____

_____

## Using Energy

People use a lot of energy to heat and light buildings and to power tools, cars, and other electric devices. A **device** is something made for a particular purpose. All devices that plug into wall outlets need electrical energy. The electrical energy is produced by changing some other form of energy.

Some of this energy comes from burning fuel. A **fuel** is a material that releases energy as heat when it burns. Common fuels include coal, natural gas, petroleum, and wood. The process of burning a fuel to produce heat and light is called **combustion**. During combustion, the fuel combines with oxygen. A chemical change occurs that releases energy stored in the fuel.

✓ READING CHECK **Use Text Features** How does the photo on this page help you understand the text?

_____

_____

## Fuels

The **primary**, or original, source of energy of almost all fuels is the sun. Plants change the energy of sunlight into plant materials that store energy, such as wood. Other fuels, such as coal, oil, and natural gas, formed when living things died and went through changes underground over a very long time. These living things were plants or animals. Their stored energy originally came from sunlight.

## Chemical Energy

Fuels burn and produce energy as heat and light. This energy comes from a chemical change. The energy is stored in the fuel as chemical energy. During combustion, substances in the fuel combine with oxygen to form new substances. These new substances do not have as much chemical energy as the original fuel.

Transportation is an important use of fuel. In a car engine, gasoline and air mix. Combustion of the mixture changes the chemical energy stored in the mixture into heat. Hot gases in the engine expand and push against engine parts. The motion of the engine parts moves the car. You can tell that combustion of gasoline releases heat by touching the hood of a car after it has been running a long time.

**Plan It!**

You are a city official who must make sure your city has enough electricity. You know you will need to use some kind of chemical energy. List the steps that must take place to get electricity to your people.

# How is **electrical power** generated from **chemical energy?**

! **Label** In the space below each part of the power plant, write what energy change occurs in the part.

steam

## Boiler

In a coal power plant, the primary source of energy is the coal. When coal is burned in the plant, chemical energy changes to heat that turns water into steam. Because the water vapor is so hot, it has a lot of energy.

_____

_____

## Turbine

The hot steam flows through a turbine. The **turbine** is a device that spins as the gas flows and changes the heat energy of the steam into energy of motion.

_____

_____

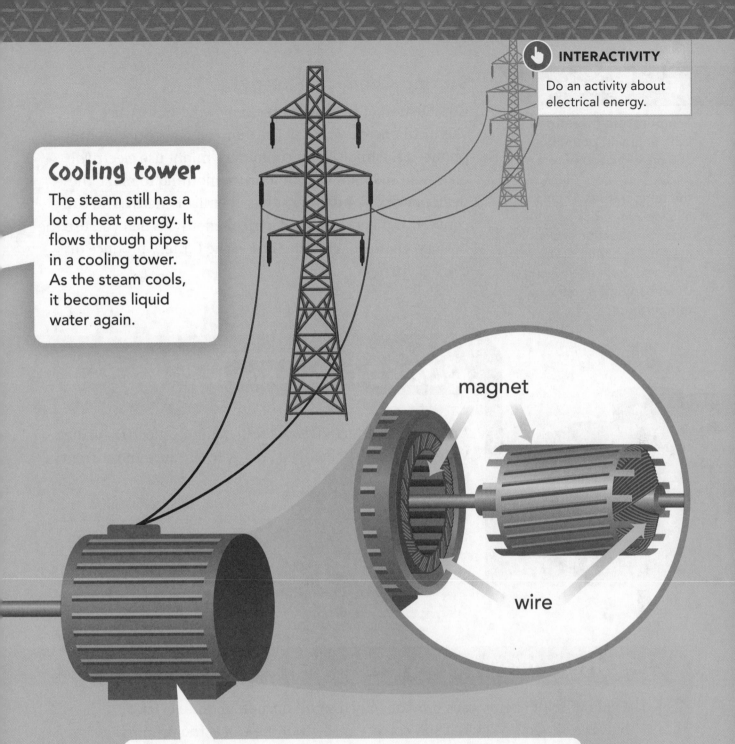

**INTERACTIVITY**

Do an activity about electrical energy.

## Cooling tower

The steam still has a lot of heat energy. It flows through pipes in a cooling tower. As the steam cools, it becomes liquid water again.

magnet

wire

## Generator

As the turbine spins, it turns a shaft that causes motion in the generator. A **generator** is a device that changes energy of motion into electrical energy. Inside the generator, a magnet is surrounded by a coil of copper wire. As the magnet turns, an electric current is generated in the wire coil.

_____

_____

## Storing Chemical Energy

Combustion of fuels is not the only way that we use chemical energy. The devices that you can carry around—a phone, a flashlight, or a computer—might use electrical energy. You do not want to burn something to make these devices work. A **battery** stores chemical energy and can convert that energy into electrical energy. When you use the battery, chemical changes inside the battery produce an electric current.

## Quest Connection

An energy-producing device will generate electric current. Where might the chemical energy to produce the current be stored?

_____

_____

## ☑ Lesson 1 Check

1. **Explain** Solar energy cells provide only a small portion of our electrical power right now. Why is it still correct to say that the sun is the primary source of most of the electricity that we use?

_____

_____

2. **Evaluate** A car uses fuel to cause it to move. What energy changes occur when this happens?

_____

_____

# Human Power

In this Quest, you will design a device that changes the mechanical energy of a moving person into electrical energy that can power a motor. Your teacher will identify the materials you can use. You must build your device by the end of this topic. Your device will help me design an exercise bike that will power a laptop computer.

1. Define the problem you must solve.

_____

_____

_____

2. What are the criteria for success? What are the constraints? Write your answers in the table.

| Criteria | Constraints |
|---|---|
|  |  |

3. Use the criteria and constraints to write a plan.

_____

_____

_____

_____

# Nonrenewable Energy Sources

**I can...**

Investigate how people extract and use natural resources.
Give examples of nonrenewable energy sources.
**4-ESS3-1**

**Literacy Skill**
Use Text Features

**Vocabulary**
fossil fuel
coal
petroleum
natural gas
nuclear fuel
uranium

**Academic Vocabulary**
outcome

▶ **VIDEO**

Watch a video about energy resources.

## CURRICULUM ▷ Connection

Have you ever heard the expression "a canary in a coal mine"? It means someone or something that warns of danger. Digging coal in a deep underground mine can be a dangerous job. One risk to coal miners is a poisonous gas, carbon monoxide. You cannot see it, and you cannot smell it. Today, miners carry electronic detectors that warn them of carbon monoxide. How did miners check for toxic gas before the detectors existed?

After a fire or explosion, mine rescuers carried a small caged bird, a canary. Because canaries are more sensitive to carbon monoxide than people, the miner would watch the bird. If carbon monoxide was present, the bird would stop singing or start swaying on its perch. The miner knew that it was time to quickly return to the surface.

**Infer** Carbon from coal and oxygen from air combine to form carbon monoxide. What process produces the gas?

# How do we find  oil?

Engineers use echoes from underground to decide where to drill for oil. What methods can you use to find a balloon buried in sand?

## Design and Build

☐ **1.** Bury the balloon that is filled with water in the sand in the box. Make sure that the sand is level and that you cannot see the balloon. Trade boxes with another group.

☐ **2.** **SEP Plan an Investigation** Write a plan to use energy to find the water buried in sand. Have your teacher review your plan before you start. Record your observations.

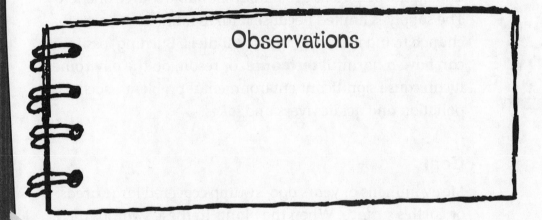

### Observations

## Evaluate Your Design

**3.** **SEP Analyze** What forms of energy did you use to search for the hidden balloon? Was your search successful?

_____

_____

**4.** **Collaborate** Compare your procedure with those of other groups. Which procedure was most successful in finding the water? Why do you think that is so?

_____

_____

_____

**Materials**

- small balloon filled with water
- large plastic box with sand
- safety goggles

**Suggested Materials**

- wooden spoon
- wooden skewer

⚠️ Wear safety goggles.

**Engineering Practice**

Engineers apply scientific ideas to solve design problems.

**Crosscutting Concepts ▶ Toolbox**

**Energy and Matter** Energy and matter flow in and out of systems. In books or Internet articles, read about the connection between fossil fuels and environmental pollution. Share the information you find with classmates.

## Fossil Fuels

Much of the energy that people use comes from fossil fuels. **Fossil fuels** are materials that formed as ancient plants and animals decayed underground. The three main fossil fuels are coal, petroleum, and natural gas. These fuels react with oxygen in the air during combustion, releasing heat and light. Fossil fuels are a nonrenewable source of energy. The supply is limited because it takes millions of years to change living materials into fossil fuels. Burning fossil fuels can have a harmful **outcome**, or result, on the enviroment. It can cause significant environmental problems, such as air pollution and acidic rivers and lakes.

## Coal

Many millions of years ago, swamps covered large areas of Earth's surface. When the plants in these swamps died, they sank to the bottom. Layer after layer of dead plants built up over a very long time. These layers were covered by soil and rock. Chemical changes transformed the plant stems and leaves into a hard, black substance, called **coal**. The amount of coal that exists in the world today will last for more than a hundred years at current rates of production. But coal is not a renewable energy source. As it is used up, no more coal replaces it.

☑ **READING CHECK** **Use Text Features** Headings are the section labels in large type. What do the headings on this page tell you about the paragraphs that follow them?

_____

_____

# Quest Connection

The energy of fossil fuels originally comes from the sun. Your Quest is to run a motor using power from human motion. How does that energy also come from the sun?

_____

_____

_____

## Petroleum

What do you buy at a gas station? Not a gas, but gasoline. The most important fuels for transportation in most of the world—gasoline and diesel—are made from petroleum. **Petroleum** is a liquid fossil fuel formed by the decay of ancient plants and animals. It is not found in as many places as coal. Saudi Arabia, Russia, and the United States produce the most petroleum. It is shipped to distant places using pipelines, trains, trucks, and large ships. Huge factories, called refineries, separate different parts of the petroleum. These are used as fuel and to make many different products that include plastics, textiles, fertilizers, and medicines.

**Reflect** These oil rigs drill and remove petroleum from beneath the ground. In your science notebook, write how this process might affect the environment.

# Where do FOSSIL FUELS come from?

It takes a long time for plants and animals to change into fossil fuels. Much of the coal and petroleum that we use today began to form long ago.

## COAL

When plants died and fell into the water, they decomposed and formed layers of peat.

After a very long time, heat from inside Earth and pressure from soil and rock changed the peat into coal.

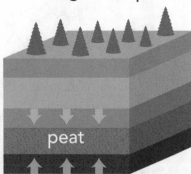

peat

The whole change took more than 10 million years.

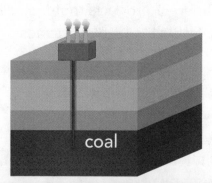

coal

! **Predict** What do you think would happen if coal did not form?

_____

_____

# PETROLEUM

When plants and animals died in the ocean, they fell to the bottom. Most of these organisms were single-celled plankton and algae.

Sediment covered them. Over a long time, these plants and animals decomposed and formed oil and natural gas.

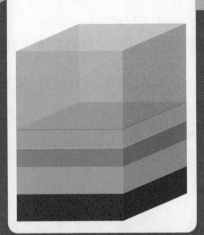

Today, these materials fill small gaps and pores in rock deep below the surface.

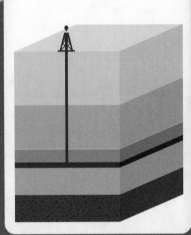

**! Infer** Why do you think coal and petroleum are different?

_____

_____

_____

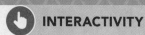
## Natural Gas

Engineers often find another fossil fuel in or near petroleum. **Natural gas** is a fossil fuel that occurs in the gas state. Like petroleum, it formed by the decay of ancient plants and animals. In many places, natural gas flows through pipes to homes and businesses. In homes, it is used for heating, cooking, and water heating. Natural gas is also an important fuel for producing electricity. Some modern vehicles use natural gas as a fuel. Because it is a gas, natural gas is harder to store and transport than coal or petroleum. It is usually stored and shipped in containers at very high pressure. Many of these containers are spheres because a sphere is very strong.

**Design It!** An engineer is evaluating use of fossil fuels for a power plant. List some criteria and constraints that would affect use of a fossil fuel.

## Nuclear Fuel

Beginning in the second half of the twentieth century, people used nuclear energy to produce electrical energy. Nuclear energy comes from changes inside particles of matter. The unstable elements that produce this energy in power plants are the **nuclear fuel**. Most nuclear power plants use the element **uranium**. Uranium is found in underground rocks. Miners dig up the rocks, and the uranium is collected from them. Uranium is a nonrenewable energy source because only a limited amount of it can be mined. Nuclear power plants work in a similar way as fossil fuel plants, but the fuel is not burned. Instead uranium atoms are split apart to produce heat energy. The heat energy makes steam that drives a turbine and generator.

............uBe a Scientist............

**Make It Turn**
Hold a toy pinwheel outdoors on a day when a breeze is blowing. Observe what happens to the pinwheel. How could wind power be used as a source of energy?

## ☑ Lesson 2 Check

**1. List** What are some examples of nonrenewable energy sources?

_____

_____

**2. Identify** What are three ways that people use natural resources?

_____

_____

_____

# How can you use a battery to produce motion?

Engineers use criteria, or standards, to evaluate whether a solution works. Their solutions are limited by constraints, such as available materials or the cost of the design. How can you design a device that uses a battery to produce motion?

**Materials**

- battery in battery holder
- insulated copper wire
- switch
- electric motor
- safety goggles

**Suggested Materials**

- movable parts from construction sets

## Design and Build

☐ 1. Decide how you will build a device that uses a battery to produce motion. List the criteria.

_____

_____

_____

☐ 2. **SEP Design a Solution** Make a diagram that shows how you will arrange the materials. Label the components. Show your diagram to your teacher before you begin.

⚠ Wear safety goggles.

**Engineering Practice**

Engineers **define design problems** and solve them through the development of an object.

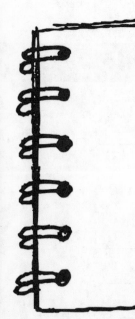

## My Design

☐ **3.** Build your device. If it does not work, revise your drawing and rebuild the device.

## Evaluate Your Design

**4. SEP Use Evidence** Does your solution meet the criteria that it makes the motor run? Provide evidence to support your answer.

_____

_____

_____

_____

**5. Hypothesize** How could you replace the battery with some type of mechanical energy to make the motor run?

_____

_____

_____

_____

# Renewable Energy Sources

**I can...**

Distinguish between renewable and nonrenewable energy sources.
Give examples of renewable energy sources.
**4-ESS3-1**

**Literacy Skill**
Use Text Features

**Vocabulary**
geothermal energy
hydropower

**Academic Vocabulary**
available

 **VIDEO**

Watch a video about geothermal energy.

## ENGINEERING Connection

The most abundant source of energy on Earth is not actually on the planet. Every day, the sun provides 10,000 times more energy to Earth than people use. Because this energy is spread out across the planet, people have developed systems to concentrate and use it. The United States already has more than 1 million solar energy systems. As engineers improve solar energy devices, this number will increase.

Solar energy in a home is used in two common ways. In one method, sunlight directly heats the house or heats water for washing and laundry. The other method uses photovoltaic cells. These devices are often placed on the roof of a building. The cells use sunlight to produce electric current. The electricity from these cells can be used immediately or stored in a battery for later use. Solar energy can also be changed to electrical energy in large facilities that then deliver it to customers.

**Write About It** Engineers are designing a solar energy system to meet all the energy needs of a home. In your science notebook, write what constraints they must consider.

# How does a windmill capture wind energy?

Scientists and engineers have developed devices that change energy from one form to another. How can you design a way to capture energy from moving air?

## Design and Build

☐ **1.** Plan a way to make a device that rotates when wind blows on it. Include a method to test the device. Show your plan to your teacher before you begin.

☐ **2.** Observe how wind direction affects the way that your device moves. Record your observations.

☐ **3.** Based on your observations, make improvements to your device. Test it again. Record your observations.

## Evaluate Your Design

**4. Infer** Use what you observed about your model and what you know about generators to describe how a windmill might produce electrical energy.

_____

_____

_____

_____

_____

_____

_____

**Suggested Materials**
- construction paper
- plastic drinking straws
- straight pins
- modeling clay
- stapler
- paper glue
- safety goggles

 Wear safety goggles.

**Engineering Practice**

Engineers apply scientific ideas to solve design problems.

## Observations

# Is renewable energy all around?

Renewable energy sources contribute more to our total power needs every year. They do not run out as we use them. Some energy can be used directly. Other forms of renewable energy are changed to electrical energy or chemical fuels before we use them.

Energy from the sun can be used directly or changed to electrical energy.

**Solar Energy**

**Biomass Energy**

Plants use energy from sunlight to grow. Plant materials can be burned as firewood or changed into liquid fuels.

As the sun heats the atmosphere, air moves around. Wind turbines change that motion to electrical energy.

Solar energy causes water to evaporate. After water condenses and falls as rain or snow, the energy of flowing rivers can be used to generate electrical energy.

**Hydropower**

**Wind Energy**

Energy from Earth's hot interior heats water beneath the surface. Heat energy obtained from beneath Earth's surface is **geothermal energy**. This warm water can heat homes and other buildings.

**Geothermal Energy**

INTERACTIVITY

Do an activity about natural resources.

## Crosscutting Concepts ▸ Toolbox

**Energy and Matter** Corn can be used to make a renewable fuel called ethanol. Corn is also an important food in many diets. How does using corn for fuel affect the supply of corn for food?

## Renewable Fuel

Plants store the energy they get from the sun as chemical energy in their cells. For a very long time, people have used the stored energy when they burned wood and other plant materials, known as biomass. Today, we also use plants to produce chemical fuels, such as alcohol. These fuels are easier to store and transport than biomass. Most gasoline fuel includes some alcohol. Biomass is a renewable energy source because new plants can be replanted many times in the same place. However, biomass is an extremely inefficient way to store energy. Much less than 1 percent of the sun's energy makes it into the biofuel. Also, a lot of land must be used to grow the biofuel.

**Compare and Contrast** Circle the text that describes the advantages of using biomass. Underline the text that describes the disadvantages.

## Hydropower

If you stand outside during a heavy rainfall, you can feel the energy of falling water. Using the energy of moving water is called **hydropower**. Hydropower relies on flowing water to create motion, such as a wheel turning. Today, hydropower is an important source of electrical energy. Dams hold water in a lake. As the water flows through openings in the dam, it turns a turbine. The turning turbine causes a generator to produce electricity. The moving water of flowing rivers can also be the source of energy to turn the turbine.

## Energy That Does Not Run Out

Biomass is a renewable energy source because we can grow more plants. However, some energy sources do not need to be replaced. They are produced continually by nature. Wind energy is completely renewable. As the atmosphere absorbs energy from the sun, temperature differences in the atmosphere cause wind to blow. While the wind may stop now and then, we can rely on it to start blowing again.

Solar energy is another source of energy that does not run out—at least for the next few billion years! As long as the sun shines, it will continue to provide energy to Earth. We use some solar energy directly to heat water or the air in a building. Solar energy can also be changed into electrical energy. Then energy can be transmitted to users far from the site of the energy cells. One limit of solar energy is that it is not available at night. When something is **available**, it is able to be had.

**Describe** How can air be used as an energy source?

_____

_____

_____

u**Be a Scientist**

**Balancing Act**
On a sunny day, put two pieces of construction paper—one white and one black—side by side in the sun. Tape them in place if there is wind. After about an hour, place one hand on top of each piece of paper. What do you observe about the paper? Explain why this happens.

## ☑ Lesson 3 Check

1. **☑ READING CHECK Use Text Features** Look at the title of each section in this lesson. How do these titles relate to one another?

_____

_____

_____

2. **Evaluate** Farmers can grow crops such as corn to be turned into fuel for vehicles. Is fuel made from corn a renewable resource? Explain your answer.

_____

_____

# How can the sun make a motor work?

In the last Quest Check-In, you powered an electric motor with a battery. How can you make your electric motor run using a solar cell rather than a battery?

**Materials**
- small solar panel
- insulated copper wire
- switch
- electric motor

**Suggested Materials**
- desk lamp

## Design and Build

☐ 1. Make a diagram that shows how you will arrange the materials to use a solar cell to run the motor. Label the components. Show your diagram to your teacher before you continue.

Engineering Practice

Engineers generate and *compare* multiple solutions to a problem.

☐ 2. Build your device. If it does not work, revise your drawing and rebuild the device.

## Evaluate Your Solution

3. **SEP Explain** How well does the solar device work compared to the battery device? Explain how you compared them.

_____

_____

_____

One important math tool is a bar graph. A bar graph can show how something changes over time. When two things are related, a double bar graph can show how one factor changes the other. A double bar graph compares two sets of data.

The blue bars in the graph show the amount of electrical energy produced from hydropower every five years between 1995 and 2015. The green bars show the amount of electrical energy produced from other renewable sources over the same time. Notice how the amount of electrical energy from hydropower changes. Then notice what happens to the amount of electrical energy from other renewable sources. The data on the double bar graph shows the connection between the electrical energy produced by hydropower and the electrical energy produced by other renewable sources.

**Draw Conclusions** What does the double bar graph show about the connection between hydroelectricity and other renewable energy sources?

_____

_____

_____

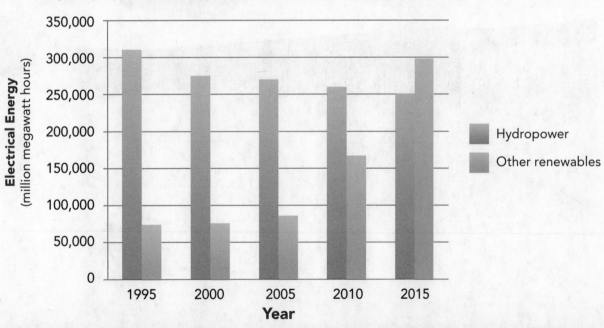

**Hydropower and other renewable electricity generation (1995–2015)**

# uEngineer It! Improve STEM

**VIDEO**

Go online to see how plastics are recycled.

# Hold *That* Phone

**Phenomenon** The earliest mobile phones were very large. People sometimes called them "bricks" because of their shape and size. Their mass was more than a kilogram! Think about how different that is from today's smart phone. Technology allows modern phones to be much smaller and use energy more efficiently.

Engineers consider many different criteria when they design a new phone. Some people want a very small phone that fits in a pocket. Other people want a phone with a large screen that can run a lot of apps. Each phone design has some features that users want, but it may not meet the needs of other users. How would you design a phone that meets your preferences?

Engineers do not change everything in a phone at one time. When they redesign a phone that is already used, first they evaluate that phone. Then they decide how to make it better.

# Improve It

Suppose that you work for a company that makes cell phones. Your job is to redesign the current phone so that it has the features people want. The first step is to decide what would make the phone better.

☐ Think about the phones that you and your friends use. What feature would you change to make the phone better?

☐ Brainstorm ways you could redesign a smart phone to add the new feature.

☐ Draw your new phone.

# Environmental Impacts of Energy Use

## I can...

Describe how the use of different natural energy resources affects the local and global environments. Evaluate how technology can improve the environmental effects of using a given energy resource.

**4-ESS3-1**

**Literacy Skill**
Use Text Features

**Vocabulary**
emission
pollutant
scrubber
greenhouse gas

**Academic Vocabulary**
impact

## STEM ⟩ Connection

As you pass a modern power plant, you are likely to see tall towers, such as those shown in the photograph. They appear to release smoke, but they are not smokestacks. What you see coming from the towers is water vapor. As the vapor cools in the air above the towers, it forms small droplets. You are actually looking at a cloud in the sky above the tower!

Power plants make a lot of steam to run turbines. The steam condenses to make hot water. In the past, the hot water often was dumped into a river or lake. In towers like these, some of the hot water evaporates from the water surface to form water vapor. Since it takes energy to make water vapor, the remaining water becomes cooler. When it has cooled enough, the water is recycled to make new steam.

**Analyze** What would be some effects on the environment of dumping hot water from a power plant into a river? Do you think this practice should be allowed?

_____

_____

_____

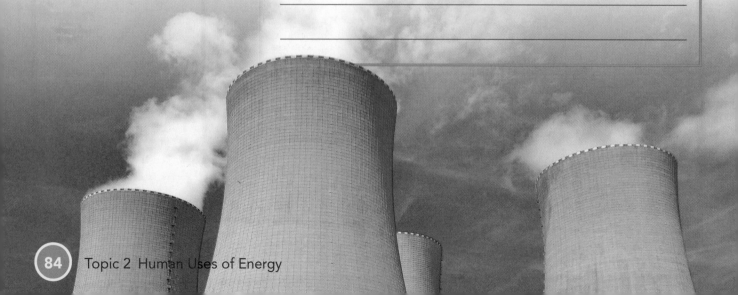

# uInvestigate Lab

# Why is oil cleanup so hard?

When crude oil spills on a beach, scientists develop ways to clean up the oil. Why is it hard to separate crude oil from sand?

## Procedure

☐ 1. Drop a spoonful of oil into a bowl of sand and mix it.

☐ 2. Make a plan to separate the oil from the sand. Show your plan to your teacher before you begin. Record your observations.

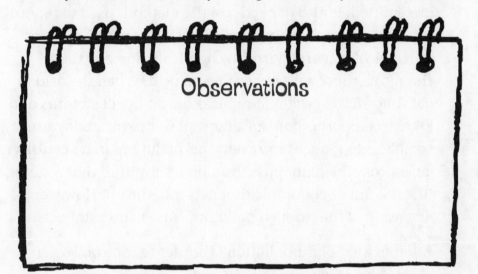

Observations

☐ 3. Think of other methods that you could use to separate the oil from the sand. Try one of those methods. Record your observations.

## Analyze and Interpret Data

4. **SEP Analyze** Why was the oil hard to separate from the sand?

_____

_____

5. **SEP Evaluate** What did your model show you about pollution on a beach?

_____

_____

**Materials**
- model oil
- sand
- bowl
- safety goggles
- plastic gloves
- spoons

**Suggested Materials**
- paper towels
- sieve

⚠ Wear safety goggles and gloves.

⚠ Do not taste lab materials.

**Science Practice**

Scientists obtain information to explain phenomena.

Have an adult help you look up the amount of carbon dioxide, or $CO_2$, in the atmosphere for the past 10 years. Make a graph with the data you collect. What patterns do you see in the data?

## Impact of Energy Production

The human use of energy has **impacts**, or effects, on the environment. These impacts occur when humans change the land to build a structure or to remove a resource. They can also occur during energy production. **Emissions** are the release of substances into the environment. Some emissions can have a harmful impact on the environment. For example, releasing a **pollutant**, or harmful substance, during energy production can poison land, water, and air.

The impact that a power plant has on the environment depends on how the power is generated and what pollutants are emitted. It also depends on the methods used to reduce harmful effects. Burning fuel in fossil-fuel plants releases particles of ash and harmful chemicals. Some of these chemicals cause rain to become an acid. When the acid gets into surface water, it reduces the ability of streams and lakes to support organisms. Most power plants today use scrubbers to reduce or prevent this pollution. In a **scrubber**, gases from the plant pass through a substance that reduces the amount of pollutants that gets into the air. However, disposing of the trapped pollutants also causes impacts.

Another kind of air pollution is harder to control. Power plants also release greenhouse gases, mainly carbon dioxide. A **greenhouse gas** is a pollutant that increases the atmosphere's ability to hold heat. Because carbon dioxide is always produced by combustion, fossil-fuel power plants are a major source of this impact.

☑ READING CHECK **Use Text Features** Choose one of the vocabulary words on the page. How does it relate to the title of this section?

_____

_____

_____

_____

## Impacts of Nuclear Power

Nuclear power plants do not produce air pollutants, but they produce solid waste that remains dangerous for thousands to millions of years. Nuclear power plants also produce large amounts of hot water.

**Analyze** How could the release of very hot water affect the environment and its living things?

_____

_____

### Science Practice
► Toolbox

**Obtaining and Evaluating Information** What are some sources of information on environmental impacts of using energy? Which source is more reliable, a government website or an oil company website? Why?

## Impact of Obtaining Fuel

Some fuels that power plants use must be mined. This process can change the land surface. Often forests and fields are removed to get to the fuel beneath them. Coal mines can leave large areas completely changed. Some mined materials dissolve in water when they are uncovered. They can wash away and pollute streams and rivers.

Drilling is also used to get fuels. Drillers must make roads and cut down forest areas to make a place for the drilling equipment. Some drilling methods use toxic materials to force the oil and gas to the surface. These materials can spill and pollute the land and water around the drilling site.

**Cause and Effect** Underline two harmful effects of obtaining fuel.

## Quest Connection

▼▼▼▼▼▼▼▼▼▼▼▼▼▼▼▼▼▼▼▼▼▼▼▼▼▼▼▼▼▼▼▼▼

Why does an energy source that does not use fuel have a smaller environmental impact?

_____

_____

_____

# How can the use of energy damage ecosystems?

Energy use can affect ecosystems in many ways. Some types of impact on the environment due to energy use are listed below.

**!** Draw a line from each description to a place that illustrates the impact.

surface mine

Disturbing land can pollute streams and rivers.

Roads can break up habitat areas.

Mining can cause a loss of habitat for plants and animals.

Fossil fuel combustion can pollute the atmosphere.

coal power plant

hydropower dam

Building dams can damage stream habitats.

## Impact of Transporting Fuels

Large pipes carry natural gas and crude oil to where the fuels are used. The largest pipes are over one meter in diameter. They carry fuel distances of thousands of kilometers. Sometimes, a pipeline starts to leak. If the leak is not noticed quickly, a lot of fuel can spill. Oil spills are very hard to clean up. Crude oil is very sticky. It covers anything it touches. Natural gas leaks add a lot of greenhouse gases to the atmosphere.

Another risk of transporting oil comes from shipping it across the ocean. Huge ships carry giant containers of crude oil from one continent to another. If a ship collides with something, a massive amount of oil can spill. The oil floats on the water, and currents can spread it over a large area.

**Apply** What is one harmful effect that the oil spill shown in the photo could cause?

_____

_____

## ☑ Lesson 4 Check

**1. Explain** What are two ways that power plants can affect the environment?

_____

_____

_____

_____

**2. Analyze** How do scrubbers help to reduce pollution?

_____

_____

_____

# Impact Inspections

You found a source of energy other than a battery for the motor. Now consider the environmental impact of that device.

1. Does using solar energy to run a motor have any negative impacts on the environment? Explain.

_____

_____

_____

_____

2. Contrast the environmental impact of the solar energy with that of a battery and the mechanical energy produced by a human.

_____

_____

_____

_____

3. What is a disadvantage of using human power compared to using a battery or solar energy?

_____

_____

_____

_____

**INTERACTIVITY**

Evaluate your design to support your Quest Findings.

**STEM** ▶

# Power from the People

*How can a device convert energy from one form to another?*

## Test Your Solution

**Phenomenon** You have learned how electrical energy can make a motor run. Design a device that uses human energy to provide power to an electric motor. Show your design to your teacher before you build the device.

Discuss how you can develop a test that compares different solutions to the problem. What criteria would you use to determine which device works best? On the card, write the steps of a test that can compare devices.

### Test Steps

_____

_____

_____

_____

_____

## Redesign and Retest

Think of a change that you can make to your device that might make it work better. How will you know whether the new design is an improvement?

_____

_____

Make the change to your design. Retest the device. Did your change improve the device? Explain your answer.

_____

_____

QUEST CHECK ✓ OFF

# Electrical Engineer

Electrical engineers work with electronics, electromagnetism, or electricity. They design, test, and produce electrical equipment that can range from small devices to large, impressive systems.

Electrical engineering is a relatively new addition to the engineering field. It has opened a whole new range of careers for engineers. An electrical engineer can work in developing solutions for problems dealing with aerospace, power generation, and automotive industries. For example, power generation engineering has become more important as interest in renewable energy has increased. Engineers who work in power engineering create more efficient ways of conducting electricity across equipment that generates energy from renewable resources.

📓 **Write About It** In your science notebook, describe some problems in the world today that an electrical engineer might be able to solve. How could he or she do it?

## ☑ Assessment

**1. Use Diagrams** This diagram shows a turbine and generator used in a hydropower plant.

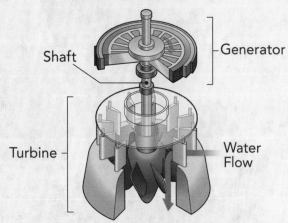

What is the function of the turbine in the power plant?

**A.** It pushes water through the dam.

**B.** It causes the generator to move.

**C.** It produces electricity that flows into power lines.

**D.** It heats the water to produce steam that turns the generator.

**2. Summarize** How were fossil fuels formed, and why are they found underground?

_____

_____

_____

_____

_____

**3. Interpret** Laura read an article about combustion of fuel to produce energy. The article stated that the energy for any fuel used in combustion comes from the sun. What does that statement mean?

**A.** The fuels used to produce power are renewable sources of energy.

**B.** All fuels originally come from plants that used sunlight or animals that ate the plants.

**C.** The fuels absorb energy when sunlight shines on them and release the energy when they burn.

**D.** Electric power in power plants can only be produced using different kinds of stored solar energy.

**4. Compare and Contrast** What is one similarity and one difference between renewable and nonrenewable energy sources?

_____

_____

_____

_____

_____

_____

_____

_____

_____

**5. Use Evidence** The graph shows the types of energy used in a recent year.

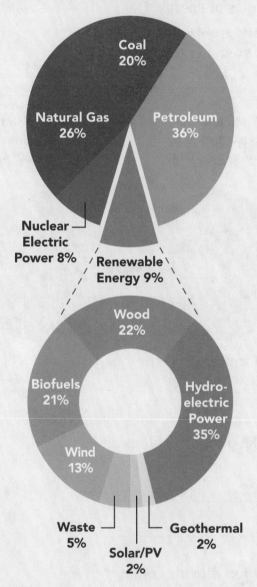

What was the largest renewable energy source during that year?

A. hydropower

B. natural gas

C. petroleum

D. wind

**6. Explain** In what way does a nuclear power plant have a smaller impact on the environment than a coal power plant?

A. Nuclear power plants are smaller than coal power plants.

B. The fuel for a coal plant is mined, but the fuel for a nuclear plant is not.

C. Nuclear power plants do not release pollutants into the atmosphere, but coal power plants do.

D. Nuclear power plants do not cause heat impacts that can harm the environment, but coal plants do.

**The Essential Question** *How do we convert energy to meet our needs?*

## Show What You Learned

Many energy sources are changed into electrical energy before we use the energy. What are some reasons that people use electrical energy instead of using other sources directly?

_____

_____

_____

_____

_____

_____

Read this scenario and answer questions 1–5.

Manny wrote a report about the environmental impacts of energy. He used the Internet to find information about greenhouse gases. Manny found these graphs on a U.S. government website. His teacher told him that information from that website is reliable.

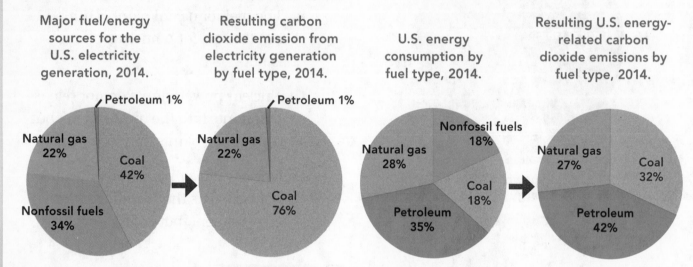

Major fuel/energy sources for the U.S. electricity generation, 2014.

Resulting carbon dioxide emission from electricity generation by fuel type, 2014.

U.S. energy consumption by fuel type, 2014.

Resulting U.S. energy-related carbon dioxide emissions by fuel type, 2014.

Manny used his knowledge of energy use and the information on the graphs to prepare his report.

**1. Use Diagrams** What conclusion could Manny make about the types of energy sources that produce carbon dioxide?.

_____

_____

**2. Interpret** The first graph shows that very little carbon dioxide comes from petroleum used to produce electricity. But the second graph shows that the largest amount of total carbon dioxide comes from petroleum. What can Manny conclude from the data?

**A.** A lot of petroleum is used to make electricity.

**B.** Burning petroleum does not always release carbon dioxide.

**C.** Most petroleum is used to produce energy that is not electricity.

**D.** Petroleum is not an important source of greenhouse gases in the atmosphere.

**3. Summarize** As the amount of greenhouse gases in the atmosphere increases, climates around the world become warmer. This is known as global climate change. What is one way that Manny found to help prevent climate change?

**A.** Use more petroleum to produce electricity.

**B.** Use more nonfossil fuel sources of energy to produce electricity.

**C.** Only use fossil fuels to produce energy in forms other than electricity.

**D.** Increase the amount of electricity that is produced and reduce other kinds of energy use.

**4. Evaluate a Plan** Coal releases more carbon dioxide than natural gas for the same amount of energy production. Manny proposed a plan to get rid of carbon dioxide emissions. His plan was to not use coal as an energy source and use only natural gas. Do you think that Manny's plan will work? Explain your reasoning?

_____

_____

_____

_____

**5. Interpret** Nuclear energy power plants produce about 20% of the electricity used in the United States. Look at the information about carbon dioxide in the graphs. What could Manny conclude about the production of carbon dioxide by nuclear power plants? Where would nuclear power be included in the first graph? Explain your answer.

_____

_____

_____

_____

_____

# How can energy resource usage change?

**Materials**
- 200 tokens
- 6-sided number cube

**Phenomenon** In the uConnect game, you modeled how energy supplies were different when the sources were nonrenewable or renewable. In real world usage, conditions sometimes change. How can you modify the game to investigate how a change in condition affects the energy supply?

**Science Practice**

Scientists obtain and combine information to explain phenomena.

## Procedure

☐ **1.** Review the uConnect game and your results. Choose one or more of these changes or make up a change of your own.

- Demand for energy increases, so users need more energy each year.
- New renewable technologies are invented, so more renewable energy is available.
- Improved technologies reduce the demand for energy by both users.
- The demand for energy changes from year to year.

   Circle which change or changes in energy supply or demand you will model.

☐ **2.** Design a solution to the new problem by writing a set of rules that show how energy is used in the model after the change.

_____

_____

_____

_____

☐ **3.** Explain how your rules model the change.

_____

_____

_____

**4.** Make a hypothesis about how the change will affect the results of energy supply and use in the game.

_____

_____

_____

_____

**5.** Play the game using your new rules. Use the table to record your data.

## Analyze and Interpret Data

**6.** **SEP Use Evidence** Did your evidence support your hypothesis? Explain.

_____

_____

_____

_____

**7.** **Evaluate** Will renewable energy sources always last longer than nonrenewable sources when you change the model? Explain.

| Turn | Supplier A | | | Supplier B | | |
|------|-------|------|-------|-------|------|-------|
| | Added | Used | Total | Added | Used | Total |
| 0 | | | | | | |
| 1 | | | | | | |
| 2 | | | | | | |
| 3 | | | | | | |
| 4 | | | | | | |
| 5 | | | | | | |
| 6 | | | | | | |
| 7 | | | | | | |
| 8 | | | | | | |

_____

_____

_____

_____

_____

_____

# Topic 3

# Waves and Information

**Next Generation Science Standards**

**4-PS4-1** Develop a model of waves to describe patterns in terms of amplitude and wavelength and that waves can cause objects to move.

**4-PS4-2** Develop a model to describe that light reflecting from objects and entering the eye allows objects to be seen.

**4-PS4-3** Generate and compare multiple solutions that use patterns to transfer information.

**3-5-ETS1-2** Generate and compare multiple possible solutions to a problem based on how well each is likely to meet the criteria and constraints of the problem.

Go online to access
your digital course.

▶ VIDEO

📖 eTEXT

👆 INTERACTIVITY

⚗ VIRTUAL LAB

🎮 GAME

☑ ASSESSMENT

## The Essential Question

### How do we use waves to communicate?

**Show What You Know**

How does sound travel from a band onstage to the crowd?

_____

_____

_____

**STEM** ▸ # Be a Message Master!

## How can information be sent securely?

**Phenomenon** Hi, I am Selena Nguyen, and I help gather information for the Central Intelligence Agency (or CIA) as an intelligence analyst. A lot of the information I deal with is confidential. Part of my job is to communicate secretly with my coworkers.

Since I have experience using secret codes to send information, a Hollywood director has asked for my help on a new movie. Two kids, Jamal and Matilda, are playing secret agents. They are trying to catch a jewel thief at a crowded museum where many large gems are on display. They think one of the museum visitors is the thief! Your Quest is to help me develop a code that the spies can use to communicate secretly in the dimly lit, noisy museum.

Follow the path to learn how you will complete the Quest. The Quest activities in the lessons will help you complete the Quest! Check off your progress on the path when you complete an activity with a QUEST CHECK ✓ OFF . Go online for more Quest activities.

## Quest Check-In 1

### Lesson 1
Identify criteria and constraints for a secret code that could be used in the museum.

**Next Generation Science Standards**

**4-PS4-3** Generate and compare multiple solutions that use patterns to transfer information.

**3-5-ETS1-2** Generate and compare multiple possible solutions to a problem based on how well each is likely to meet the criteria and constraints of the problem.

## Quest Check-In Lab 3

### Lesson 3
Try a different code. Design a way to communicate using only light.

## Quest Check-In 4

### Lesson 4
Compare and improve your secret codes.

## Quest Check-In Lab 2

### Lesson 2
Develop a method for communicating in code using only sounds.

## Quest Findings

Choose a secret communication method and demonstrate how it works. Explain why you chose this design.

# How do we describe waves?

**Phenomenon** It is easy to spot waves moving toward a beach, but there are other waves people cannot see. Using a model can help make invisible waves easier to understand or explain. How can you make a model of a wave?

**Materials**
• index cards

**Suggested Materials**
• drawing paper
• colored pencils

## Procedure

☐ **1.** Think about what you know about waves in the water. Write each idea you have on a separate index card.

☐ **2.** **SEP Develop a Model** Build a model you can use to teach younger students about waves. Choose materials and use your cards for your model.

☐ **3.** Use your model to describe waves to other students.

### Science Practice

Scientists *develop models* to describe natural processes.

## Analyze and Interpret Data

**4.** **SEP Use Models** You may have used what you already observed about water waves to help you construct your wave model. How might your model help you ask questions about waves you cannot see?

_____

_____

_____

_____

_____

_____

_____

_____

# Use Evidence from Text

People gather facts by reading text. Follow these suggestions to help you find and use evidence.

- Read closely, paying attention to important information.
- Underline or circle this information to keep track of where it is in the text.
- Use this information as evidence to support a claim.

Read the text passage to find out what lasers are and how they work.

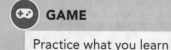

**GAME**

Practice what you learn with the Mini Games.

### A Bright Idea

Lasers are used in scanners at the store, in music players, and in certain surgeries. The word *laser* stands for "light amplification by stimulated emission of radiation." This is a complex phrase, but it helps to break it into parts. To amplify something means to make it stronger or bigger. An emission is something that is released. A laser is a release of light that is stronger than light from a light bulb.

To make one type of laser, scientists send light energy into a ruby. The ruby's particles gain and release energy. This causes the energy to bounce around inside the ruby crystal. Some of the particles gain energy over and over. This is how the light energy is amplified. Scientists use mirrors around the ruby to guide the released light into a focused beam.

☑ **READING CHECK** **Use Evidence from Text** What evidence supports the claim that lasers need an outside source of energy? Underline the evidence you used for your answer.

# Properties of Waves

**I can...**

Describe the basic properties of waves. Describe how waves can cause objects to move.

**4-PS4-1**

**Literacy Skill**
Use Evidence from Text

**Vocabulary**
wave
amplitude
wavelength
frequency
transverse
crest
trough
longitudinal

**Academic Vocabulary**
transfer

**VIDEO**

Watch a video about the properties of waves.

## SPORTS ⟩ Connection

Surfing is a very popular sport in towns near the ocean. To catch a wave, a surfer must paddle at the same speed that the waves travel. Just before the tallest part of the wave is below the surfboard, the surfer jumps up to a standing position. The surfer rides the wave toward the sandy shore.

The most daring surfers try to catch the biggest, fastest waves. Boats can pull surfers to catch waves that are going too fast. People surf huge waves this way. Big waves start farther from shore where the water is deep. When waves reach shallow water, the bottom of the wave drags along the ocean floor. The bottom of the wave travels more slowly than the top. This causes the wave to break.

**Infer** Why does a surfer have to paddle at a certain speed to surf a wave?

_____

_____

# uInvestigate Lab

# How does a wave carry energy?

Scientists run experiments as examples and use this information to develop a model. How can you use an experiment to develop a model of how a wave carries energy?

## Procedure

☐ 1. **SEP Develop a Model** Choose materials to make a model wave. Plan how to use the materials to make your model. Have your teacher approve your plan.

_____

_____

☐ 2. Make a plan for measuring two waves with different wave speeds and test it. Choose and use additional materials if you need them.

☐ 3. Draw your observations of the two waves from step 2. Include labels and distances between peaks on the waves.

## Analyze and Interpret Data

4. **SEP Explain** Did the height or peak-to-peak distance change when you gave one wave more energy than another?

_____

_____

_____

_____

5. **SEP Use Models** How did your models show how waves carry energy?

_____

_____

**Suggested Materials**
- assortment of ropes
- assortment of long springs
- measuring tape
- stopwatch or timer
- string

 Be aware of physical safety.

**Science Practice**

Scientists develop models based on evidence.

**Investigating Human Sounds** Investigate the production of sound waves using your voice. Write an explanation for what happens when you try each of the steps below.

- Hum with your nose and mouth open.
- Hum with your nose pinched closed and mouth open.
- Hum with your nose open and mouth closed.
- Hum with your nose pinched closed and your mouth closed.

## Waves

Waves are around us all the time. Light and sound are types of waves. Ripples on a lake or tremors from an earthquake are also types of waves. A **wave** is a disturbance that carries energy and travels in a repeating pattern. The disturbances that cause waves are vibrations. When an object vibrates, it travels back and forth. One back and forth motion causes one complete wave. The energy that causes the vibration is the energy carried by the wave.

Light waves can travel through empty space, but other wave types need a material to travel through. This material is called a medium. For example, sound waves need a medium. When someone calls your name, the sound travels as a disturbance in air. Wave speed is how fast a wave travels. It is different for different wave types and wave mediums. Think about a speedboat. Its vibrations make water waves and sound waves at the same time. The sound of the boat reaches your ears before the water waves do. Light waves travel even faster than sound waves. Light could travel around Earth seven times in less than one second!

☑ READING CHECK **Use Evidence from Text** Use the information on this page to explain why it is silent in outer space.

_____

_____

*Quest* Connection

▼ ▼ ▼ ▼ ▼ ▼ ▼ ▼ ▼ ▼ ▼ ▼ ▼ ▼ ▼ ▼ ▼ ▼ ▼ ▼ ▼ ▼ ▼ ▼ ▼

How can you use waves to send a message across a room?

_____

_____

_____

## Wave Characteristics

INTERACTIVITY

Complete an activity about wave characteristics.

Wave characteristics depend on the vibration that causes the wave. For example, a hit from a drumstick causes a drum's surface to move back and forth. The drum's surface then pushes the air near it. This makes a sound wave in the air. The greatest height of a wave from its resting position is called its **amplitude**. In the drum example, the amplitude would be the greatest distance the surface travels away from its resting position. High amplitude sound waves are louder than low amplitude sound waves.

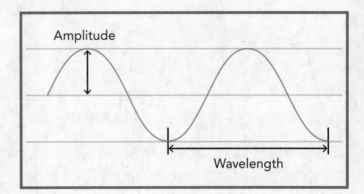

Scientists define **wavelength** as the distance between similar points on a wave. It can be measured from the lowest point of the wave to the next lowest point of the wave.

**Frequency** is the number of wave repetitions in a certain amount of time. If a drum head moves back and forth very quickly, it makes waves with higher frequency. The sound wave the drum makes will have the same frequency as the vibration of the drum head. High frequency sound waves have a higher pitch. The frequency of a wave is also connected to its length. More frequent waves will be shorter even if they are in the same medium.

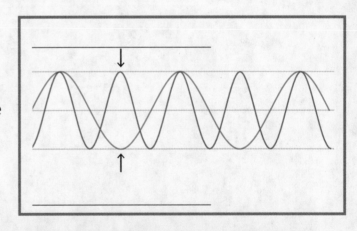

**Identify** Label the wave with higher frequency. Label the wave with lower frequency.

**Plan It!** We see lightning before we hear thunder. Write a plan to prove that light travels faster than sound through air.

_____

_____

_____

# How does a wave move?

Waves can cause particles to move in patterns that repeat. There are two patterns that describe oscillating wave movement.

A **transverse** wave is a wave that moves perpendicular to the direction of the particles. The energy of the wave moves perpendicular to the particles too.

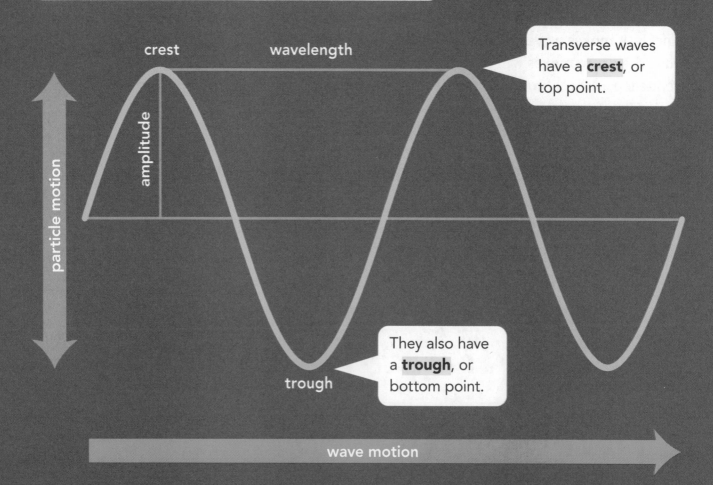

crest

wavelength

Transverse waves have a **crest**, or top point.

amplitude

particle motion

trough

They also have a **trough**, or bottom point.

wave motion

A **longitudinal** wave is one that moves in the same direction as the particles. Longitudinal waves compress and expand as they travel. It is easy to see the wave's energy move in a longitudinal wave.

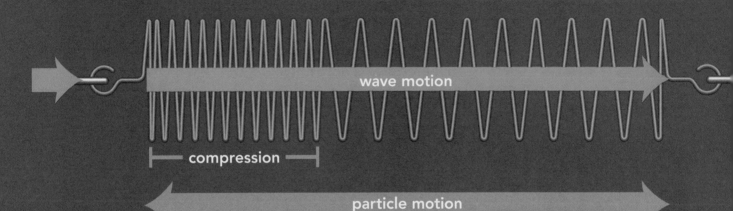

wave motion

compression

particle motion

wave motion (continued)

rarefaction — compression

particle motion

**Identify** Label the wavelength, amplitude, crest, and trough on this transverse wave.

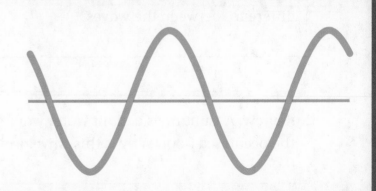

## Wave Energy

Waves are a transfer of energy. If you send a wave along a spring, you will see the coils of the spring move back and forth. The coils return to their original position after the wave has passed. The word **transfer** means "to relocate." Waves transfer energy through a medium but do not transfer the medium particles. This is why anchored boats only move up and down when waves pass under them. They are not pushed toward the shore.

The energy of a wave will spread out if the wave spreads out. You can see this happen when you toss a pebble into a pond. The wave gets smaller as it moves outward. Where did the energy go? The energy is still conserved, but it is spread out over a larger area. If you add up all of the energy when the wave makes a large circle, it will be the same as the energy when the wave first started.

**Predict** A diver jumps into a pool. What happens to the size of the waves as they spread through the pool?

_____

_____

_____

## Literacy ▸ Toolbox 🔧

**Use Evidence from Text**
When you read a claim, you can look for facts to support it. Find the evidence in the passage that supports this claim: Waves transfer energy through a medium, not into the individual particles.

## ✓ Lesson 1 Check

1. **Describe** A scientist compared two waves. One wave had more repetitions per second than the other. How would you describe the difference between the waves?

_____

_____

2. **Review** A tsunami is a giant water wave caused by an earthquake at the ocean sea floor. Why is this wave dangerous when it reaches land?

_____

_____

# Communicating Tent to Tent

CIA agents send and receive messages from all over the world. Waves are a good way to send messages. Suppose you and a friend are in tents that are far apart at a campground. It is nighttime, and others are sleeping. Loud noises or bright lights might wake them up. How can you and your friend communicate with each other?

What criteria (goals) and constraints (limits) do you and your friend have to keep in mind when communicating?

_____

_____

_____

_____

What are some ways you can send messages from tent to tent using waves?

_____

How will you be able to understand messages that you receive?

_____

_____

Do you think it will be easy or difficult to communicate this way? Explain your answer.

_____

_____

_____

# uEngineer It! Design STEM

**INTERACTIVITY**

Learn about different types of codes.

# Crack That Code!

**Phenomenon** A code is a system of signals or symbols that represent words or letters in communication. Codes have been part of secret communication for a long time. To understand a code, you must know what each symbol means. Coded messages must be decoded, or turned back into understandable language.

People who are blind use Braille code to read. Braille replaces letters and numbers with patterns of raised dots. Another well-known code is Morse code. Morse code uses dots and dashes. Unlike Braille code, Morse code messages can be sent by waves. A code that replaces a letter with a symbol is called a cipher. Braille and Morse code are ciphers. Ciphers are meant to be learned, but many other codes are not. Those codes help people communicate in secret.

**Interpret Diagrams** How would you write the word *code* in Morse code?

_____

English Braille Alphabet

A B C D E F G H I J
K L M N O P Q R S T
U V W X Y Z

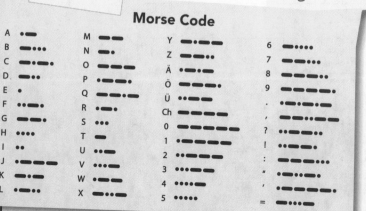
### Morse Code

# Design It

When you are designing a code, you need to consider how people will send, receive, and use it. For example, if a coded message must be sent a long distance, Morse code might be a better choice than Braille code. While Braille needs to be on a printed page, Morse code can be sent using waves.

Paul Revere and other American patriots designed a simple code to send a message from Boston to Charlestown, two towns separated by a wide river. Read about the purpose of the code and Paul Revere's design solution.

## Paul Revere's Clever Code

**Purpose of code** To send a secret message to patriots in Charlestown about how the British would travel to Concord (by land or sea)

**Solution** The code was sent using lights hung in the tall steeple of Boston's North Church.

1 lantern = British will arrive by land
2 lanterns = British will arrive by sea

**Design a Solution** One reason Paul Revere's code was successful was because it was simple. Develop a code to send a complex message using only ten characters or less. Explain your code, and then write the encoded message on the line.

**My code**

_____

_____

_____

_____

**My encoded message**

_____

_____

_____

# Patterns of Waves

**I can...**

Model waves using patterns in wave properties.

4-PS4-1

**Literacy Skill**
Use Evidence from Text

**Vocabulary**
wave period
circular wave
plane wave
superposition

**Academic Vocabulary**
appear

▶ **VIDEO**

Watch a video about patterns of waves.

## LOCAL-TO-GLOBAL ⟩ Connection

Have you ever wanted to hear your voice on the radio? You could use a ham radio. With a license and simple training, anybody can use this device. It can connect people as close as next door and as far away as another country. If you contact someone far away, you will need a big antenna in order to receive signals.

Ham radios use specific wave frequencies. Radio stations use other wave frequencies. Ham radio operators need a microphone, a tuner, and a speaker to hear other broadcasts. A ham radio can be very simple, or it can be complex and powerful. Getting involved in ham radio is a great way to meet people, and to learn some science!

**Describe** Who is one person you would contact with a ham radio? What would your radio need in order to reach that person?

_____

_____

_____

_____

# uInvestigate Lab

**HANDS-ON LAB**

4-PS4-1, SEP.2, SEP.6

**Materials**
- tray
- water
- ruler
- water dropper
- apron

# What patterns can waves make?

Scientists perform experiments to collect evidence and form conclusions. How can you use disturbances in water to gather evidence about wave patterns?

⚠ Wear safety apron.

**Science Practice**

Scientists **gather evidence** to construct an explanation.

## Procedure

☐ 1. Place the tray on a flat surface and pour water into it until it is about half full.

☐ 2. Use the materials to make two different wave patterns in the water.

| Wave 1 | Wave 2 |
|---|---|
| **Draw a model** <br> What wave pattern did you observe? | **Draw a model** <br> What wave pattern did you observe? |
| | |

## Analyze and Interpret Data

3. **SEP Construct an Explanation** Choose one of the wave patterns you observed. How do you think this pattern was made?

_____

_____

_____

_____

Lesson 2 Patterns of Waves    117

This swing is oscillating.

**ʋBe a Scientist**

**Ripples**

Pour water into a large bowl. When the water is still, tap the surface with your finger. How could you change the frequency of these water waves?

## Patterns in Wave Characteristics

The frequency, amplitude, and wavelength of waves follow a pattern. This means that they repeat, and they can be predicted. If you can observe the properties of part of a wave, you can figure out what the rest of the wave is doing. One important pattern in waves is that they can oscillate. When an object oscillates, it moves back and forth between two points like the swing you see here. Some other objects that oscillate are pendulums and rocking chairs. A **wave period** is the amount of time it takes for a wave to complete one back-and-forth motion.

Some wave patterns depend on each other. Remember that waves with high frequencies have shorter wavelengths. This makes sense because waves that occur less often have crests that are farther apart. This means that they are less frequent than waves that have a shorter wavelength.

**Write About It** Write a paragraph in your science notebook that compares the motion of a swing to an oscillating wave. Use vocabulary words from this lesson in your description.

## *Quest* Connection

How could you use sound wavelengths that are long and short to send a message?

_____

_____

_____

## Wave Patterns

In order for waves to **appear**, or show up, a disturbance must happen in a medium. Different disturbances cause waves with different patterns. For example, the woman in the photo has thrown a stone into the lake. Waves have formed at the point where the stone landed in the water. Multiple waves will spread out in all directions from the point, causing circles of waves. The circles get larger, but the distances between them stay the same. These waves that are caused by a disturbance at a single point are called **circular waves**.

If you push on the surface of the water with your hand, waves will form. The waves will move straight across the water in parallel lines from one location to another, not as a circle.

A **plane wave** is a wave that is made when a line of matter is disturbed. Plane waves move in parallel lines that travel in the same direction. Plane waves can look similar to stripes when viewed from above.

**☑ READING CHECK Use Evidence from Text** What wave pattern forms when someone skips rocks on the surface of a pond? Use evidence from the text to defend your answer.

_____

_____

_____

### Crosscutting Concepts ▸ Toolbox

**Patterns** Matter and energy interact to form wave patterns. How does matter affect wave patterns?

# How do Wave patterns move?

## Circular Wave

Circular waves transfer energy outward in a circular shape. Put an **X** where you think the source, or starting point, of the wave is.

one wavelength

Circular Wave wavelength measurement

_____

# Line Wave

A force acts on a line wave from the left. Draw an arrow for which direction the wave's energy would likely move.

|- - - - - - - - -| one wavelength

**Line Wave wavelength measurement**

_____

Both line waves and circular waves have wavelengths. The wavelengths are labeled on each wave. Use a ruler to measure and record the wavelengths of each.

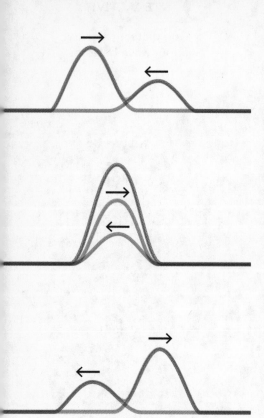

## Waves Can Combine

When more than one wave moves through a medium, they can meet. When this happens, the waves add together as they travel through each other. This is called **superposition**. When the crests of two waves meet, their two amplitudes add together. The wave is taller for a moment. When the crest of one wave meets an equal trough of another wave, the wave is destroyed briefly. An equal crest and trough cancel each other out, so the medium is still for a moment.

**Interpret Diagrams** How does the diagram provide evidence that waves travel through each other?

_____

_____

_____

_____

_____

## ✅ Lesson 2 Check

**1. Describe** Describe line waves and circular waves. How is each wave made?

_____

_____

_____

_____

_____

**2. Explain** How could two waves moving toward each other suddenly disappear?

_____

_____

# How can you send a message with sound?

Engineers come up with ways to transmit messages in different situations. How can you make a method of communication using only sound?

**Suggested Materials**
- musical instruments
- whistle

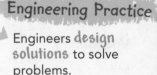

⚠ Be aware of physical safety.

## Design a Solution

☐ 1. Pick an object that makes a sound, or a sound that you can make that is easy to alter into a pattern. Describe which sound you will use.

_____

☐ 2. Design a communication system that uses only sound to send a coded message. Describe your system. Show your description to your teacher, and then use it to send a message.

**Engineering Practice**

Engineers **design solutions** to solve problems.

## Evaluate Your Solution

3. **Evaluate** Was your code easy to send and receive? Explain.

_____

_____

4. **SEP Analyze** How secure do you think a sound message is? Why?

_____

_____

5. **Infer** In what situations, or under what criteria, would using sound to communicate be better than using other methods?

_____

_____

# Waves and the Electromagnetic Spectrum

**I can...**

Model how light reflection allows objects to be seen.

4-PS4-2

**Literacy Skill**
Use Evidence from Text

**Vocabulary**
ray
reflect
refract
absorb

**Academic Vocabulary**
system

▶ **VIDEO**

Watch a video about waves and the electromagnetic spectrum.

## STEM Connection

Oxygen and water are common chemicals on Earth. Each planet has chemicals that are common on its surface. Other planets are too far away for scientists to collect samples of the gases, liquids, and solids that make them unique. Instead, scientists use light waves.

Some light from stars bounces off planets when it reaches them. The light that bounces off an object is called its spectrum. Planets also take in a lot of the light that hits them. Scientists understand how different materials take in light. By observing what light a planet takes in and what light bounces off the planet, scientists can identify a planet's chemicals. For example, even before scientists sent a space probe, they knew that the atmosphere of Mars was mostly carbon dioxide. Carbon dioxide takes in certain wavelengths of light.

📔 **Make Meaning** The pattern of light that bounces off a planet carries information. Scientists use this information to draw conclusions. What are some other ways light might be used to carry information? Write your ideas in your science notebook.

**Mars**

# How is light reflected?

Scientists study light to see how it moves and changes. How can you make a model to understand how light reacts when it hits a shiny surface?

## Procedure

☐ 1. **SEP Plan an Investigation** Use the materials to show how light moves and changes. Write a plan that includes taking measurements.

☐ 2. **SEP Carry Out an Investigation** Have your teacher approve your plan, and then conduct your investigation.

☐ 3. Draw a diagram of your observations. Be sure that it includes the measurements you took.

## Analyze and Interpret Data

4. **SEP Explain** Use evidence from your model to explain how light moves and changes when it hits a shiny surface.

_____

_____

_____

_____

**Materials**
- light source
- black construction paper
- white construction paper
- scissors
- tape
- mirror
- protractor
- string

⚠ Be careful using scissors.

⚠ Do not shine light toward eyes.

**Science Practice**

Scientists **develop models** to help explain natural processes.

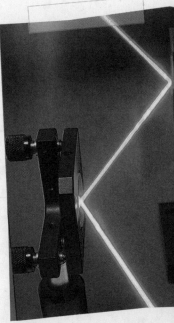

**Light Reflection**

Shine a flashlight or other light source at a smooth sheet of aluminum foil and watch it reflect. Now alter the foil by crumpling it into a ball and opening it up again. What does the light look like now when reflected off the foil? Explain why there is a difference.

## Properties of Light Waves

Light waves are a type of transverse wave. Light waves transfer energy, but they do not need a medium to travel through. Light can be modeled as traveling in rays. A **ray** is a line of energy that continues in one direction until it hits an object. Light rays can be reflected, refracted, or absorbed. When rays **reflect**, or bounce, off of a surface, they move in a new direction. Light rays bend, or **refract**, when they enter a new medium. The way light refracts depends on the type of matter it passes through. A prism is a geometric object that bends light. When white light refracts through a prism, it separates into different colors like those in the photo.

When light hits an object but is not reflected or bent, it is absorbed. To **absorb** means "to take in." Light that is absorbed by something is no longer visible.

**Explain** Why does black clothing get warmer than white clothing in sunlight?

_____

_____

## Quest Connection

The eye can see different colors. How could you use colors to make a pattern to be used as part of a code?

_____

_____

_____

## Seeing Objects

Light waves allow you to see objects. Light must reflect off an object before you can see it. The human eye works as a **system**, or a group of parts that work together as a whole. Some of the parts that make up the eye system are the pupil, the lens, and the retina. The pupil is the black hole in the center of the eye that lets light in. The pupil can move to let more or less light in. The lens is the part of the eye that bends and focuses light into images you can see. The retina is the part of the eye that receives the image from the lens. The retina sends electrical messages about light to your brain to be decoded.

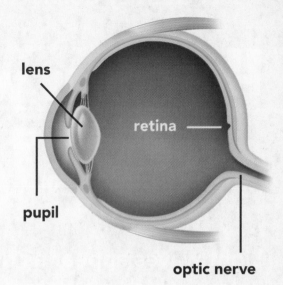

lens

retina

pupil

optic nerve

☑ READING CHECK **Use Evidence from Text** What evidence in the text shows that the eye is a system?

_____

_____

_____

**Design It!**

You are an engineer designing a machine that can recognize objects visually. Sketch a design of a system that shows all of the parts the machine will need. Show the path that light will take before the machine can recognize it.

# How does your eye see color?

Light waves appear as different colors, which are determined by their wavelengths.

Waves from a source of white light, such as the sun, contain all of the colors of the rainbow.

The color yellow is reflected off the banana.

retina

lens

The retina gathers the light that comes into your eye. Certain cells in the retina determine the differences between the wavelengths of light. The retina sends an electrical signal to the brain, which interprets the banana as yellow.

The optic nerve connects the eye to the brain.

optic nerve

**Draw** a second object that is a different color than the banana. Then draw the process of how your eye sees the color of that object.

**Angles** Light rays can hit objects at different angles. When something is perpendicular, it is at a 90-degree angle to a surface. Draw a light ray that is perpendicular to an object.

## Light and Matter

One property of matter is how much light can pass through it. Matter can be transparent, translucent, or opaque. Opaque matter lets no light through. An object that is translucent lets some light through, but not all light. An object that is transparent lets almost all light pass through, and you can see through it clearly. Whether matter is opaque, translucent, or transparent can depend on how much matter there is. Remember that light travels as waves. If a light wave does not interact with anything, it keeps moving. Solids are more likely to absorb light and be opaque. Particles in solids tend to be very close together. Matter with more space between particles, such as gases, tends to be translucent or transparent.

**Identify** A particular curtain makes a room completely dark when it is closed. How can you describe the curtain?

opaque

translucent

transparent

## Waves You Cannot See

The electromagnetic spectrum is a range of waves from tiny gamma rays to huge radio waves. The light we can see is only a small part of the electromagnetic spectrum. This includes wavelengths that make up the colors of the rainbow: red, orange, yellow, green, blue, indigo, and violet. Visible wavelengths are between 380 and 780 nanometers (one millimeter = 1 million nanometers). Humans cannot see electromagnetic waves outside this range. X-rays, microwaves, and radio waves are all invisible to humans.

**Infer** The high frequency of X-rays causes them to interact with matter. Some dense materials, such as bones, absorb more X-rays than the materials around them. This is why X-rays can be used to make images of bones while they are still inside people. Would X-rays be useful for sending messages long distances?

_____

_____

_____

**INTERACTIVITY**

Complete an activity about X-rays.

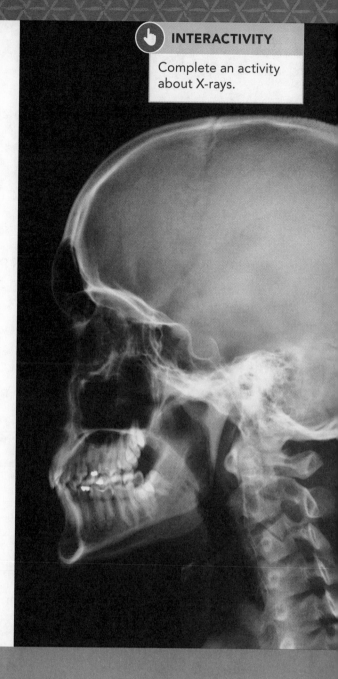

## ☑ Lesson 3 Check

**1. Review** Why does your eye see a banana as yellow?

_____

_____

_____

**2. Explain** Why are you not able to see objects in the dark?

_____

_____

_____

# How can you send a message with light?

Engineers develop ways to use light to communicate when sound will not work or travels too slowly. How can you make a pattern for communication using only light?

**Suggested Materials**

- flashlight
- lamp
- colored gels or cellophane
- cardboard

⚠ Be aware of physical safety.

⚠ Do not shine light toward eyes.

## Design Your Solution

☐ **1.** How can you use the materials to make a light pattern?

_____

_____

_____

_____

_____

### Engineering Practice

Engineers **design solutions** to solve problems.

☐ **2.** Construct a communication system that uses only white light to make a pattern. Describe your system. Show your plan to your teacher. Then test it by sending a short message to a partner.

_____

_____

_____

_____

_____

_____

_____

☐ 3. Construct a second communication system using light and color. Describe your system and show it to your teacher. After your teacher approves your plan, test your system.

_____

_____

_____

## Evaluate Your Solution

4. **Evaluate** Did your communication systems work well? Use your observations to support your claim.

_____

_____

5. **Evaluate and Revise** Compare your experiences with the second communication system with those of your classmates. How is your system different from others? How could you improve the system you came up with?

_____

_____

_____

_____

6. **Analyze** Think about the properties of light waves. What might interrupt your message?

_____

_____

_____

# Waves and Information

Demonstrate how high-tech devices use waves to send and receive information.

**4-PS4-3, 3-5-ETS1-2**

**Literacy Skill**
Use Evidence from Text

**Vocabulary**
signal
transmitter
antenna
receiver
digital
analog

**Academic Vocabulary**
range

▶ **VIDEO**

Watch a video about waves and information.

## CURRICULUM ⟩ Connection

Modern technology allows people to talk to someone on the other side of the planet in seconds. Long-distance communication used to be much harder. Smoke signals were one form of communication used in ancient times. Someone would build a fire, and smoke would billow into the sky. Then the person would cover and release the smoke in a pattern to signal other people. A mail service called The Pony Express began in the 1860s. It delivered letters by riders on horseback. Messages could travel farther, but they took days to arrive. In the 1890s, Guglielmo Marconi invented a wireless telegraph that sent messages using radio waves. This was the first time in history invisible waves sent messages across long distances. This increased the distance and speed of long-distance communication.

**Draw Conclusions** Why do you think Marconi built these towers?

_____

_____

# How can information from waves be translated?

**Materials**
• grid paper

Scientists and engineers code information to transmit it from one place to another. How can you use a grid to encode a wave?

**Science Practice**

Scientists design solutions to solve problems.

## Procedure

☐ **1.** Draw a transverse wave on the grid paper. Mark a horizontal center line on the wave.

☐ **2.** Write a code to tell someone how to draw your wave. Use the information on the grid paper to help you.

_____

_____

_____

_____

☐ **3.** Trade your code with another student. Using a new piece of grid paper, try to draw the other person's wave using only the code provided.

## Analyze and Interpret Data

**4. Evaluate** How well did your coding method work? Was your partner able to remake your wave? What could you change about your coding method to make it easier for them to remake?

_____

_____

_____

_____

_____

**Signal Finder**
Find a radio and tune it
to a channel with a weak
signal. Move the antenna
in different ways. Were
you able to get a stronger
signal? Why do you think
that is?

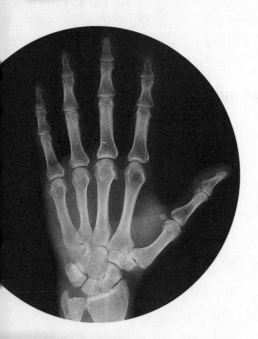

## Waves Outside the Visible Spectrum

A **range** includes all the possibilities between two
end points. The range of light wave frequencies that
humans can see is very limited. The range of light wave
frequencies we *cannot* see is much larger! People use these
invisible waves in many ways. X-ray waves have a very
short wavelength. They are used to photograph bones.
Microwaves, which have longer wavelengths, are used to
heat food. Radio waves are very useful for communication.
Radio waves can send a **signal**, or a message with
information. Radio waves carry signals from radio and
television stations, cell phones, and Internet satellites.

**Identify** What are some signals that you can receive or
send yourself?

_____

_____

_____

## Radio Waves

Many devices use radio frequency signals to do different
things. All of those devices include similar parts that work
as a system. First, a signal must travel from one device to
another. The **transmitter** is the part of a device that sends
out radio signals. The **antenna** is the part of a device that
takes in the radio waves. The **receiver** then converts the
radio waves into a usable message. Receivers turn signals
into music, images, or data to make web pages.

☑ READING CHECK **Use Evidence from Text**
Summarize the evidence that supports the claim that a
radio is a system.

_____

_____

_____

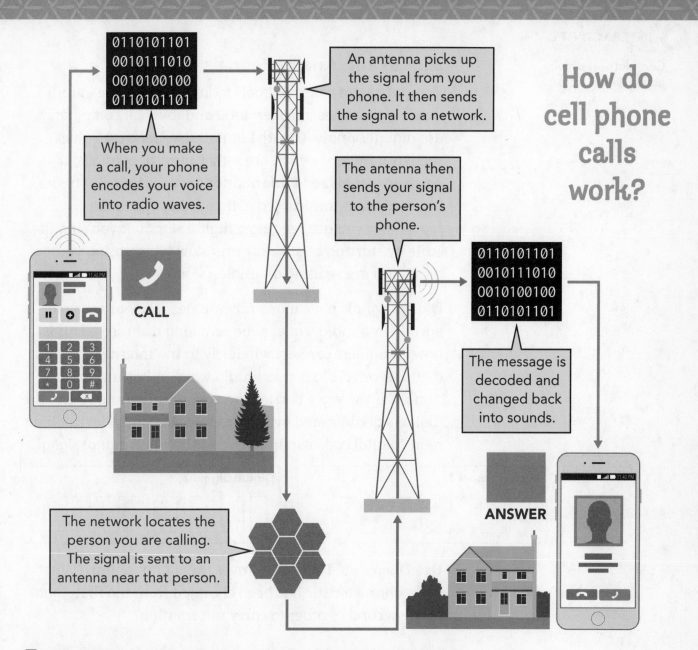

# How do cell phone calls work?

When you make a call, your phone encodes your voice into radio waves.

An antenna picks up the signal from your phone. It then sends the signal to a network.

The antenna then sends your signal to the person's phone.

The message is decoded and changed back into sounds.

The network locates the person you are calling. The signal is sent to an antenna near that person.

CALL

ANSWER

0110101101
0010111010
0010100100
0110101101

0110101101
0010111010
0010100100
0110101101

📓 **Write About It** Satellite phones are used in places without cell phone antennas. This technology would not be possible without radio waves or other electromagnetic waves. Find out more about satellite phones to understand why this is true. Write a summary of what you learn in your science notebook.

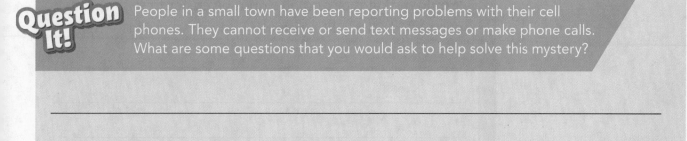

**Question It!** People in a small town have been reporting problems with their cell phones. They cannot receive or send text messages or make phone calls. What are some questions that you would ask to help solve this mystery?

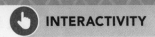
## Digital and Analog Signals

Computers are common tools today. They can be found inside cell phones, refrigerators, and toys. All computers use digital signals. **Digital** signals use clear-cut values such as numbers, which are sometimes called digits. **Analog** signals send information in a continuous stream. Think about a musical scale. If you sing each note separately, you are sending a digital signal. If you sing the scale by starting at one note and slowly increasing your pitch, you are sending an analog signal.

Digital signals have many advantages. They are easy to encode into radio waves to be sent long distances. This is how computers connect wirelessly to the Internet. They use digital receivers to convert radio wave pulses into digital signals. If the wave carries encoded information, so will the digital signal formed by the receiver. Also, any device that reads digital code can understand the same digital signal.

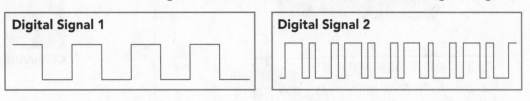

**Use Diagrams** These two waves are digital signals. What wave characteristic has been changed from the first signal to the second in order to carry information?

_____

## Quest Connection

Would a digital or analog signal be easier to send through a crowded, dimly lit museum? Explain your reasoning.

_____

_____

_____

## Technology Mimics Life

Think about the communication technologies discussed in this topic. Can you think of ways that they are similar to human systems? A good comparison would be our eyes and ears. Our ears and eyes collect different kinds of waves. Specific parts of those organs pick up the signals. Then the signals are decoded by our brains. When we speak, we broadcast wave signals to the world. Technology extends the range of our ability to detect waves.

**Apply Concepts** How is a microphone similar to an ear?

_____

_____

## Engineering Practices ▸ Toolbox

**Design Solutions** When engineers design solutions, they use ideas from many different sources. Designing machines based on life forms is called *biomimicry*. How can engineers use life forms to help them design wave technology?

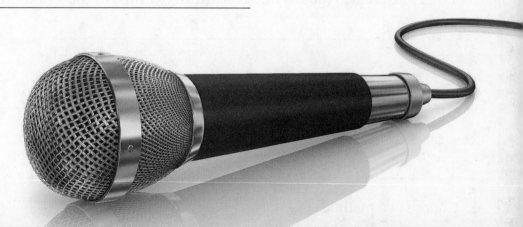

## ☑ Lesson 4 Check

1. **Describe** What are three necessary parts of a radio communication system?

_____

_____

2. **Apply Concepts** Morse code uses dots and dashes to communicate information. Could Morse code be sent easily as a digital signal? Explain your answer.

_____

_____

_____

# Compare Codes

As an intelligence analyst, I often have to choose how to communicate in a given situation. Every situation is different, so which type of communication works best will change. Compare and contrast the different communication methods you have explored based on how they fit the situation in the movie.

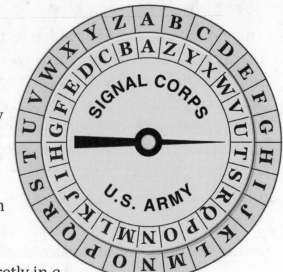

1. In the spy movie, the kids have to communicate secretly in a dimly lit museum full of visitors. One visitor might be the thief! List some criteria (goals) and constraints (limits) of the situation.

_____

_____

_____

_____

2. Choose two methods of communication that you have developed during the Quest. Make a chart that describes how each method of communication would work or fail under the given criteria.

3. Choose one method to improve. How could you change this method to work even better under the criteria and constraints of the situation?

_____

_____

_____

# Why are antennas tall?

**Phenomenon** Transmitters and receivers need antennas. You may have seen antennas placed on tall metal structures around where you live. Why do you think antennas are placed on tall structures? A good way to answer this question is to gather what you know and then make a science-based claim.

What are some uses for radio waves?

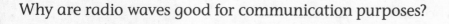

_____

_____

_____

Why are radio waves good for communication purposes?

_____

_____

_____

Radio waves travel faster through air than they do through solid materials. What might make radio communication faster?

_____

_____

_____

**Solve It with Science** Make a science-based claim that answers the question "Why are antennas tall?"

_____

_____

_____

## STEM ▸ Be a Message Master!

*How can information be sent securely?*

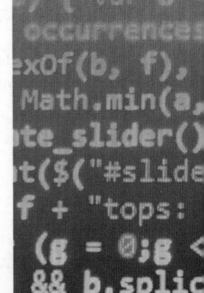

**Phenomenon** Lights, camera, action! It is time to complete the Quest! The movie director needs to know how the young spies will communicate. Explain your secret communication method and demonstrate how it works.

### Describe Your Method

Explain how your code will work and how you will communicate it.

_____

_____

_____

_____

_____

_____

_____

Show your method to a classmate. Work together to send and receive a coded message.

# Intelligence Analyst

An intelligence analyst is an expert who looks at data. Intelligence analysts gather a lot of knowledge about a specific subject. They use their knowledge to help understand new information and to make predictions. One major place that intelligence analysts work is the CIA, or Central Intelligence Agency. At the CIA, analysts prepare reports to tell the government officials if there are threats to national security. Their job requires them to keep secrets necessary to protect the United States.

Intelligence analysts should be skilled at collecting and interpreting data. They need to be able to see patterns in information, solve codes, and understand world events. They also need to be able to communicate with people all over the world. It helps if analysts know several languages. Finally, intelligence analysts need to be willing for much of their work to be kept secret.

**📓 Write About It**
In your science notebook, describe how you could build the skills needed to be an intelligence analyst.

**1. Identify** Name each labeled part of the wave.

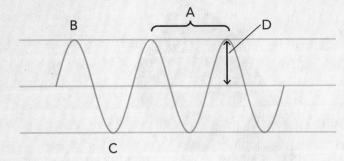

A. _____

B. _____

C. _____

D. _____

**2. Review** What are the characteristics of a digital signal?

_____

_____

_____

_____

_____

_____

_____

_____

_____

**3. Apply Concepts** Isaac is looking at a red apple on an apple tree. Which of these choices explains why the apple is red?

A. White light hits the object, and red light is reflected into your eye.

B. White light hits the object, and red light is absorbed into the object.

C. Red light hits the object, and white light is reflected into your eye.

D. Red light hits the object, and red light is reflected into your eye.

**4. Vocabulary** Which is **not** involved in radio wave communication?

A. transmitter

B. signal

C. receiver

D. lens

**5. Summarize** Describe the structures of the eye that help you see objects.

_____

_____

_____

_____

_____

_____

**6. Develop a Model** Draw a diagram that shows how light rays from the sun allow you to see an object.

**7. Identify** A sound wave compresses particles in the same direction as the wave is moving. What kind of wave is a sound wave?

_____

_____

_____

_____

**8. Explain** What are two properties of waves, and how can they change?

_____

_____

_____

_____

_____

_____

**The Essential Question** *How do we use waves to communicate?*

## Show What You Learned

Explain three ways people use waves to communicate. Give an example of when each communication method could be used.

_____

_____

_____

_____

_____

_____

_____

_____

_____

Read this scenario and answer questions 1–5.

Small groups of cells send out electrical pulses to make your heart beat. These pulses happen over and over. They also carry energy. This means that the electrical signals sent through your heart can be described by waves. When doctors want to see if a person's heart is beating normally, they measure the electrical waves using an EKG machine. They place several electrodes from the machine on the person's chest. The electrodes receive the signal sent out by the heart. The EKG machine records the wave pattern on a grid. Doctors compare the EKG pattern from a patient to a normal heartbeat pattern to see if they match. Here are several EKG wave patterns.

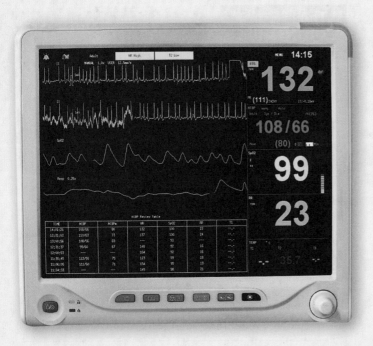

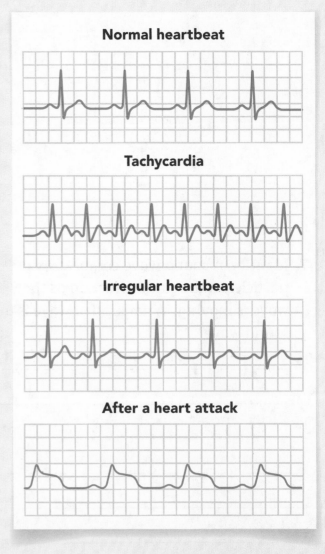

Normal heartbeat

Tachycardia

Irregular heartbeat

After a heart attack

1. **Interpret Graphs** What changes occur to the electrical signal sent through a person's heart when he or she has the heart condition tachycardia?

   A. Its wavelength increases.

   B. Its amplitude increases.

   C. Its frequency increases.

   D. It does not change.

**2. Use Evidence** After a heart attack, a person's heartbeat is very weak, very slow, and often irregular. What evidence in the post-heart-attack EKG points to these symptoms?

_____

_____

_____

**3. Classify** Are the EKG machine electrodes a type of antenna? Why or why not?

_____

_____

_____

**4. Develop a Model** Draw a model to represent the electrical signal of a person who is suffering from a slow heartbeat.

_____

**5. Explain** Some hospital patients are hooked up to an EKG machine continuously. Doctors can read their heart signal on a computer screen. The screen shows information in different colors to help doctors find the information they need quickly. How does the screen use waves to encode information in different colors?

_____

_____

_____

# How can you model a light or sound wave?

**Suggested Materials**
- string
- rope
- toy spring
- tape

**Phenomenon** Scientists analyze light, sound, and other types of waves. How can you make a model that represents a light or sound wave?

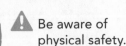

## Procedure

☐ **1.** Decide whether to model a light wave or a sound wave and write your choice.

_____

⚠ Be aware of physical safety.

☐ **2.** Decide which materials would be best to make your wave model. Write a plan to build your model wave.

_____

_____

_____

**Science Practice**

Scientists **develop models** to describe natural processes.

☐ **3.** Show your plan to your teacher. Once you have approval, model the type of wave you chose. Record the wave properties you can observe in your model.

### Observations

# Analyze and Interpret Data

**4.** Draw a diagram of your model. Label the parts of the diagram that show the properties you observed.

**5. Compare and Contrast** What are two ways your wave model is similar to the wave you are trying to represent? What are two ways your wave model is different?

_____

_____

_____

_____

_____

_____

_____

_____

# Earth's Features

**Next Generation Science Standards**

**4-ESS2-1** Make observations and/or measurements to provide evidence of the effects of weathering or the rate of erosion by water, ice, wind, or vegetation.

**4-ESS2-2** Analyze and interpret data from maps to describe patterns of Earth's features.

**3-5-ETS1-1** Define a simple design problem reflecting a need or a want that includes specified criteria for success and constraints on materials, time, or cost.

Go online to access
your digital course.

▶ VIDEO

📖 eTEXT

👆 INTERACTIVITY

📱 VIRTUAL LAB

🎮 GAME

☑ ASSESSMENT

# The Essential Question

## How can you use maps to understand Earth's features?

**Show What You Know**

The movement of water shapes landforms over millions of years. If you were drawing a map of this area, how would you show the features seen here?

_____

_____

# Does ✖ Mark the Spot? That's Up to You!

## How can we use Earth processes to find buried treasure?

**Phenomenon** Hello! I am Salena Patrick, a geologist. I am an expert on landforms. I recently found a bottle with a map inside that shows there are hidden treasures buried deep within three land areas. There was also a clue that says the treasures are buried in locations that will one day be exposed through changes in Earth's surface.

In this problem-based learning activity, you will study maps, build landform models, test how those landforms may change over time, search for treasure, and present your findings.

Follow the path to discover what you need to do to complete the Quest. The Quest Check-In activities will help you complete the Quest. You can check off every step you complete with a QUEST CHECK ✓ OFF. Go online for more Quest activities.

## Quest Check-In 1

### Lesson 1
Learn how to read different types of maps. Find out how understanding parts of maps will help you locate the buried treasure.

## Quest Check-In 2

### Lesson 2
Learn about the patterns of some landforms, where they occur, and how they are made.

**Next Generation Science Standards**

**4-ESS2-1** Make observations and/or measurements to provide evidence of the effects of weathering or the rate of erosion by water, ice, wind, or vegetation.

**4-ESS2-2** Analyze and interpret data from maps to describe patterns of Earth's features.

## Quest Check-In Lab 4

### Lesson 4

See how the effects of weathering and erosion shape landforms. Learn how these processes can help you find the treasure.

## Quest Check-In Lab 3

### Lesson 3

Discover how rocks, minerals, and soil form and how they create Earth's landforms.

## Quest Findings

Use what you have learned about maps, models, and Earth's features to describe changes your landform underwent and how you discovered the treasure.

# uConnect Lab

# How can rain affect land?

When geologists investigate landforms, they want to know how the feature formed. How can you model changes that rain causes in landforms?

## Procedure

☐ **1.** How will different amounts of rain affect differently sized soil mounds? Write your prediction.

_____

_____

☐ **2.** Set up your "land" in the milk jug. Carefully, turn each cup upside down in the jug. Jiggle the cups to release the mounds of dirt.

☐ **3.** Make a plan to test your prediction. Write your plan. Show it to your teacher before you begin. Record your observations.

## Analyze and Interpret Data

**4. SEP Use Evidence** How can rain affect land? Write your conclusions based on the evidence from your investigation.

_____

_____

_____

_____

_____

_____

_____

**Materials**
- bottom half of a gallon milk jug
- 3 plastic cups with different amounts of soil
- water

**Suggested Materials**
- watering can
- metric ruler
- graduated cylinder
- plastic spoon

**Science Practice**

Scientists **investigate** to provide evidence that supports scientific ideas.

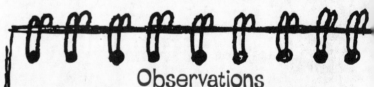

## Observations

|  | Water amount #1 | Water amount #2 |
|---|---|---|
| Small mound |  |  |
| Medium mound |  |  |
| Large mound |  |  |

# Draw Conclusions

One important reading skill is drawing conclusions. It is like playing a mystery game. Here's how you do it.

**GAME**

Practice what you learn with the Mini Games.

- Collect clues when reading by finding important information.
- Underline the clues as you read them.
- Use the clues to understand what the text means.

Read the following passage to find out why engineers moved a whole lighthouse.

## Lighthouse on the Move

Cape Hatteras sticks out into the Atlantic Ocean from the coast of North Carolina. In 1870, people put up a lighthouse at the tip of the cape to help ships avoid running into it. The lighthouse stood 1,000 meters from the shore. Over the years, powerful storms and constant waves wore away the coastline. By the 1990s, the lighthouse was almost surrounded by water. The lighthouse needed to be moved. The National Park Service built a base in a new spot and moved the lighthouse to it in one piece. Engineers raised the lighthouse onto a moving platform. Slowly, the lighthouse made the trip to its new, safe location. On November 13, 1999, the lighthouse lit up again. Today, its beacon continues to keep ships safe at sea.

✓READING CHECK **Draw Conclusions** The lighthouse is currently 488 meters from the ocean. Draw a conclusion about how far the lighthouse may be from the ocean in 100 years.

_____

_____

_____

# Maps and Data

## I can...

Read maps to identify and compare Earth's surface features.
**4-ESS2-2**

**Literacy Skill**
Draw Conclusions

**Vocabulary**
symbol
legend
compass rose

**Academic Vocabulary**
features

▶ **VIDEO**

Watch a video about maps and data.

## SPORTS ⟩ Connection

If you run on a school track, getting lost is difficult. You just go around and around. On a cross-country race, getting lost can be a serious problem. Race organizers solve this problem by printing a map of the course. The map shows the path the race follows and the finish line. It also shows checkpoints and places to stop for water. Whether for a cross-country race or a cross-the-country vacation, maps are the tools that get you from here to there and back again!

**Apply** Look at the features on the map. How can this map help runners observe such a large park on a small sheet of paper?

_____

_____

# How do tools help us?

Geologists sometimes use tools to find their way in unfamiliar places. New students at a school also must find their way in an unfamiliar place. What are two different ways you could help new students at your school find their way around the school—to the gym, the playground, the cafeteria, the library, and even the principal's office?

**Science Practice**

Scientists analyze and interpret data to make sense of phenomena using logical reasoning.

## Procedure

☐ **1.** Think of two different tools to help new students find their way around your school. Write your ideas.

_____

_____

☐ **2.** How could you test your tools?

_____

_____

_____

_____

☐ **3.** With your teacher's permission, test your tools. Record your data.

_____

_____

## Analyze and Interpret Data

**4. SEP Evaluate** Based on your data, which tool is most useful? How could you change it to make it more useful?

_____

_____

_____

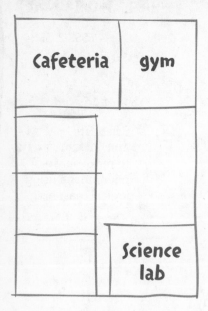

Cafeteria | gym

Science lab

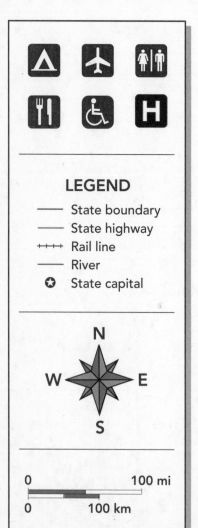

LEGEND

—— State boundary
—— State highway
++++ Rail line
—— River
✪ State capital

N
W E
S

0                    100 mi
0            100 km

## Read a Map

The map shows the rooms in a school. For a map to be useful, it must have enough information. For example, a school map could include the location of the gym, cafeteria, and science lab.

Maps often have a legend, symbols, a compass rose, or a map scale.

- **Symbols** are small pictures, letters, lines, or colors that appear on a map. They should need little or no explanation. Draw a box around the symbols.
- A **legend**, or key, tells what map symbols stand for.
- A **compass rose** shows the directions north (N), east (E), south (S), and west (W). It is placed on the map with N pointing toward north.
- A map scale shows the distance a map covers. The scale on a map of a large area would be in miles or kilometers. A scale of a room would be in feet or meters. Circle the map scale.

☑ READING CHECK **Draw Conclusions** How would a map scale be useful?

_____

_____

# Quest Connection

▼▼▼▼▼▼▼▼▼▼▼▼▼▼▼▼▼▼▼▼▼▼▼▼▼▼▼

**Draw** What might you include in a legend if you were making a map of an area that has both mountains and coastlines? Draw your map legend.

## Types of Maps

A physical map shows an area's natural physical features, such as hills, valleys, rivers, lakes, waterfalls, and bays—usually by using different colors. A **feature** is a characteristic or part of something. In the map of the United States, several larger rivers are shown with blue lines. Water is usually shown as blue. The brown and darker green colors show areas where the land is higher, such as hills and mountains. The lighter green colors show areas that are flatter, such as plains.

**Apply** Circle part of the map where there are mountains. Put a box around where there are plains.

A political map shows countries, states, and cities. Capital cities on political maps are often marked with a star. Road maps show roads and highways in an area. Roads can be drawn using different colors or types of lines to show different kinds of roads. Road maps need to be changed when new roads are built or when old ones are closed.

Most of today's maps are drawn using information collected by space satellites. GPS, or the Global Positioning System, constantly sends out signals that a device uses to pinpoint almost exactly where it is.

**Science Practice**
► **Toolbox**

**Construct Explanations**
Scientists use reliable sources of information to make an explanation. How does technology help you observe large and small areas to gather information?

# How can you see the same place in different ways?

These maps are all maps of San Francisco. Each map shows different information. Look at each map and see what information it includes.

**Street Map** Use a marker to trace the most direct route to go from Daly City to the bridge that crosses the San Francisco Bay.

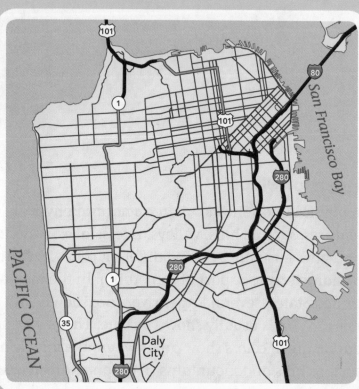

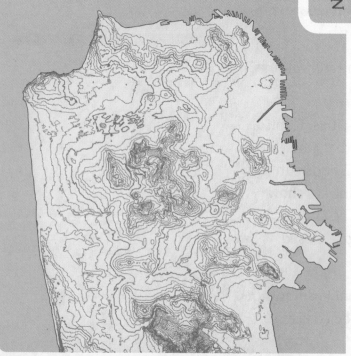

**Topographic Map** This map shows the land surface of San Francisco using contour lines. Contour lines that are closer together show steeper land. Contour lines farther apart show flatter land. Circle one of the highest points in San Francisco. Is San Francisco flat or hilly? How do you know?

_____

_____

_____

_____

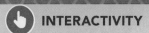

## Satellite Map A satellite
map shows an image of a place
taken from a satellite. Map features,
such as roads, are highlighted on
the satellite image. Describe how
a satellite map is different from the
other maps.

_____

_____

_____

_____

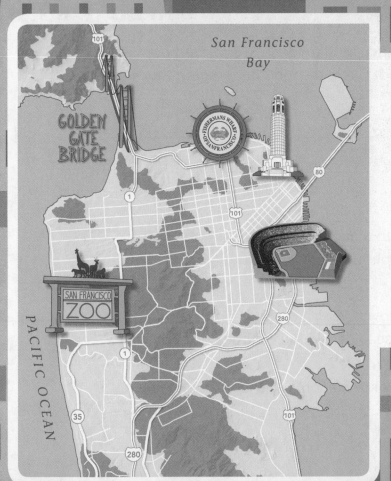

## Local Attractions Map
What types of attractions are there to
see in San Francisco?

_____

_____

_____

_____

_____

## Literacy ▸ Toolbox

**Draw Conclusions** You draw a conclusion when you make a statement that summarizes what you think specific a collection of data or observations means. What conclusions can you draw about growing vegetables in Virginia?

## Resource Maps

Resource maps show what can be produced in or taken from an area. They may feature natural resources, such as forests, animals, plants, coal, silver, and gold. Resource maps could also show items made in the state or energy produced there. This map shows crops and livestock in Virginia.

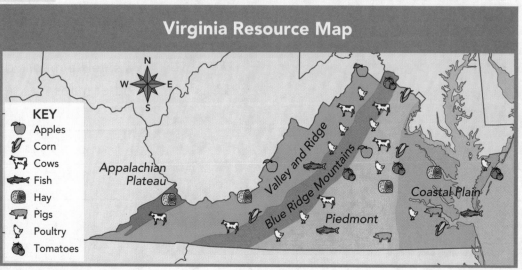

## ☑ Lesson 1 Check

1. **Analyze** Use the Virginia Resource Map to identify and compare where cows and pigs are farmed. Circle the tools on the map that were most useful.

_____

_____

_____

2. Jake finds a 100-year-old map in a book. He thinks it is a map of Elmdale, where he lives. Jake does not see many roads or other places he knows on the map.

Jake gets a current map of his town. Which of these features normally marked on a map could Jake use to determine whether both maps are of Elmdale? Circle all that apply.

Elm Lake                Elmdale Police Station        Duncan Creek

Burdock Swamp        Hubbard's Hill                Hendricks Public Library

Maple Lane Park      Rickard Canyon              Bell's Farm

# Quest Check-In

# The Making of a Legend

The Quest map in the bottle shows different areas of land. You will need to use symbols to represent land areas shown on the map. The drawing shows the area where the hidden treasures are buried.

1. Draw a physical map to show what this area would look like if you were looking at it from directly above. Include a legend with your map.

2. Place a star on the map next to the three areas where you think the treasures might be buried.

3. Suppose you gave your legend to some friends who did not have the map. How would the legend help them understand the kinds of features that are on the map?

_____

_____

_____

_____

_____

# uEngineer It! Design STEM

**INTERACTIVITY**

Go online to determine criteria for building a bridge across a canyon.

# Take a Hike!

**Phenomenon** Desert terrain can be extremely difficult to cross. The desert is very dry and often very hot during the day. The temperature can become very cold at night or at certain times of the year. High winds can produce sandstorms.

Deserts are very sandy or rocky, so building on them is also difficult. Sandy soil tends to collapse over time. A road built on sand will crumble much faster than one built on more solid ground. Engineers must develop unique solutions to build any kind of structure in a desert.

A popular desert park wants to open a new hiking trail for visitors. The trail will bring visitors over difficult terrain to see some unique desert features. The engineers who will build the trail must come up with some unique solutions. The trail must be easy to walk on. It must also be built without disturbing the environment too much.

# Design It

The design team at the park has asked for your help in designing the desert trail. They want the trail to be made of natural materials that can withstand both the extreme heat and cold. The materials should be relatively inexpensive. The trail should blend in with the surrounding environment so that it does not disturb the view of the desert.

☐ **1. Identify** What are the criteria for the trail?

_____

_____

_____

☐ **2. Identify** What are the constraints?

_____

_____

_____

☐ **3. Choose** What materials would you use to build the trail?

_____

_____

**4. Design** Draw a design for a sample section of your hiking trail. Be sure to include labels on features of your trail that will help it meet the criteria for success.

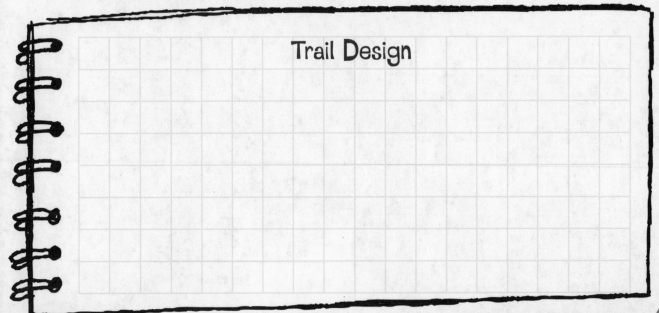

Trail Design

# Patterns of Earth's Features

**I can...**

Identify patterns in Earth's surface features.

**4-ESS2-2**

**Literacy Skill**
Draw Conclusions

**Vocabulary**

canyon
butte
fault
trench

**Academic Vocabulary**

patterns

▶ **VIDEO**

Watch a video about patterns of Earth's features.

## ENGINEERING ▷ Connection

Can you imagine how different your life would be if you only had limited electricity? Some places might face that situation if dams were not built. The water that moves through dams can be used to make electricity. In that way, a dam is good for most people. But dams can also change Earth's features. When water approaches a dam, it slows. As a result, the sediments—bits of rock and other materials—that the water carries settle here. The buildup of sediment before the dam can change the water's flow. In this way, the path of the river can change.

📓 **Write About It** What effects do you think might occur if a river's path changes?

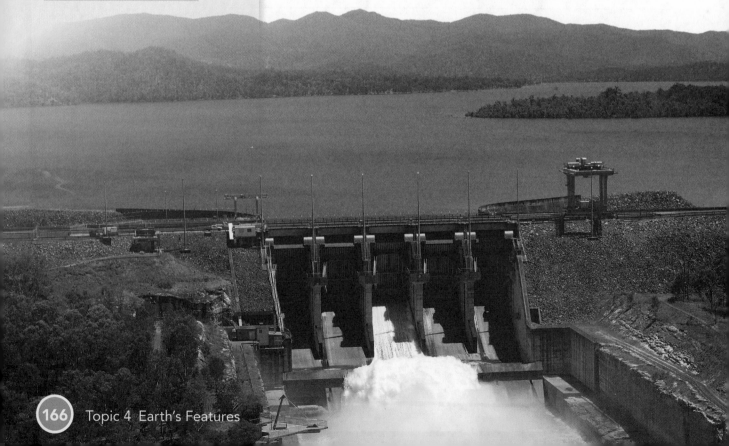

# uInvestigate Lab

# Where are major landforms?

**Materials**
- 2 rectangular sponges

Geologists study how huge pieces of Earth's surface, called plates, move. How can you model the movement of these plates?

**Science Practice**

Scientists use models to develop explanations.

## Procedure

☐ **1.** Predict how Earth's plates and landforms are related.

_____

_____

☐ **2. SEP Use Models** Use the sponges to model how plates might interact. Draw three diagrams to show different ways you can make the sponges interact. Use arrows to show how the sponges moved.

## Analyze and Interpret Data

**3. SEP Draw Conclusions** What conclusions can you make about the movement of Earth's plates and how they shape landforms? Explain your ideas.

_____

_____

**INTERACTIVITY**

Complete an activity about landforms.

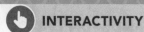

## Science Practice
▶ Toolbox

**Cite Evidence** The movement of Earth's plates causes volcanoes to appear. What evidence suggests that it is the movement of Earth's plates that causes volcanoes to form?

## Patterns of Mountains

Mountains are a type of landform found on Earth's surface. Mountain ranges are lines of mountains connected by high ground. **Canyons**, found in mountain ranges, are deep, narrow areas surrounded by a mountain's steep sides. Another landform, a **butte**, is a single hill that has steep sides and a flat top. A plateau is a large area of raised flat land that extends over a great distance. Cliffs are steep rock faces at the edge of a body of water.

Geologists study mountains because they are one kind of landform that occurs in pattterns across Earth's surface. A **pattern** is something that appears or occurs again and again in the same way. For example, mountains and volcanoes are common along the edges of Earth's plates. Earth's surface is divided into these plates, which are made up of rock. The plates move up and down and sideways. As the plates crash together, mountains and volcanoes form.

**☑ READING CHECK Draw Conclusions** Discuss with a partner how you think the Himalaya, a mountain range, formed.

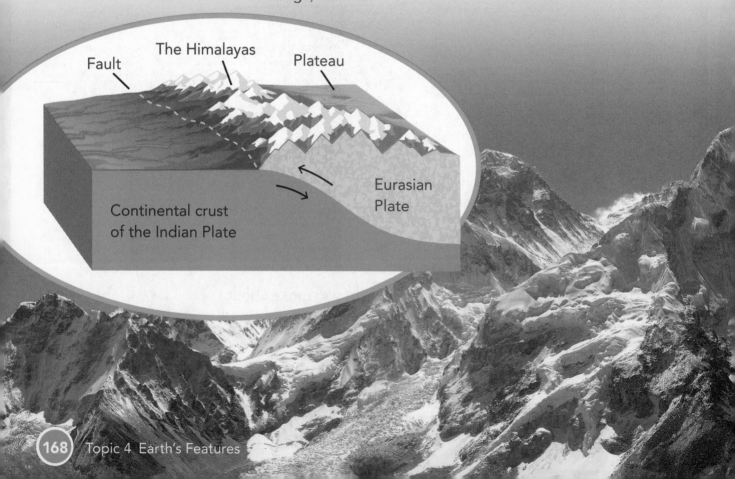

Fault

The Himalayas

Plateau

Continental crust of the Indian Plate

Eurasian Plate

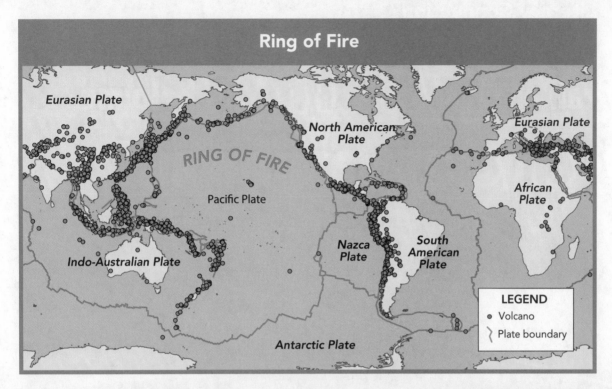

## Ring of Fire

**Eurasian Plate**

**North American Plate**

**RING OF FIRE**

**Eurasian Plate**

**African Plate**

**Pacific Plate**

**Indo-Australian Plate**

**Nazca Plate**

**South American Plate**

**Antarctic Plate**

**LEGEND**
- Volcano
- Plate boundary

## Patterns of Earthquakes and Volcanoes

Patterns of earthquake activity and volcanoes are closely related. Both occur along **faults**, or cracks in Earth's crust. Large faults often occur at plate boundaries. Smaller faults can occur in the middle of plates. Both earthquakes and volcanoes are the result of plates moving along these faults. Volcanoes form at places where magma, or molten rock, reaches Earth's surface. Volcanoes and earthquakes are common along a section of Earth called the Ring of Fire, which is the plate boundaries surrounding the Pacific Ocean.

### Crosscutting Concepts ▸ Toolbox

**Patterns** Finding patterns helps scientists to organize and classify. Analyze the Ring of Fire map. Describe a pattern of Earth's features the map shows.

## Quest Connection

How do the features of a mountain differ from the features of a plateau?

_____

_____

_____

# How can a physical map help me locate different landforms?

Appalachian Mountains

Coastal Plain

Mid-Atlantic Ridge

Physical maps show the shape of landforms.

! Describe how to use the map scale.

## LEGEND

| Feet | Meters |
|---|---|
| 8,200 | 2,500 |
| 4,000 | 1,220 |
| 100 | 30 |
| -1,000 | -305 |
| -4,000 | -1,220 |
| -8,000 | -2,440 |

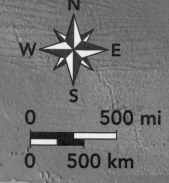

N
W E
S

0        500 mi

0        500 km

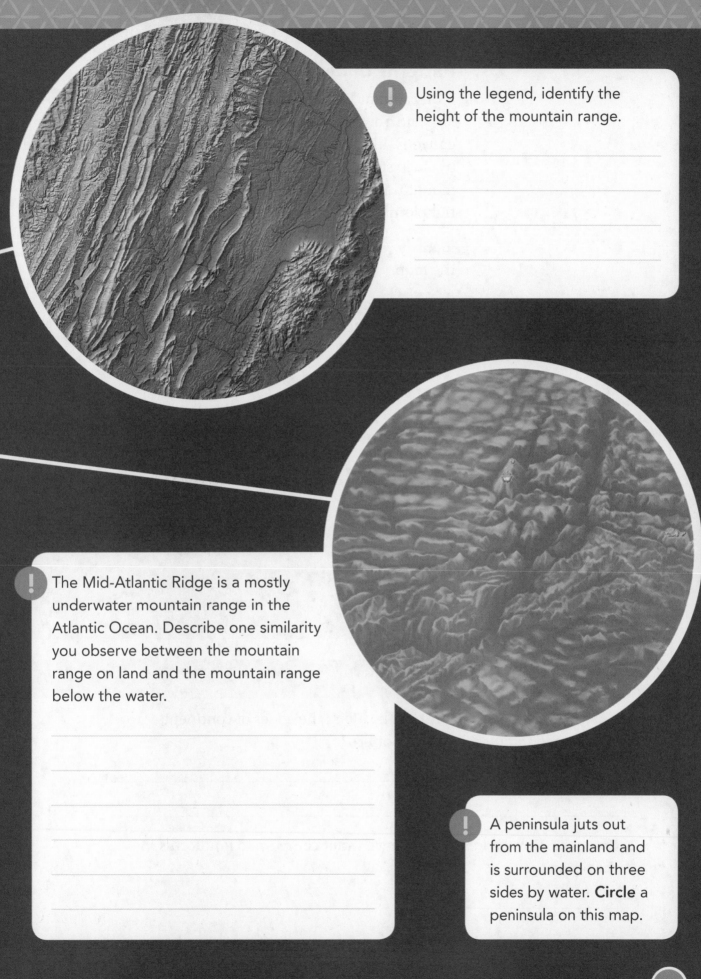

! Using the legend, identify the height of the mountain range.

_____
_____
_____
_____
_____

! The Mid-Atlantic Ridge is a mostly underwater mountain range in the Atlantic Ocean. Describe one similarity you observe between the mountain range on land and the mountain range below the water.

_____
_____
_____
_____
_____
_____

! A peninsula juts out from the mainland and is surrounded on three sides by water. **Circle** a peninsula on this map.

## Patterns Under the Ocean

Many similar landforms lie under the oceans. **Trenches** are long, narrow, sunken areas in the ocean floor. Underwater canyons, like those above ground, are low areas surrounded by steep sides. Seafloors have ridges, which are like mountain ranges, and broad basins, which are like large, flat plains.

**Identify** Circle each kind of feature in a different color on the map.

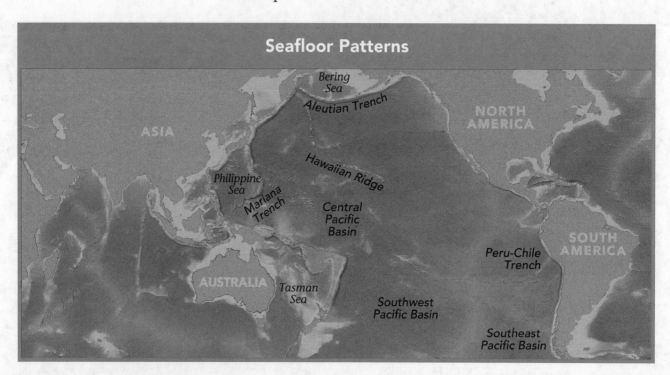

Seafloor Patterns

## ☑ Lesson 2 Check

1. **Analyze** Most mountain ranges lie along the edges of continents. Why do mountains follow this pattern?

_____

_____

2. **Compare** How do landforms above water compare to landforms in the ocean?

_____

_____

# A Changing Landscape

The Quest map in the bottle showed many landforms, including mountains, plateaus, and cliffs along the coast. Think about the features and patterns of these landforms.

1. Draw and label each landform in a space below.

2. **Compare and Contrast** How are these three landforms different?

_____

_____

_____

_____

# Rocks, Minerals, and Soil

## I can...

Describe how rocks and soil form.
Identify the properties of minerals.

**4-ESS2-1**

**Literacy Skill**
Draw Conclusions

**Vocabulary**
igneous
sedimentary
metamorphic

**Academic Vocabulary**
characteristic

▶ **VIDEO**

Watch a video about rocks, minerals, and soil.

## ENGINEERING ▶ Connection

Can you see any rocks in the glass that makes up the windows of your home or school? Engineers often use rocks or minerals for developing products. You may be surprised to learn how many things that you use every day are made using these resources. Computers, cell phones, television sets, microwave ovens, and toasters contain materials made from rocks and minerals. The form of the rock may be different from a rock you find on the ground. For example, the glass of cell phones contains the element lead and quartz, a mineral found in rocks. Electrical circuits inside cell phones may have silicon, platinum, palladium, niobium, gold, arsenic, aluminum, zinc, and copper. All of these materials come from rocks!

📓 **Make Meaning** What other everyday items do you use that you think might contain rocks or the minerals in rocks?

# uInvestigate Lab

## How can you classify minerals?

**HANDS-ON LAB**

4-ESS2-1, SEP.3

Geologists use properties of minerals to identify and classify them. How can you classify minerals according to properties?

**Materials**
- mineral samples
- hand lens
- magnet
- nail

## Procedure

☐ **1.** Choose three mineral samples. Write their names in the table.

☐ **2. SEP Investigate** Use the hand lens to make careful observations of each mineral. Choose three properties to test. Write them in the table. Then test the minerals. Record your observations.

**Science Practice**

Scientists **investigate** to provide evidence that supports scientific ideas.

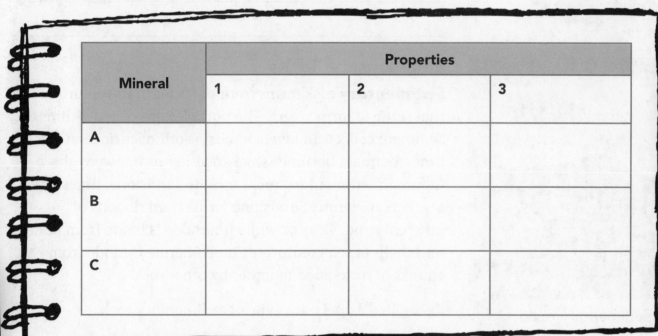

| Mineral | Properties | | |
|---|---|---|---|
| | 1 | 2 | 3 |
| A | | | |
| B | | | |
| C | | | |

## Analyze and Interpret Data

**3. SEP Explain** How did the hand lens help you observe and classify the minerals?

_____

_____

_____

Lesson 3  Rocks, Minerals, and Soil    **175**

igneous rock

## Igneous Rocks

Rocks are sorted by certain **characteristics**, or features. Rocks are often sorted by their main characteristic, which is how they formed. Rocks form in three main ways. **Igneous** rocks form from molten rock, or magma. Magma heats up below or inside Earth's crust. Under heat and pressure, it can break through to Earth's surface as lava. When lava or magma cools, igneous rock forms.

☑ READING CHECK **Draw Conclusions** Igneous rock is found along plate boundaries. Why do you think that is?

_____

_____

_____

_____

sedimentary rock

## Sedimentary Rocks

**Sedimentary** rock forms from particles in the environment that settle to form layers. The particles are called sediment. Sediment collects in layers in basins or flat surfaces. Over time, sediment becomes stuck together as if it were glued. Common sedimentary rocks include sandstone, limestone, and conglomerate. Sandstone forms from ribbons of different sand. Gray or white limestone is made from bones and shells of sea creatures. Conglomerate is made from chunks of rock glued together by other rock.

**Recognize** Label each type of sedimentary rock.

_____   _____   _____

## Metamorphic Rocks

Rock can be changed by heat, pressure, or both. Rock that forms this way is called **metamorphic** rock. When either sedimentary, igneous, or other metamorphic rock is put under great pressure and very high temperature, the rock changes form. It usually develops new crystals. For example, marble is made when limestone or chalk is heated and squeezed. Metamorphic shale is slate, which breaks along neat, smooth lines. Igneous granite becomes the metamorphic rock gneiss (sounds like "nice").

**Identify** Draw an arrow in the white box to show the possible direction of the pressure that changed shale into this metamorphic slate.

### Science Practice
► Toolbox

**Make Observations**
What would you observe if you felt each of the rocks?

metamorphic rock

## Quest Connection

In general, sedimentary rock wears away more quickly, and igneous and metamorphic rock wears away more slowly. Which type of rock might make up a coastal cliff? Explain your answer.

_____

_____

_____

_____

Visual Literacy Connection

# How do rocks change?

Igneous, sedimentary, and metamorphic rock are formed in different ways. Over millions of years, these rocks continually change from one type to another type of rock. This process is called the rock cycle. The diagram shows one possible path rocks can take through the rock cycle. Follow the diagram and label each blank with the type of rock that is formed.

metamorphic
igneous
sedimentary

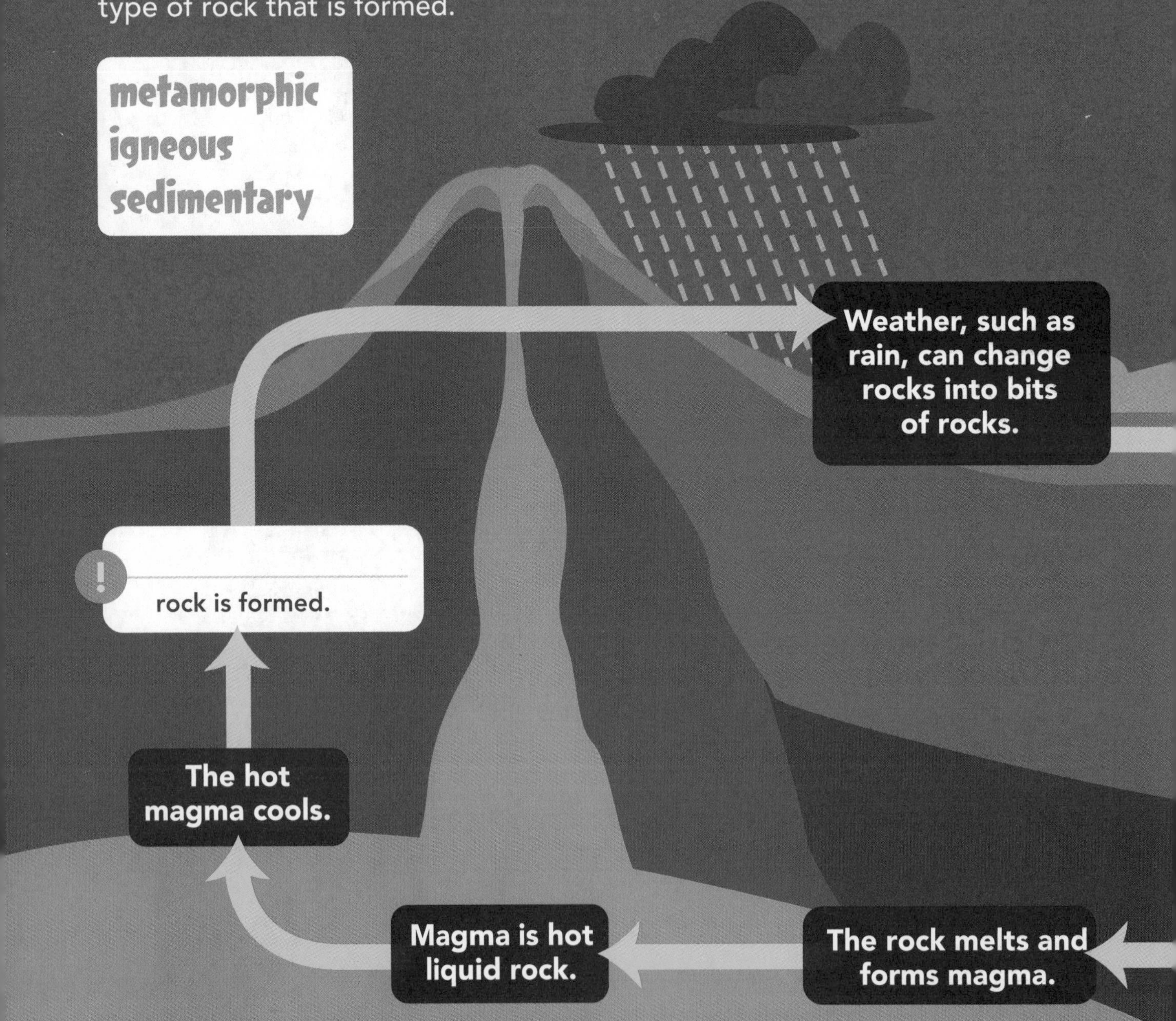

Weather, such as rain, can change rocks into bits of rocks.
! ______ rock is formed.
The hot magma cools.
Magma is hot liquid rock.
The rock melts and forms magma.

**!** **Connect** How does the rock cycle diagram help you identify types of rocks and the ways each type of rock is formed?

_____

_____

_____

_____

_____

**The rock particles can be moved and settle in new places.**

**The particles combine together.**

**!** _____ rock is formed.

**Heat and pressure change the rock.**

**!** _____ rock is formed.

**Identify Rocks** How can you know what rocks are made of? Try the vinegar test. A drop of vinegar on marble or limestone will bubble. That's because they both contain a substance called calcium carbonate. Drop vinegar onto several different rocks. Record what you observe.

## Minerals

Rocks are made of one or more minerals. Minerals have properties, including color, texture, luster, streak, cleavage, and hardness. Some propeprties are easily observed. Luster is how a mineral's surface reflects light. A glassy luster is shiny, like glass. A metallic luster looks like polished metal. Luster can also be waxy, pearly, chalky, and other lusters.

A mineral's streak is its color in powdered form. This powder can be seen by rubbing a mineral across a streak plate. Minerals that break along smooth, flat surfaces have cleavage. Most minerals break in definite patterns. Some minerals with perfect cleavage break into flat, smooth layers. Other minerals do not have cleavage. They break into nonflat shapes or splinter. Hardness is how easily the surface of a mineral can be scratched. A mineral with greater hardness can scratch a mineral with lower hardness.

Minerals can be sorted into metals and gems. Gold and silver are metals. Diamonds are gems. Minerals can be soft or hard. Talc is the softest mineral. Diamond is the hardest mineral and may be used to make cutting tools. All minerals have a crystal, or organized, structure.

**Compare and Contrast** How are these minerals different?

_____

_____

## Soil

Soil is a mixture of rock particles, air, water, and decomposing matter. The main rock particles in soil are sand, silt, and clay. They come from parent material, which is broken down rock. The type of rock particles in the soil affects how the soil drains. Water pours quickly through sandy soil and less quickly through clay soil. Air enters soil as animals dig through it. As more organic matter, called humus, mixes in the soil, the soil becomes topsoil. Rich topsoil supports plant growth. If you dug down 15 meters or more into soil, you would most likely discover several layers of soil types. A cross section of soil, such as in the illustration, is called a soil profile.

**Predict** What might happen if you tried to grow crops in soil with little topsoil?

_____

_____

_____

_____

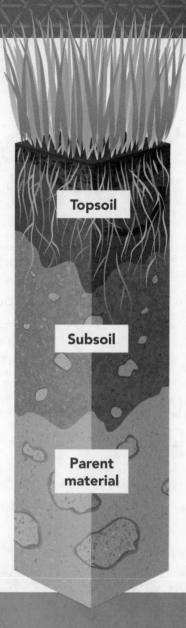

Topsoil

Subsoil

Parent material

## ☑ Lesson 3 Check

1. **Connect** How are soil, rocks, and minerals related? Include what rocks are made of.

_____

_____

_____

2. **Classify** Think about the properties of minerals. How might you sort those properties? Explain how you sorted.

_____

_____

_____

# How can you make a model of a landform?

Remember that the hidden treasures are buried deep within plateaus and coastal cliffs or near a mountain. In this lab, you will design and make a model of a rocky land form—a mountain, plateau, or cliff. You will use this model in the next Check-In to test how water affects your chosen landform.

**Suggested Materials**

- mineral samples
- cardboard
- paper plates
- craft sticks
- foam and plastic cups
- white glue
- bottom half of a gallon milk jug
- sand
- soil
- rock samples
- water

## Design and Build

☐ **1.** Choose one of the rocky landforms to model—mountain, plateau, or coastal cliff. Discuss ways to use any of the materials to design and construct a model of your landform. Draw your ideas for the designs.

**Engineering Practice**

Engineers **investigate** to provide evidence that supports scientific ideas.

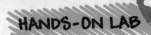
☐ **2.** Consider which materials will best show the characteristics of your landform. Make a list of those materials and tell why they best represent your landform.

_____

_____

_____

☐ **3. SEP Develop a Model** Build your model. Sketch or take a photo of your model. Save this for your Quest Findings.

# Evaluate Your Design

**4.** Think about where your landform can be seen on the map from Lesson 1's Quest Check-In. What patterns of Earth's features might you expect to see around your landform?

_____

_____

**5. Compare and Contrast** How is your land model similar to and different from an actual landscape?

_____

_____

_____

**6. CCC Stability and Change** How might the rocks and your landform change over time?

_____

_____

_____

_____

_____

# Weathering and Erosion

Use evidence to show how weathering and erosion change Earth's surface.

**4-ESS2-1**

**Literacy Skill**
Draw Conclusions

**Vocabulary**
weathering
erosion

**Academic Vocabulary**
evidence

▶ **VIDEO**

Watch a video about weathering and erosion.

## STEM › Connection

Engineers design solutions to protect both land and people. One solution they have designed is a sea wall that can be built along a coastline. Most sea walls are built using concrete or large rocks. When rough seas threaten a town, a sea wall stops the water to prevent flooding. It also stops ocean waves from carrying away soil and sand. In these examples, a sea wall prevents problems. Other times, a sea wall can cause problems—especially with the environment. It can block the movement of sand along the coast, which is important in keeping the coast from washing away. It can also block animals, such as sea turtles, from coming onto a beach to lay their eggs.

📖 **Write About It** What do you think might be some factors that designers and engineers would have to consider when they plan a sea wall?

# How can a rock wear away?

Geologists know that some rocks can break down because of water. What data can you gather about how water can break down rock?

**Materials**
- clear jar with lid
- hand lens
- water
- sandstone sample
- limestone sample
- chalk
- safety goggles

⚠ Wear safety goggles.

## Procedure

☐ 1. Write a prediction about which rock sample will be affected more by water.

_____

_____

☐ 2. **SEP Plan** Write a procedure to test your hypothesis. Use all of the materials. Remember to include a control in your procedure. Show your procedure to your teacher before you begin.

☐ 3. Record your observations.

**Science Practice**

Scientists investigate to provide evidence that supports scientific ideas.

## Analyze and Interpret Data

4. **SEP Draw Conclusions** What conclusions can you draw from your investigation?

_____

_____

_____

_____

_____

_____

_____

_____

Observations

## Chemical Weathering

Ocean waves, rushing rivers, pouring rain, and blustering winds can change rocks. **Weathering** is the process that wears away or breaks down rock. The two basic types of weathering are chemical and physical. Chemical weathering can happen when rain mixes with chemicals in the air and interacts with the rock. Chemical weathering can also happen when plants rot and produce chemicals. Those chemicals can interact with rock. In both examples, the surface of the rock can become rough or pitted. Deep pits, or holes, in rock are evidence that chemical weathering has taken place. **Evidence** is observable information that you can use to answer questions. Chemical weathering causes rock materials to turn into new kinds of materials.

☑ **READING CHECK** **Draw Conclusions** What do you think happened to the statue in the picture to make it change color?

_____

_____

_____

---

**uBe a Scientist**

**Weathering** Materials other than rocks can be weathered. Rub a piece of wood with coarse sandpaper. What do you see? Tap the wood dust onto a piece of paper. What conclusion can you draw from this investigation?

## Physical Weathering

Physical weathering happens when wind, water, ice, or plants cause rock to flake or crack. The force of these materials causes rock to wear away or break into smaller pieces. As the wind blows, small particles of sand and other materials hit the rock, cutting and shaping it. Some plant roots can grow inside rock, forcing the rock to crack. Flowing water can cause rocks to hit one another and break apart. Water can also enter cracks in rock. If temperatures are cold enough, the water will freeze. The frozen water in the cracks expands and pushes against the rock, breaking it. Another way that ice weathers rock is in the form of glaciers. Glaciers are large sheets of slow-moving ice that cut and crack rock as they scrape over land.

### Science Practice
► Toolbox

**Ask Questions** What questions would you ask if you were to design a way to prevent the physical weathering of an important stone monument?

## Quest Connection

Describe how weathering affects mountains, plateaus, and cliffs by the coast.

_____

_____

_____

_____

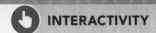
## Erosion

Particles of weathered rock can be removed from the land by gravity, wind, water, and ice. **Erosion** is the process in which these weathered particles are removed from land. Rivers, streams, and water from rain and snow pick up broken particles and rock bits. Constant waves against the land can erode cliffs and shorelines. Erosion can cause slow changes over time.

Ice can also remove particles. Most often the ice that erodes land is in the form of glaciers. Gravity pulls those glaciers downward, causing particles to be picked up in the process.

Strong winds can remove rock and soil that have been loosened by physical and chemical weathering. Wind erosion can destroy landforms or make new ones.

**Synthesize** How are the processes of weathering and erosion related?

_____

_____

_____

_____

## Movement of Particles

Water, wind, and ice carry particles from places where they were weathered. Winds can move small particles over great distances—sometimes halfway across a continent. Waves can carry sand onto beaches, off of beaches, and along beaches. They can carve structures, such as sea caves, along the shore.

**Explain** Why do you think some of the rock on this rock structure weathered and eroded while other parts did not?

_____

_____

_____

Tiny rock particles are always moving along with the movement of water. Glaciers like the one in the photo do not appear to be moving. But they move slowly, carrying particles with them to new places.

## Deposition

As particles are moved by water, wind, and ice, they settle in new locations. Deposition is the process in which particles removed by erosion are deposited in a new place. Deposition happens when wind or water slows or when ice melts.

As particles are deposited in one place over time, the particles can build up, producing new landforms. For example, many deposited particles and other sediment can form a delta at a place where a river flows into a large body of water.

**Identify** Draw arrows to show the direction in which river water flowed and deposited particles to form this delta.

## Changes in Landforms over Time

Weathering and erosion, along with the movement and deposition of particles, are happening all the time. For example, a large rock can take thousands of years to become an arch-like structure. This large rock can be weathered away by water and wind. The weathered rock particles are removed from the rock by erosion. Then the particles get carried away and settle over time in a new location. All these processes are ongoing and continue to shape landforms.

**Compare and Contrast** Describe how weathering and erosion are different. How did these processes form the river?

_____

_____

_____

_____

## ☑ Lesson 4 Check

Lucia planted a garden on a gentle slope. She cleared the area of five large rocks. She planted seeds. It rained on her garden about twice a week. After a few weeks, Lucia noticed a layer of mud on the concrete below the garden. Many of her plants were not growing.

1. ☑ **READING CHECK** **Draw Conclusions** What happened to Lucia's garden?

_____

_____

2. **Use Evidence from Text** What evidence supports your conclusion about Lucia's garden?

_____

_____

# How does water affect landforms?

You know what causes weathering and erosion. Now you have the chance to demonstrate these processes as part of your Quest. Along the way, you may uncover the hidden treasure! You will use the model you made in the previous Check-In Lab. How will water affect your model?

**Materials**
- land model
- water
- plastic spray bottle
- cardboard cutouts

**Suggested Materials**
- paper towel

## Test Your Design

☐ 1. Predict what will happen to the landform model if it were weathered and eroded.

_____

_____

☐ 2. **SEP Use Models** Develop a procedure to model weathering and erosion of your landform. Have your teacher approve your plan. Then carry out your procedure. Sketch or take photos to show what happens along the way.

**Engineering Practice**

Engineers investigate to provide evidence that supports scientific ideas.

## Evaluate Your Design

3. **Compare and Contrast** Compare what happened to your landform with classmates who modeled a different landform.

_____

_____

_____

4. **SEP Use Evidence** Provide evidence of any effects of weathering or erosion you observed.

_____

_____

# EXTREME science

## Powerful Plants

Plants are more powerful than we think. Did you know that plants can cause damage to rocks? Rocks have little protection against the powerful roots of plants. Like wind and water, plants can weather rock!

Any time a plant seed falls into a crack in a rock, the seed may sprout. Roots of sprouting plants grow into cracks of rocks. The roots force bits of rock to crumble. The more the rock crumbles, the stronger the hold the plant has on the rock. This is an example of physical weathering. [Some plant roots produce strong chemicals that break apart the rock. The plants take minerals from the rocks, making the rocks weaker. This is an example of chemical weathering.

☑ **READING CHECK** **Draw Conclusions**

What might you expect to happen to a stone wall with many cracks over 200 years? Draw what you think the results would be.

| Today | 100 years in the future | 200 years in the future |
| --- | --- | --- |
|  |  |  |

**INTERACTIVITY**

Organize your data to support your Quest Findings.

# Does X Mark the Spot? That's Up to You!

## How can we use Earth processes to find buried treasure?

## Plan and Prepare a Presentation

**Phenomenon** Produce a presentation that shows how a mountain, plateau, or coastal cliff is weathered and eroded. First, make notes to list what you will show. Then decide what visuals you will use as evidence for each stage of the process. Use the sketches you have drawn or the photos you have taken during Quest Check-Ins to provide evidence of your findings.

Provide a description of your evidence. Your audience should understand that what your presentation shows actually took place over millions of years.

## Construct Explanations

What evidence did you use to explain that weathering and erosion can change a landform over time?

_____

_____

# Geologist

Geologists study the Earth. They figure out how Earth's features form and change. They study mountain formations, volcanoes, and earthquakes. They learn about rocks, minerals, petroleum, coal, soil, and more. A geologist's job often involves collecting samples and analyzing data. Most geologists have a specialty, meaning they focus on a narrow topic. Some study volcanoes, wearing heat-protection gear as they sample bits of hot lava. Other geologists map ocean currents or test to see if land is stable enough to build on. Some collect and test rock samples.

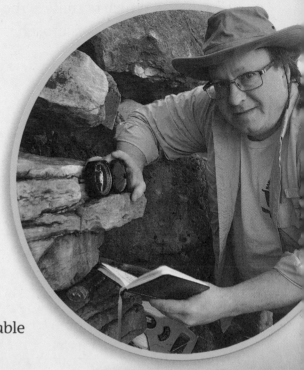

Geologists may work in mining or engineering or may teach and carry out research at universities. At times, geologists use instruments, such as rock hammers or drills. They make charts, draw maps, and write reports. Geologists work in offices, labs, and often outdoors. So, if you love science AND enjoy the outdoors, you might make a great geologist!

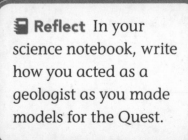

**Reflect** In your science notebook, write how you acted as a geologist as you made models for the Quest.

## ☑ Assessment

**1. Vocabulary** Which of these is the process by which rock is broken into particles?

    **A.** sediment

    **B.** deposition

    **C.** erosion

    **D.** weathering

**2. Use Diagrams** Identify and label the parts of the diagram.

    **A.** _____

    **B.** _____

    **C.** _____

    **D.** _____

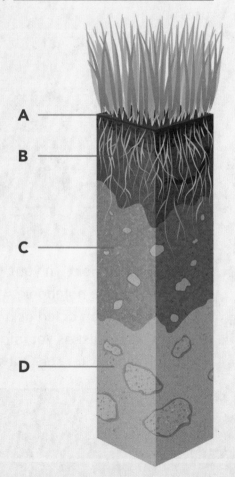

**3. Explain** What are some differences between renewable energy resources and nonrenewable energy resources?

_____

_____

_____

_____

_____

**4. Describe** Which of these describes a process in the rock cycle?

    **A.** Igneous or metamorphic rock is broken into particles, or sediment.

    **B.** Sedimentary rock is formed from cooling magma under Earth's surface.

    **C.** Metamorphic rock forms when rock particles collect in a shallow sea.

    **D.** Sedimentary rock crystals form as the rock cools and becomes solid.

**5. Summarize** Where is somewhere on Earth that you might find volcanoes? Why are they found in this place?

_____

_____

_____

_____

_____

_____

**6. Apply** What processes produced this land feature?

_____

_____

_____

_____

_____

_____

**7. Describe** What information do you need to draw a topographic map? Be specific.

_____

_____

_____

_____

_____

_____

**Word Bank**

| sedimentary | cycle | heat |
|---|---|---|
| igneous | weathered | |

**8. Summarize** Fill in the blanks using the word bank above to complete this paragraph.

Earth has three types of rock. They are connected in a pattern called the rock _____. _____ rock forms when molten material beneath Earth's surface rises and cools. That rock may get _____ into particles. Those particles collect and over time are cemented together to form _____ rock. At times, great _____ and/or pressure can cause rock to form metamorphic rock.

**The Essential Question** *How can you use maps to understand Earth's features?*

**Show What You Learned**

Explain how you can use maps to locate specific landforms. Describe the tools that help you use the maps correctly.

_____

_____

_____

_____

_____

_____

Field geologists were preparing to study processes in a natural environment. They used the topographical map to help them prepare for their field work. Study the map. Then answer the questions.

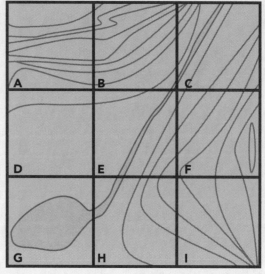

1. **Plan an Investigation** The geologists plan to study how long it takes for particles to become separated from the parent material. They will also study what causes the particles to separate. What phenomenon are the geologists studying?

   **A.** earthquakes

   **B.** deposition

   **C.** weathering

   **D.** sedimentation

2. **Plan an Investigation** In the second phase of their study, the geologists will ask what removes the particles and how much material is removed over a certain period. What phenomenon will the geologists study in this part of their field work?

   **A.** erosion

   **B.** deposition

   **C.** weathering

   **D.** sedimentation

3. **Patterns** Hiking through which path would be a steeper cllimb?

   **A.** from E through F

   **B.** from H through G

   **C.** From D through A

   **D.** from D through G

**4. Cause and Effect** The geologists took a sample of rock and dirt from the bottom of the lake in box G. They then asked what all of the rocks and dirt were made from. They found that most of the youngest material on the lake bottom was the same type of material that the surrounding mountains were made of. Use vocabulary words to explain this phenomenon.

_____

_____

_____

_____

**5. Collect Data** The geologists want to study how quickly weathering and erosion are currently happening on the mountains. What kinds of data should they collect?

  **A.** the height of the mountains

  **B.** how deep a lake at the bottom of the mountain is

  **C.** average yearly rainfall and temperature

  **D.** what kinds of vegetation can grow there

# uDemonstrate Lab

# How can you identify minerals?

**Phenomenon** When geologists need to identify unknown mineral samples, they compare the properties of the sample to the known properties of minerals. How can you identify mineral samples?

**Materials**
- 6 mineral samples
- hand lens
- streak plate
- nail
- penny

## Procedure

☐ **1.** Study the table of known mineral properties.

**Science Practice**

Scientists **investigate** to provide evidence that supports scientific ideas.

### Properties of Minerals

| Mineral | Color | Luster | Streak | Hardness |
|---|---|---|---|---|
| Calcite | white/clear | glassy | white | 3 |
| Feldspar | varied | glassy | white | 6 |
| Hornblende | dark green to black | dull/glassy | pale gray | 5.5 |
| Mica (muscovite) | ruby, green, brown, black | pearly/ glassy | white | 2.5 |
| Pyrite | gold | metallic | green to brown to black | 6.5 |
| Rose quartz | pink | glassy | white | 7 |

☐ **2.** Make a plan to identify the six mineral samples. Use the tools to help you test for each property.

☐ **3.** Show your plan to your teacher before you start.

☐ **4.** Conduct your tests. Record your observations.

**Observations of Mineral Samples**

| Sample | Color | Luster | Streak | Hardness | Identity of Mineral |
|--------|-------|--------|--------|----------|---------------------|
| Mineral **A** | | | | | |
| Mineral **B** | | | | | |
| Mineral **C** | | | | | |
| Mineral **D** | | | | | |
| Mineral **E** | | | | | |
| Mineral **F** | | | | | |

## Analyze and Interpret Data

**5. CCC Patterns** How does knowing the properties of minerals help you identify unknown samples?

_____

_____

_____

_____

**6. SEP Explain** How could you test cleavage in minerals?

_____

_____

_____

# Earth's Natural Hazards

**Next Generation Science Standards**

**4-ESS3-2** Generate and compare multiple solutions to reduce the impacts of natural Earth processes on humans. **3-5-ETS1-2** Generate and compare multiple possible solutions to a problem based on how well each is likely to meet the criteria and constraints of the problem.

Go online to access
your digital course.

▶ VIDEO

📖 eTEXT

👆 INTERACTIVITY

📱 VIRTUAL LAB

🎮 GAME

☑ ASSESSMENT

## The Essential Question

## What impact do natural hazards have?

### Show What You Know

This volcano was not active for a very long time. What do you think might have happened to cause the volcano to erupt?

_____

_____

_____

# Protect the City! Hazard Incoming!

## How can we reduce the impacts of natural hazards?

**Phenomenon** Hello! I am Geraldine Pascoe, a volcanologist. My job is to study volcanoes. Scientists report that there have been earthquakes near a city. This means that the volcano could erupt soon. The earthquake could also damage a dam, causing floodwaters to surge toward the city.

City officials need our help. In this problem-based learning activity, you will find ways to prevent the impact of these natural hazards on the people of the city.

Follow the path to learn how you can complete the Quest. Check your progress as you complete each activity with a **QUEST CHECK ✓ OFF**. Go online for more Quest activities.

## Quest Check-In 1

### Lesson 1

Learn how volcanoes affect cities. Decide what challenges they present and develop solutions to those challenges.

**Next Generation Science Standards**

**4-ESS3-2** Generate and compare multiple solutions to reduce the impacts of natural Earth processes on humans.

**3-5-ETS1-2** Generate and compare multiple possible solutions to a problem based on how well each is likely to meet the criteria and constraints of the problem.

**VIDEO**

Watch a video about a volcanologist at work.

## Quest Check-In 2

**Lesson 2**

Discover ways that the weather produces natural hazards. Apply what you learn to solve the problem of flooding.

## Quest Check-In Lab 3

**Lesson 3**

Develop two solutions to reduce the impacts of natural hazards and decide which would be most effective.

## Quest Findings

Present your solutions for reducing the impact of a natural hazard on the city.

# How can you reduce the impact of rapidly sliding soil?

Engineers try to find ways to limit damage from natural hazards. How can you limit the damage from soil sliding down a slope?

## Procedure

☐ **1.** In the plastic container, build a slope with the newspaper, the modeling clay, and the soil. Add water to slope. Record your observations.

☐ **2.** Think of a way to prevent what happened. Rebuild your slope. Choose additional materials. Test again with water.

☐ **3.** Record your observations.

### Observations

## Analyze and Interpret Data

**4. Evaluate** What was the most successful part of your model? How could you apply this to the real world?

_____

_____

_____

**5. SEP Analyze** Compare your solution to another group. Did their solution work better than yours?

_____

_____

**Materials**

- safety goggles
- plastic container
- newspaper
- modeling clay
- soil
- water

**Suggested Materials**

- straws
- scissors
- pipe cleaners
- coffee stirrers
- tape
- construction paper
- rocks
- cardboard houses
- water bottle

⚠ Wear safety goggles.

⚠ Be careful using scissors.

**Engineering Practice**

Engineers **compare solutions** to figure out how to solve a problem.

# Cause and Effect

As you read, you might notice that one event can lead to another event happening. This is a cause-and-effect relationship. The cause is the reason something happens. The effect is what happens. Use these strategies to find cause-and-effect relationships.

- Look for key words that show cause and effect, such as *because, cause, reason, result, since,* and *so.*
- Remember that one effect can have several causes, or several effects may result from one cause.

Read this passage about flooding in Texas.

## Week-Long Rain Floods Texas

Over one week, rainfall in central Texas reached record-setting amounts. Austin-Bergstrom Airport reported 22.3 centimeters of rain on May 26. The rain caused air travel delays. In some areas, the rain caused flash floods on roadways. Drivers were warned to stay home because of deep water on the roads. Rivers overflowed, and lake water flooded neighborhoods. Some people became trapped. Rescue crews used small motorboats to collect people from their homes and take them to safety. If the rains had continued, then flood damage would have been even worse.

✓ **READING CHECK** **Cause and Effect** What was the cause of the air travel delays and deep water on roads?

_____

_____

_____

_____

**GAME**

Practice what you learn with the Mini Games.

# Tectonic Hazards

## I can...

Describe how volcanic eruptions, earthquakes, and tsunamis can impact people.

**4-ESS3-2**

**Literacy Skill**
Cause and Effect

**Vocabulary**
fault
earthquake
tsunami
volcano
eruption

**Academic Vocabulary**
hazard

 **VIDEO**

Watch a video about tectonic hazards.

## CURRICULUM › Connection

Countries that border the Pacific Ocean are especially at risk from ocean hazards. Huge waves can form after an ocean earthquake. The waves can move across thousands of kilometers of ocean water. By the time the waves reach shore, they can be enormous! Some waves can be more than 10 meters high, 30 meters wide, and last for more than 10 minutes. After the waves hit the shoreline, they can travel inland for several kilometers and destroy coastal communities.

The earthquakes that cause these waves cannot be predicted. However, some places have systems that provide warning after the earthquake happens. The system helps to save lives. Countries also use special ocean buoys to warn people of giant waves.

**Draw Conclusions** Why do scientists monitor earthquakes to help predict these ocean hazards?

_____

_____

NOAA — TSUNAMI

# uInvestigate Lab

## How can a *large wave* affect land?

Scientists study big waves to find ways to reduce the damage they cause. How can you model large waves and how they affect land?

## Procedure

☐ **1.** Predict what you think will happen if a huge wave hit a town on an ocean shore.

_____

_____

☐ **2.** Choose materials to build a model shore in the plastic container. Write a plan to use the model shore to test your prediction.

☐ **3.** Show your plan to your teacher before you begin. Record your observations.

### Observations

**Materials**
- safety goggles
- large, clear plastic container, 28 cm × 18 cm × 6 cm
- water, 2 L
- square piece of foam

**Suggested Materials**
- sand
- newspaper
- mud
- duct tape
- model trees
- modeling clay
- small model boat

 Wear safety goggles.

**Science Practice**

Scientists develop and use models to gather evidence.

## Analyze and Interpret Data

**4. SEP Draw Conclusions** If the wave you produced was larger, how would it affect your model beach?

_____

_____

**Earthquake Evidence**

Make three rectangles from modeling clay. Each rectangle should be a different color. The rectangles should be the same size— 5 cm × 8 cm × 2 cm. Stack the rectangles on top of each other. Cut through the stack from top to bottom at an angle. Slide the upper stack up by 2 cm. Then cut the clay in half lengthwise. What do you observe? How does this model earthquake activity?

## Earthquakes

Earth's surface is a thin layer of rock called the crust. The crust is the top part of large pieces of rock called tectonic plates. The plates usually move slowly—just centimeters per year. Tectonic plates push, pull, or slide past each other at their edges. The plates continuously move, which causes stress along faults. A **fault** is a crack in the crust where the two sides slide past each other. Eventually, that stress is released, and an **earthquake**, or a shift within Earth, happens. The shift causes the crust to shake.

✓ **READING CHECK** **Cause and Effect** Underline the text that explains the cause of an earthquake.

The San Andreas fault in California is more than 1,300 km (800 mi) long and 16 km (10 mi) deep. The San Andreas fault moves side to side similar to the blocks in this diagram.

With other faults, blocks slip away from or under each other. The Tohoku earthquake happened because one plate slid under another plate edge.

## Hazards of Earthquakes

A **hazard** is a danger to humans resulting from an event. The hazards of earthquakes are measured by the Modified Mercalli Intensity Scale, which rates the damage they do. An earthquake's energy is measured on a magnitude scale. It is written as a number following a capital letter *M*. A high magnitude measurement means greater hazards for people nearby. Earthquakes below M3.0 happen frequently, but people usually do not feel them. An M5.0 earthquake can rattle buildings, knock pictures off walls, and cause minor damage. Anything greater than M6.0 is a serious earthquake. Buildings crumble, bridges fall, and roads are torn apart. Another major hazard from earthquakes is fire.

The M9.1 Tohoku quake in 2011 in Japan caused a destructive tsunami. A **tsunami** is a massive wave that can cause damage when it reaches land. Earthquakes that rupture the ocean floor can cause tsunamis and damage a long way from the earthquake's center.

### Literacy ▸ Toolbox

**Cause and Effect**
An effect is what happens. Identify at least 5 possible effects if a M5.0 earthquake happened where you live.

## Quest Connection

**Describe** What might be one way to reduce damage in a school from a M5.1 earthquake?

_____

_____

_____

# What happens during a tsunami?

A tsunami describes a series of huge ocean waves that are caused by shifts of land underwater.

The movement of the seafloor causes the movement of the ocean to form large waves.

The large waves of the tsunami move in all directions away from the source of the plate shifting underwater.

When two tectonic plates slide past each other underwater, a large movement of water takes place.

Sea level

WAVE DIRECTION

WAVE DIRECTION

fault

earthquake focus

## Facts about tsunamis

- Tsunamis can move at speeds up to 1,000 kph (600 mph).
- In deep ocean, tsunamis may only be 30 cm (about 12 in) high.
- In Tohoku, Japan, a tsunami wave traveled inland and flooded areas up to 39 m (128 ft) above sea level.

**!** **Record your own tsunami facts in this space.**

_____
_____
_____
_____
_____
_____
_____
_____
_____
_____

When the waves reach the coast, they move slower and increase in height.

**Flooding** can continue inland covering areas with water and debris.

Earth's crust

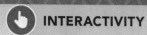
## Volcanoes

A **volcano** is an opening in Earth's crust that allows super-heated materials from beneath the crust to reach the surface. Volcanoes erupt in different ways. One volcano exploded with such power that it tossed 8 ton rocks as far as 1 km (0.6 mi) away. Others, like Hawaii's Mauna Loa, ooze burning lava. An **eruption**, or release of volcanic material, can take minutes, hours, or even longer. Hawaii's Kilauea has been erupting continuously since 1983!

The hazards from volcanic eruptions are sometimes obvious. Lava pours over an area. Buildings, plants, and trees caught in the lava will burn. When the lava cools, it forms rock. Removing lava rock from roads or other facilities is difficult. A cloud like the one shown is a different hazard. While lava moves slowly, the ash cloud moves quickly. Sometimes the ash cloud flows down the side of the volcano, destroying everything in its path. Ash and hot gas may move at speeds up to 700 kph (450 mph). Buildings or trees may be destroyed. People and animals can get burned from the hot ash or gas. Melted ice on the volcano can mix with cloud materials. The result is a river of mud that erodes soil, pollutes rivers, and can destroy towns and villages.

**Write About It** In your science notebook, describe what you might see if you visited a town near an erupting volcano.

## ✔ Lesson 1 Check

**1. Cause and Effect** How might a volcano affect people who live near it?

_____

_____

_____

**2. Explain** How can an earthquake impact humans?

_____

_____

# Beware: Hot Ash!

A minor earthquake occurred near a volcano. Since then, the volcano shows signs that it might erupt again. Smoke and steam have been coming from the volcano every day. There is a city 8 km (5 mi) away from the volcano. Past eruptions filled the air with gases and ash. Breathing was difficult. Everything in the city was covered in ash. Building roofs collapsed. How can the people in the city near the volcano reduce the hazards from the current volcano if it erupts?

1. Identify two problems that the people in the city might face if the volcano erupts.

   _____
   _____
   _____

2. What are two ways that the people could help reduce these impacts from the volcano?

   _____
   _____
   _____
   _____

3. Compare solutions with a partner. Whose solutions do you think would work better? Why?

   _____
   _____
   _____
   _____

**INTERACTIVITY**

Go online to see how earthquakes and other hazards affect people.

# Warning!

**Phenomenon** When an earthquake strikes, damage to homes may occur over a large area. On January 17, 1994, a powerful M6.7 earthquake occurred northwest of Los Angeles, California. Shakes from the Northridge Earthquake damaged thousands of buildings. More were damaged by the fires caused by broken gas lines after the shaking stopped. Bridges collapsed, and a dozen highways could not be driven on. Each road and building had to be looked at by experts to decide whether it was safe. Many buildings had to be torn down because they were unsafe.

Earthquakes present many problems for hazard-control engineers. They look for ways to reduce damage from earthquakes.

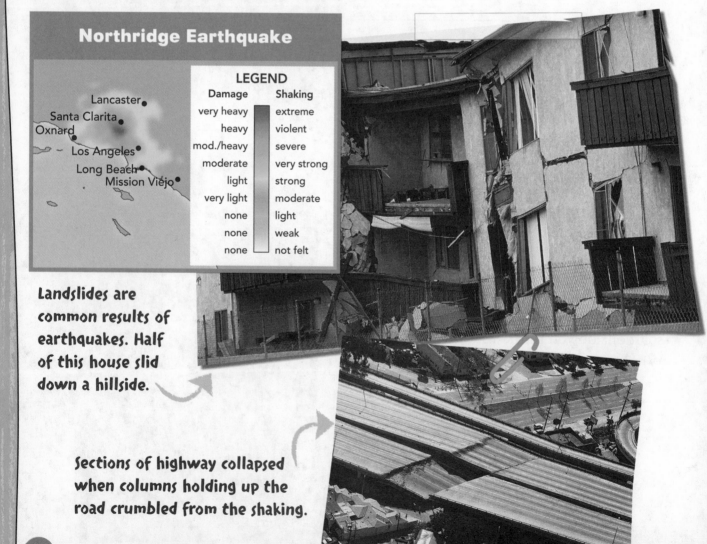

**Northridge Earthquake**

Lancaster
Santa Clarita
Oxnard
Los Angeles
Long Beach
Mission Viejo

| LEGEND | |
|---|---|
| **Damage** | **Shaking** |
| very heavy | extreme |
| heavy | violent |
| mod./heavy | severe |
| moderate | very strong |
| light | strong |
| very light | moderate |
| none | light |
| none | weak |
| none | not felt |

Landslides are common results of earthquakes. Half of this house slid down a hillside.

Sections of highway collapsed when columns holding up the road crumbled from the shaking.

# Design It

Suppose you were an expert about natural hazard control. A powerful earthquake has occurred along the Hayward Fault in northern California. You are asked to identify areas along the Hayward Fault that need reinforced structures to protect them from future earthquakes. The chart shows the reports of damage to different towns from the earthquake. This information can help identify which areas are at the greatest risk for future earthquake damage.

| Location | Damage |
|---|---|
| San Jose | building foundations cracked, roads damaged, 2 bridges collapsed, airport runways cracked, 37 homes damaged |
| Pleasanton | 134 houses destroyed or partially damaged, roadways damaged |
| Walnut Creek | pictures fallen from walls, 2 chimneys damaged, windows shattered |
| Mountain View | buildings have minor damage, school walls cracked, windows broken |
| San Mateo | 2 sections of the bridge across the bay collapsed |
| Stockton | shaking felt, several windows broken |

Your task is to design an earthquake danger map. Your map will use different colors to show different levels of possible danger from future earthquakes. Decide which towns need reinforced structures the most.

| Earthquake center | | | | |
|---|---|---|---|---|
| ⬤ | | | | |

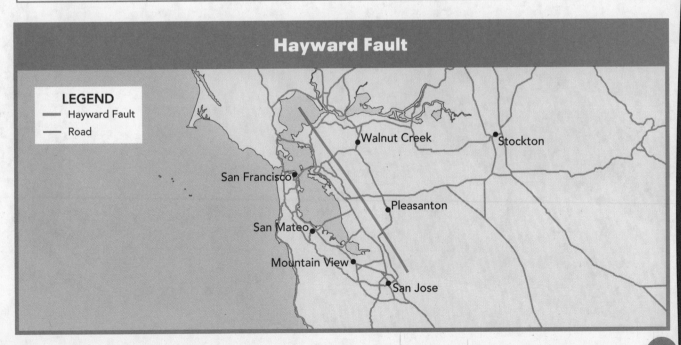

# Weather Hazards

**I can...**

Describe how weather hazards can affect humans.

**4-ESS3-2, 3-5-ETS1-2**

**Literacy Skill**
Cause and Effect

**Vocabulary**
flood
drought
avalanche
landslide

**Academic Vocabulary**
outcome

▶ **VIDEO**

Watch a video about weather hazards.

**SPORTS** ▷ **Connection**

Skiers, snowboarders, and snowmobilers look forward to new snow. New snow falls on old snow. But if it piles up too quickly, ice, snow, and rock may suddenly slide down the mountain. This same thing can be caused by rapid melting, earthquakes, and changes by humans or other animals. Athletes should stay in areas marked safe by ski patrols. They should also wear safety lights. If they are caught in the rapidly falling snow, people should climb toward the surface.

☑ **READING CHECK Cause and Effect** Underline the causes of a sudden slide of snow, ice, and rock down a mountain.

# How does snow *sliding quickly down* a mountain impact people?

Scientists study and model snowfalls on mountains to prevent hazards. How can you model the impact of hazardous snow conditions?

## Procedure

☐ 1. When modeling snowpack on a mountainside, which materials would you use for each layer of snow?

| Hard snowpack | Light middle layer | Recent snowfall |
|---|---|---|
|  |  |  |

☐ 2. **SEP Develop a Model** Write a procedure to model what happens to humans and trees when snow and other materials suddenly slide down a mountainside.

☐ 3. Show your plan to your teacher before you begin. Record your observations.

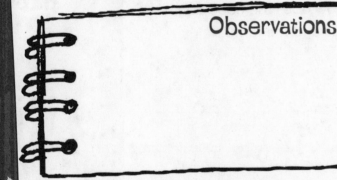

## Observations

## Analyze and Interpret Data

4. **SEP Explain** How might the sudden, rapid fall of snow down a mountainside affect people?

_____

_____

_____

### Materials

- safety goggles
- plastic container
- foam board
- coarse sand, 1 cup
- fine sand, 1/2 cup
- light-weight perlite, 1/2 cup

### Suggested Materials

- protractor
- model trees
- modeling clay
- gravel
- model human figures

 Wear safety goggles.

### Science Practice

Scientists use models to test cause-and-effect relationships.

# How much rainfall is enough?

Rain is important to human life and to other living things. Too much or too little rain, though, can be a big problem.

A **flood** is the flow of water over land that is not normally covered with water. A nearby river has flooded. Water pours over the farm's fields.

! How does the flood affect the soil and the farm?

_____

_____

_____

_____

_____

! How does the flood affect the plants?

_____

_____

There has been no rain for months. The farm suffers from a **drought**, a long period of very dry weather.

! How do you think a drought can affect plant and animal life?

_____

_____

_____

_____

_____

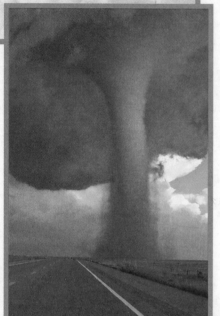

## Blizzards, Hurricanes, and Tornadoes

A blizzard is a snowstorm with high winds. Driving in a blizzard can be dangerous, electric power can be cut off, and trees and buildings can cave in under the weight of the snow. People can be harmed by extreme cold.

Tornadoes are funnel-shaped wind storms that reach from clouds all the way to the ground. A mild tornado can uproot trees and other plants. A powerful tornado can destroy whole neighborhoods.

Hurricanes begin over warm ocean water. Warm, moist air over the ocean rises. It is replaced by cooler air, which heats and rises. Huge storm clouds form. The clouds carry massive amounts of water, which then falls as rain. As the storm gets stronger, wind speed increases. The wind can tear apart buildings and snap the tops off trees. The rain can cause flooding. Hurricanes can also cause a rise in the local sea level, causing water to wash ashore and flood coastal towns. This hazard is called a storm surge.

✓ **READING CHECK** **Cause and Effect** Circle the text that tells two causes of flooding from hurricanes.

## Quest Connection

How might flooding affect the city near the volcano?

_____

_____

_____

_____

## Landslides and Avalanches

Avalanches and landslides are similar. An **avalanche** is the sudden sliding of snow, ice, and rock down a slope. A **landslide** is the sliding of rock and soil down a slope. Earthquakes or heavy rain can cause soil and rock to loosen. The ground shifts and flows downhill. The **outcome**, or result, of a landslide can be damage to buildings, roads, and property. Sometimes a landslide can block a river, causing a temporary dam and a lake to form. When the dam breaks, the flood can wash away towns along the river. This happened in Wyoming in 1925, when the town of Kelly washed away.

**Compare** How is the damage caused by a landslide and an avalanche similar?

_____

_____

_____

_____

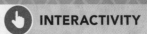
**INTERACTIVITY**

Complete an activity about weather events.

### Math ▸ Toolbox

**How much water?**
A blizzard dumps 1.5 m of snow on a mountain. How much water is it? 10 cm of snow equals about 1 cm of water. How much water fell during the blizzard? Be sure to convert all numbers to centimeters!

## ☑ Lesson 2 Check

1. **Describe** How can a tornado affect people?

_____

_____

2. ☑ READING CHECK **Cause and Effect** A large hurricane strikes the East Coast of North America. What are three impacts the hurricane might have on people?

_____

_____

_____

_____

# Water Warnings

The city near the volcano had an earthquake recently. This broke the dam, which caused the local river that flows through the city to flood. Now the roads are all underwater, and people cannot get from one side of the city to the other. Large areas of the city have lost electric power. The water supply is now polluted.

1. Research to find at least two additional ways flooding impacts people.

_____

_____

_____

_____

_____

2. Choose two of the impacts on people. Brainstorm ways that the city could reduce the impacts from flooding.

_____

_____

_____

_____

_____

QUEST CHECK ✓ OFF

# SOLVE it with Science

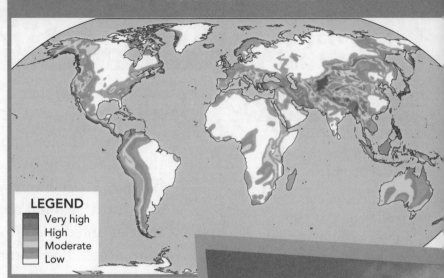

## Where is the greatest earthquake risk?

**LEGEND**
Very high
High
Moderate
Low

**Phenomenon** Earthquakes occur all the time as Earth's plates move, settle, and move again. The United States Geological Survey (USGS) locates several million earthquakes around the world every year. Most earthquakes are very small, so no one feels them. We know they happen because seismographs record them worldwide. Seismographs are instruments that measure how much Earth's surface shakes during an earthquake. Earthquake damage increases as the strength of the earthquake increases. Where are the largest earthquake hazards?

A good way to answer this question is to look at a map of predicted hazards based on where earthquakes have occurred in the past. Study the map and answer the questions.

Which continent has the highest earthquake hazards? Which continent has the lowest?

_____

Which parts of the United States have the highest earthquake hazards?

_____

_____

Now apply what you know. Earthquakes usually occur at the boundaries between tectonic plates. What can you infer about the places where there are high seismic hazards?

_____

_____

# Impacts of Natural Hazards

## I can...

Explain how natural hazards can negatively affect humans.

Describe some solutions that reduce the impact of natural hazards.

**4-ESS3-2, 3-5-ETS1-2**

**Literacy Skill**
Cause and Effect

**Vocabulary**
wildfire

**Academic Vocabulary**
potential

 **VIDEO**

Watch a video about the costs in injuries and damage from natural hazards.

## ENGINEERING > Connection

Engineers develop improved techniques and materials that make the impact of natural disasters less likely to happen. These improvements help make sure that the structures we build are strong enough to reduce human injuries and deaths from natural forces, such as wind, snow, water, fire, and moving earth.

In the past, one of the greatest dangers from earthquakes was the collapse of buildings. Today, engineers plan for safer structures by using seismic designs. These designs include new buildings that bend and adjust to the shaking from earthquakes. Some buildings sit on huge rubber bearings that allow the base of the building to sway without moving the building above it. Other buildings have a sturdy framework called cross braces, outside the structure. In the U.S., buildings are required to meet earthquake safety measures if they are in active earthquake zones.

**Identify** Circle features of this building that you think help prevent damage from natural hazards.

**Write About It** In your science notebook, tell how you would make a building that is less likely to be harmed by natural hazards.

# Where should you build an earthquake-safe structure?

**Materials**
- thin cardboard
- thick cardboard, 2 pieces
- scissosrs
- tape

**Phenomenon** Engineers look for places that will not be badly damaged by an earthquake. How can you use a model to investigate what happens to a building at different distances from an earthquake?

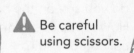
⚠ Be careful using scissors.

## Plan Your Procedure

☐ **1.** Build a model of a tall building from the thin cardboard.

☐ **2.** Place the 2 pieces of thick cardboard side by side to represent 2 tectonic plates.

**Engineering Practice**
Engineers *build models* to compare solutions.

☐ **3.** Write a procedure to test your building in at least 3 places. Show your plan to your teacher before you begin. Record your observations. After each test, repair your building, if needed.

### Observations

## Evaluate Your Plan

**4. SEP Interpret** Where is the safest place to build your structure? Why do you think that is so?

_____

_____

_____

_____

**Soil in Runoff**

Next time rain falls, line a strainer with paper towels. With an adult, find a place where water is running in a stream through a yard or park. Place the strainer in the water's path. After 5 minutes, remove the paper towel and let it dry. What do you see on the paper? How much of the matter collected is soil?

Wildfires in national parks destroy animal habitats and pollute the air with smoke.

## Short-Term Effects of Hazards

Major weather events can have widespread and long-lasting effects. Think about a drought that has been happening in the Great Plains. The immediate problems from the drought are loss of crops, soil erosion, and difficulty feeding livestock. Planting native grasses and trees could solve the soil erosion and livestock feed problems. But during a drought, grasslands and forests dry out. One lightning strike can cause a **wildfire**, a fire that burns out of control. Wildfires can burn huge areas of forests and grasslands. In one year, wildfires affected nearly 3.5 million hectares (8.7 million acres) in the United States. That is more than twice the size of Connecticut!

While firefighters battle the fire, people in the area must leave their homes. However, land can recover quickly from a wildfire. The ash provides the soil with nutrients. If rains come, grasses and low shrubs return. Communities harmed by wildfires take much longer to replace.

✓ **READING CHECK Cause and Effect** Circle the effects of drought in the text.

**Plan It!** A local road runs beside a steep hillside. Every time a lot of rain falls, rocks and soil fall onto the road. Develop a plan that offers two suggestions about how to stop the effects of this hazard.

_____

_____

_____

_____

_____

_____

_____

after the eruption

30 years later

## Long-Term Effects of Hazards

Tectonic hazards may cause long-term effects that are difficult to fix. For example, volcanic eruptions produce lava, ash, and debris. Lava forms rock, which can only be removed by blasting. Ash and debris released by the eruption may cover large areas up to a depth of several meters. Hot ash kills plants and animals caught by the eruption. Over time, the land may recover—but very slowly. In the case of Mount St. Helens, recovery has taken more than 30 years. A new lake replaced the one that filled with ash. The area now has low-lying shrubs and grasses. Trees will take longer to grow.

**Explain** Why does recovery in an area take so long after a volcano?

_____

_____

_____

### Science Practice ▸Toolbox

**Cause and Effect** A single cause can have multiple effects, both good and bad. One positive effect of a wildfire is that forest debris is cleared and new growth occurs. What would be a positive effect of a volcano erupting?

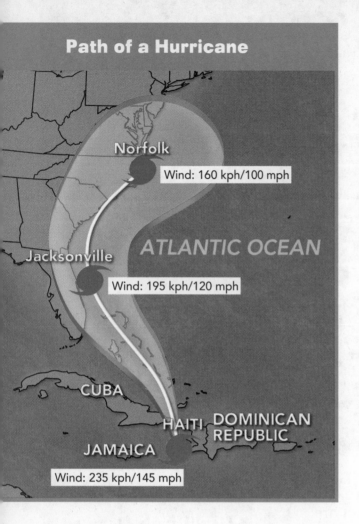

## Path of a Hurricane

Norfolk
Wind: 160 kph/100 mph

ATLANTIC OCEAN

Jacksonville
Wind: 195 kph/120 mph

CUBA

HAITI  DOMINICAN
REPUBLIC

JAMAICA
Wind: 235 kph/145 mph

## Predict Natural Hazards

Scientists try to predict when a natural hazard will happen. Predicting is easier to do with hurricanes and volcanic eruptions than with earthquakes, tsunamis, or landslides. Weather satellites track hurricanes from when they first form. Scientists watch the speed and the direction of the storm. They can make maps similar to this one to show the path of a hurricane. They can warn people when **potential**, or possible, hazards are likely to happen. For volcanoes, scientists use seismograms to track the movement of magma toward Earth's surface. However, even with constant watching, scientists are unable to predict when an earthquake will occur.

**Conclude** How does predicting hazardous weather help protect people?

_____

_____

_____

## Quest Connection

How can tracking the path of a hurricane help scientists predict where it will go next?

_____

_____

_____

_____

## When Hazards Strike

INTERACTIVITY

Complete an activity about a fun wilderness adventure.

There is no way to stop natural hazards from happening. So people should be prepared if a hazard does happen. Both federal and local governments look for solutions to problems caused by hazards. For example, cities and towns put salt on roads to stop ice from forming during winter storms. Some places provide shelters where people can stay safe during a hazard. Local governments and various organizations also provide shelters after a hazard. People who have lost homes can find clothing, a place to stay, and food for a longer period. Government agencies and organizations also provide electricity, clean water, and other necessities for those people who cannot return home.

## ☑ Lesson 3 Check

1. **Explain** What are two solutions that reduce the impact of natural hazards?

_____

_____

_____

2. Choose a natural hazard. Identify two ways that the hazard can negatively affect humans.

_____

_____

_____

# How can you reduce hazard damage?

You have learned about some natural hazards and possible solutions to reduce the damage they cause. Now you need to apply what you have learned to the hazards facing the city. Then you can generate and compare solutions to reduce the impacts of natural Earth processes on humans.

**Materials**
- plastic container

**Suggested Materials**
- water
- sand
- mud
- rocks
- model trees
- model houses
- people figurines
- vinegar
- baking soda
- measuring cup

## Design Your Model

☐ **1.** Design a solution to reduce the impact of a natural hazard. Choose to test a solution for either a flood or a volcano. Record the hazard.

_____

☐ **2.** Generate two solutions that can reduce the impact of the hazard you chose.

_____
_____
_____
_____

☐ **3.** Design and build a model to test each solution. What criteria of your solution will you test with your model?

_____
_____
_____

**Engineering Practice**

Engineers design and evaluate solutions to problems.

☐ **4.** Show your model to your teacher before you begin. Carry out your tests. Record your observations.

| Solution 1 | Solution 2 |
| --- | --- |
| | |

## Evaluate Your Solutions

**5. SEP Use a Model** Will your solutions reduce the impact of the hazard? Use evidence from your tests to support your answer.

_____

_____

_____

**6. Compare** Compare your two solutions. How were they similar? How were they different?

_____

_____

_____

_____

# Protect the City! Hazard Incoming!

## How can we reduce the impacts of natural hazards?

**Phenomenon** It is time to decide which solution you will recommend to the city officials.

### Organize Your Ideas

Review the solutions you tested. Which solution do you think would be best for reducing the effects of natural hazards on people? Why?

_____

_____

_____

_____

_____

_____

_____

Create a presentation for the city about your chosen solution. Be sure to include why you chose the solution and how it will reduce the impact of the natural hazard. Make sure your presentation shows both possible solutions and compares them to each other.

# Volcanologist

A volcanologist studies volcanoes and works to predict possible eruptions. This is an on-the-site, face-of-danger job. Lava reaches temperatures between 700°C and 1,200°C (1,300°F to 2,200°F). Volcanologists take samples of hot lava, ash, and debris. Evidence from lava rock helps volcanologists determine what is happening under Earth's crust.

Volcanologists work all around the world, often in remote locations. They are geology specialists. They also study chemistry, physics, biology, and advanced math. They use computer technology to study and evaluate data from volcanoes throughout the world. If you like extreme science, volcanologist might be the job for you!

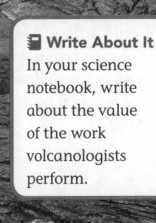

**📓 Write About It**
In your science notebook, write about the value of the work volcanologists perform.

**1. Cause and Effect** Write an effect of each cause.

| Cause | Effect |
|---|---|
| hurricane | |
| earthquake | |
| tsunami | |

**2. Vocabulary** Which sentence describes an avalanche?

**A.** Rocks, shrubs, and soil blow onto lower land.

**B.** Snow rushes downhill and carries rocks and debris with it.

**C.** The ground shakes and splits open, damaging buildings and roadways.

**D.** A huge cloud of hot ash, gas, and debris fills the air.

**3. Explain** A large volcano erupts about 1,600 kilometers (1,000 miles) away from your location. Local officials warn that the volcano eruption could cause problems in town. How can a distant volcano eruption cause problems near you?

_____

_____

_____

**4. Analyze** A farmer needs to grow crops, but he worries about problems from a potential drought. What is one problem that could be caused by a drought?

_____

_____

_____

_____

_____

Use the diagram to answer question 5.

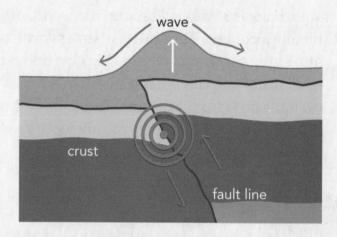

**5. Interpret** What is happening in this illustration?

**A.** An earthquake has caused a thunderstorm in the ocean.

**B.** An earthquake occurred and caused a tsunami.

**C.** A tsunami has forced a shift in two tectonic plates.

**D.** A volcanic eruption has caused an earthquake.

**6.** Match the cause to the effect.

_____ **A.** lightning    **1.** ash cloud

_____ **B.** flooding    **2.** wind damage

_____ **C.** tornado    **3.** wildfire

_____ **D.** volcano    **4.** erosion

**7. Explain** Why does it take time for grass to appear after volcanic ash covers the land?

_____

_____

_____

_____

_____

_____

**8. Cause and Effect** Which choice explains why farmers were able to grow more crops after a volcanic eruption than before it.

**A.** The eruption deposited ash in the farm fields, delivering minerals.

**B.** The eruption lowered the temperature so the crops were not as hot.

**C.** The eruption caused an increase in rain clouds that formed in the area.

**D.** The eruption reduced the number of animals in the area, so they were not eating as many crops.

**9. Explain** What are two ways that a blizzard can negatively impact people?

_____

_____

_____

_____

_____

_____

_____

_____

_____

**The Essential Question** *What impact do natural hazards have?*

**Show What You Learned**

How can natural hazards affect people?

_____

_____

_____

_____

_____

_____

_____

_____

Read this scenario and answer questions 1–5.

Lucia's family lives near the coast. They are familiar with the hazards of hurricanes. A category 5 hurricane with winds up to 260 kph (160 mph) was heading toward Lucia's home. A storm surge of 3 m (118 in.) was expected to come ashore. Lucia's father boarded up the windows with large pieces of plywood. Lucia put the lawn chairs, the hose, and her bike in the house and locked it. Lucia's family left the area as soon as the evacuation order was given. The table shows the total rainfall in several cities over a period of 24 hours during the storm.

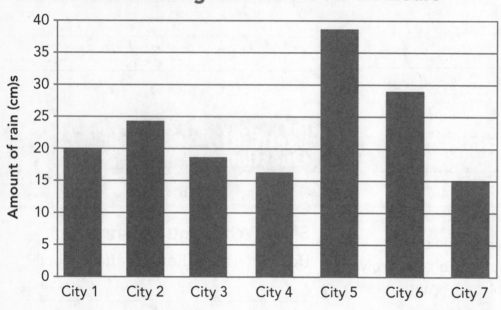

**Rainfall During Hurricane Over 24 Hours**

1. **Identify** Which of these is an immediate potential hazard of the hurricane that Lucia's family should be prepared for?

   **A.** fire damage

   **B.** soil erosion

   **C.** heavy flooding

   **D.** cold temperatures

2. **Cause and Effect** Identify two causes of the hazard you identified in question 1.

_____

_____

_____

_____

3. **Identify** Each of the cities on the chart could face flooding. The emergency managers can build temporary dams, but they only have enough resources to build two in time. They want to help the areas at highest risk for flooding. Which two cities should receive the temporary dams?

   **A.** cities 1 and 2

   **B.** cities 1 and 5

   **C.** cities 3 and 6

   **D.** cities 5 and 6

4. **Explain** What solutions did Lucia's family use to protect their home from the hurricane?

_____

_____

_____

_____

5. **Cause and Effect** What effect of the hurricane was the family protecting against by taking the actions you listed in question 4?

_____

_____

_____

_____

# How can homes be designed to be more

earthquake resistant?

**Phenomenon** When engineers plan homes, they think about the hazards that might happen to that home. How can you build a model house that can survive an earthquake?

## Design and Build

☐ **1.** Review all the suggested materials and design two houses using different materials for each house. List the materials and draw a simple sketch of how they will be used.

| Materials 1 | Materials 2 |
|---|---|
| | |
| **House 1** | **House 2** |
| | |

☐ **2.** Show your designs to your teacher and build each house.

**Materials**
- safety goggles
- stopwatch
- large plastic container

**Suggested Materials**
- foam sheets, spongy
- hole punch
- pipe cleaners
- toothpicks
- glue
- cardboard
- straws
- paper clips
- safety pins
- string
- construction paper
- scissors
- Staples

 Wear safety goggles.

 Be careful using scissors.

**Engineering Practice**

Engineers **compare solutions** to figure out how to solve a problem.

3. Plan a test to see whether each house is earthquake resistant. Record your observations.

## Observations

| House 1 | House 2 |
|---------|---------|
|         |         |

## Evaluate Your Design

4. **Compare** Which model survived the "earthquake" best? Why do you think it did?

_____

_____

_____

5. **Evaluate** Based on your observations, how might you improve your earthquake-resistant house?

_____

_____

_____

# The History of Planet Earth

**Next Generation Science Standards**

**4-ESS1-1** Identify evidence from patterns in rock formations and fossils in rock layers to support an explanation for changes in a landscape over time.

▶ VIDEO

📖 eTEXT

👆 INTERACTIVITY

🧪 VIRTUAL LAB

🎮 GAME

☑ ASSESSMENT

## The Essential Question

What evidence can you find that Earth's surface has changed?

**Show What You Know**

What do you think caused the different colors in these rock layers?

_____

_____

_____

_____

# Dig for the Truth

How can rocks and fossils describe a location?

**Phenomenon** Hi, I'm Rocco Romano, a museum fact checker. I received a core sample of rock layers from a discovery team working on an island. The core sample comes from a cave where the discovery team found a bone. They think that the bone might be from an ancient dwarf elephant! The museum needs your help to see whether the team's core sample matches the core sample where other dwarf elephant bones were found.

In this problem-based learning activity, you will examine evidence from the core sample. You will compare evidence from the sample to another core sample from where the dwarf elephant bones were found. If the core samples match, then the team will have more evidence to support their claim about the bone.

Follow the path to learn how you will complete the Quest. The Quest activities in the lessons will help you complete the Quest! Check off your progress on the path when you complete an activity with a  . Go online for more Quest activities.

**Next Generation Science Standards**

**4-ESS1-1** Identify evidence from patterns in rock formations and fossils in rock layers to support an explanation for changes in a landscape over time.

## Quest Check-In 1

### Lesson 1

Apply what you know about patterns in rock formations to describe what the island looked like during the rise and fall of the dwarf elephants.

## Quest Check-In Lab 2

### Lesson 2

Analyze the core sample. Investigate if patterns in the core sample match those in other core samples from where dwarf elephant bones were found.

## Quest Findings

Complete the Quest! Examine your evidence. Write a summary of findings for the discovery team. Explain whether or not the evidence supports the team's claim about the bone.

# uConnect Lab

# Where are fossils found in rock layers?

Scientists put pieces of evidence together to help them figure out big questions. How can you construct an explanation for where scientists find different kinds of fossils?

## Procedure

☐ 1. Work with a partner to write what you know about the three types of rock.

_____

_____

_____

_____

☐ 2. Pick a color of construction paper to model each type of rock. Then use the construction paper to model rock layers in a rock column. Label your layers.

☐ 3. Look at the Pictures of Fossils sheet. Use these examples to draw fossils on your rock column. Make sure to draw the fossils only where you think they would be found.

## Analyze and Interpret Data

4. **SEP Explain** Explain why you chose to draw your fossils on certain layers and not others.

_____

_____

_____

_____

_____

**HANDS-ON LAB**

4-ESS1-1, SEP.6

**Materials**
- yellow, red, and blue construction paper
- Pictures of Fossils sheet

**Science Practice**

Scientists **construct explanations** using evidence and observations.

# Sequence

When you read, you can identify events that take place. Then you can sequence the events, or put them in order. Here is how to do it:

 **GAME**

Practice what you learn with the Mini Games.

- Look for signal words such as *after, before, then, next, finally,* and *later.*
- Use the signal words and other clues to put events in the order they happened.

Read the following passage. Look for signal words to understand the sequence of events.

## How Limestone and Marble Form

Limestone is a type of rock that forms over millions of years. It is made up of sediments, tiny pieces of rock or sand mixed with plant and animal matter. First, algae, ocean plants, corals, and other animals die, and their remains settle on the ocean floor. Then, the pressure of the ocean compresses the plant and animal matter into rock. Over time, the limestone goes through more changes. Heat and pressure inside Earth compress the limestone rock into marble. Some of the marble floors you see in buildings are the remains of ancient plants and animals!

☑ **READING CHECK** **Sequence** Underline the sequence words in the paragraph. Summarize the sequence of events that result in the formation of limestone.

_____

_____

_____

_____

# Patterns in Fossils and Rock Formations

## I can...

Identify patterns in fossils and rock formations.

**4-ESS1-1**

**Literacy Skill**
Sequence

**Vocabulary**
fossil
strata

**Academic Vocabulary**
horizontal

▶ **VIDEO**

Watch a video about patterns in fossils and rock formations.

## STEM Connection

What would you do if you were working at a construction site and discovered fossils? In California, during construction of a subway line, workers found the tusk and teeth of an ancient elephant. Scientists had to help find and remove any fossils at the site before construction of the subway could continue. Scientists can use radar to help them see below the ground without digging. Radar is a type of radiation using radio waves that can pass through the ground. The radio waves reflect, or bounce off, materials. Fossils reflect radio waves differently than the surrounding rock. The reflection pattern is used to map what is in the rock. Then the dig can begin. This way the fossils can be uncovered without harming them. While they work, scientists gather rock core samples. The samples give clues about what Earth was like when the rock was formed.

📓 **Make Meaning** In your science notebook, describe how scientists can use technology to find evidence. Besides radar, what other tools help scientists find fossils?

# What patterns do fossils follow?

Scientists construct explanations to describe natural occurrences on Earth. How can you construct an explanation to describe fossil patterns?

**Materials**
- Fossil Cards sheet
- scissors

⚠ Be careful using scissors.

## Procedure

☐ **1.** Cut out the fossil cards. Each card contains pictures of fossils that are found in different rock layers.

☐ **2.** Find the card with the number 1 in the lower left-hand corner. Place this card on your desk.

☐ **3.** Examine the other fossil cards. Sequence the cards using the fossils. Place the next card on top of the first card. Keep going until all of the cards are in order.

**Science Practice**

Scientists **construct explanations** with evidence to support it.

## Analyze and Interpret Data

**4. SEP Explain** How did you determine the sequence of the fossils?

_____

_____

_____

_____

_____

**5. CCC Patterns** Based on your evidence, what patterns do you think you will see in other rock layers?

_____

_____

_____

_____

**Modeling Fossils**

Press a sugar cube into a flat piece of clay. Make holes in the clay on opposite sides of the cube. Let the clay dry. Pour water through the holes until the sugar cube dissolves. Examine the clay. How does this model show how fossils are formed?

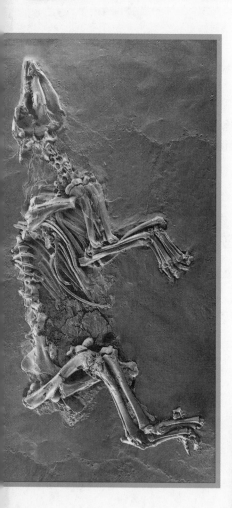

## Fossils

Scientists found the fossil in the photo in a layer of rock. **Fossils** are mineralized remains or evidence of plants and animals that lived long ago. Body fossils form when the body of a dead plant or animal is covered in sediments. The soft tissue of the organism decays. Over time, minerals replace the hard tissues, such as bones.

Cast and mold fossils are imprints of an organism's body, left in the rock. Trace fossils are impressions such as footprints, burrows, or nests made by once-living organisms.

✓ **READING CHECK** **Sequence** Describe the sequence that forms a body fossil.

_____

_____

Fossils provide clues about the environments where organisms lived. They can show whether an organism lived on land or in the water. They can also show whether the climate was warm or cold.

**Infer** What was the environment like where this organism lived? What clues are you using as evidence?

_____

_____

_____

## Quest Connection

What can a fossil's location tell scientists about the organism?

_____

_____

_____

## Rock Formations

When an organism dies, matter from its body breaks down into small particles. Those particles build up and help form rocks. The particles, along with pieces of rock, are called sediments. New layers of sediment are deposited over older layers. These different layers harden into rock and form **horizontal** patterns, or patterns that are parallel to Earth's surface. Most fossils are found within sedimentary rock. Scientists compare the ages of fossils and rock layers, or **strata**, by examining the order of the layers. Sometimes scientists take core samples of the rock layers, such as the ones shown in the photo.

**Use Evidence** What evidence in the photograph shows that the core samples came from sedimentary rock?

_____

_____

## Rock Strata Can Change

Many changes affect rock layers on Earth. Sometimes movement occurs along a crack in the surface of Earth. This crack is known as a fault. When this happens, the rock layers can shift. Rocks can get pushed up, moved apart, or even turned over. As a result, an older rock layer may be closer to the surface than a younger layer.

Rock layers also change when magma from deep underground pushes into the layers. The magma cools and hardens into igneous rock. The igneous rocks are younger than the rocks around them. Heat and pressure can also change sedimentary rocks into metamorphic rocks. Scientists have to carefully study all evidence to know how old rock layers are.

**Explain** In a core sample, will the lowest layer always be the oldest? Explain your answer.

_____

_____

_____

T: 675.5

B: 678.21 m.

**INTERACTIVITY**

Complete an activity about how mountains can change.

## Literacy ▸ Toolbox 🔧

**Sequence** Understanding a sequence of events helps you understand what caused something to happen. Can you sequence the events that led to the rainbow-colored mountains of Peru?

## A Colorful Change

Sedimentary rocks change when conditions on Earth change. Rainbow Mountain in Peru is a beautiful example. For millions of years, the plains of South America flooded and drained over and over. Each flood or dry period left behind different sediments. The sediments hardened into horizontal rock layers with different colors. Later, movement of the Earth's crust pushed the sediment layers straight upward. Similar to how iron rusts and turns red, minerals in the layers became even more colorful when they combined with the air. Wind smoothed the jagged rocks of Rainbow Mountain over time.

Over millions of years, some of the plains of western Peru transformed into large mountains, such as Rainbow Mountain.

**Draw Conclusions** How could scientists figure out which rock layer is oldest at Rainbow Mountain?

_____

_____

_____

_____

_____

## Geologic Time Scale

Fossils appear in rock strata in a certain order. They form predictable patterns. By studying rock strata, scientists have been able to construct a fossil record. This record tells how organisms have changed over time. From the fossils, scientists developed a geologic time scale. This scale spans the entire history of Earth. It divides time into unequal sections. Some different organisms lived during each section of time. Certain fossils can tell a geologist right away how old a rock is.

**Interpret Diagrams** How long ago did dinosaurs go extinct?

_____

_____

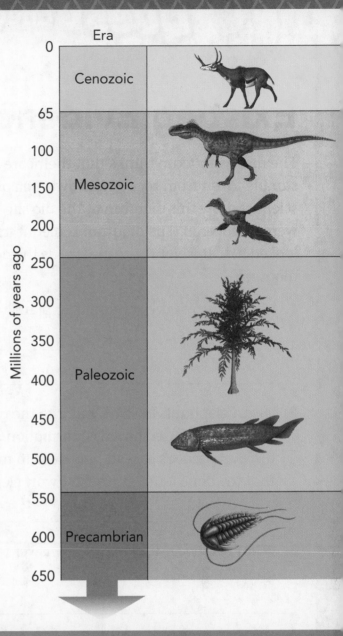

Era

Millions of years ago

| | |
|---|---|
| 0 | |
| | Cenozoic |
| 65 | |
| 100 | |
| 150 | Mesozoic |
| 200 | |
| 250 | |
| 300 | |
| 350 | |
| 400 | Paleozoic |
| 450 | |
| 500 | |
| 550 | |
| 600 | Precambrian |
| 650 | |

## Lesson 1 Check

1. **Infer** What are some features of ancient organisms that a fossil might reveal?

_____

_____

2. **Identify** What patterns can be seen in fossil and rock formations?

_____

_____

_____

# Existing Evidence

The discovery team thinks that their core sample may match a reference sample taken from rock where dwarf elephant bones were found. A scientist drew this diagram at the dig site where dwarf elephant bones were discovered. The diagram is meant to show only what the rock strata looked like. It is not the same size as the actual dig site. Examine the diagram.

1. Which layer is the youngest? Explain.

_____

_____

2. Dwarf elephants looked similar to the elephants that are alive today but smaller. Based on this information, which layer would the discovery team's core sample need to match to help provide evidence that the bone found is from a dwarf elephant?

_____

3. What evidence supports your answer to question 2?

_____

_____

_____

_____

_____

_____

_____

# Canyonlands

Did you know that a hike into a canyon can let you see the past? Rivers carve canyons after rock layers form. The walls of the canyon expose rock layers and evidence about the past. The diagram shows the dimensions of a steep canyon.

Use a metric ruler to answer the following questions.

1. Measure the thickness of each layer in centimeters. Use the scale provided to find the actual thickness of each layer.

2. How much thicker is the Paleozoic layer than the Mesozoic layer?

_____

3. How deep is the canyon?

_____

| Layer | Measurement in centimeters | Actual thickness of layer in meters |
|-------|----------------------------|-------------------------------------|
| Paleozoic | | |
| Mesozoic | | |
| Cenozoic | | |

4. How can patterns in a canyon rock formation provide evidence of changes in a landscape over time?

_____

_____

_____

Scale
1 cm = 100 m

Cenozoic

Mesozoic

Paleozoic

Precambrian

The Precambrian layer continues below the bottom of the canyon.

▶ **VIDEO**

Go online to see what you can design as a museum fact checker.

# Making a Good Impression

**Phenomenon** Even if an organism decomposes before rock forms, it can still leave an imprint. An imprint is a mark or outline of an object on a surface. All living things are made of carbon. When an organism dies, it leaves a layer of carbon on the rock below. The rest of the organism decomposes, but the carbon layer on the rock remains. This carbon imprint can be preserved by sediments just like other fossils. The carbon layer can show the leaves of plants.

# Model It

Make your own model of a carbon imprint fossil!

1. Choose a plant that lived long ago. Press an item that looks similar to that plant into clay. Then paint your model and let it dry.

2. Place your model on a piece of cardboard. Place another piece of cardboard over your model. Flatten your model by pressing it down or using heavy books.

- ☐ Remove the cardboard over your model. Describe what your imprint looks like after it has been flattened.

- ☐ How is your imprint different from your original model? How is it the same?

- ☐ What does the paint in your model represent?

- ☐ What do the cardboard and books represent?

- ☐ How does your model show how a carbon imprint is formed?

# Evidence of Change from Fossils and Rock Formations

## I can...

Use patterns in fossils and rock formations to explain how a landscape has changed over time.

**4-ESS1-1**

**Literacy Skill**
Sequence

**Vocabulary**
key bed

**Academic Vocabulary**
sample

 **VIDEO**

Watch a video about evidence of change on Earth.

## ENGINEERING › Connection

Have you ever dug a hole in the sand at the beach? Were you trying to see how deep you could dig? Engineers dig very deep holes in the earth to see what is there. Many engineering challenges occur when drilling deep holes. Engineers must figure out how to keep their drill from breaking or melting. They also need to figure out how to keep the hole from collapsing.

So far, the deepest hole on Earth is the Kola Superdeep Borehole in Russia. From 1970 to 1994, engineers drilled through layers of rock and reached a depth of over 12 kilometers. Scientists were amazed to find microscopic plankton fossils over 6.5 kilometers underground.

**Describe** What kinds of things would you want to see if you were digging deep into Earth's surface?

_____

_____

# How can rock layers show change?

Earth is constantly changing. Earthquakes and molten magma below Earth's surface cause Earth's crust to change in different ways. How can you make a model to show some of these changes?

## Procedure

☐ **1.** Plan how you can use some or all of the materials to model the process of fossil formation. Write your plan.

_____

_____

_____

☐ **2. SEP Develop a Model** Have your teacher approve your plan before you begin. Then build your model.

☐ **3.** Think of how an event can change rock layers. Write a plan to model this event. What change will you model? Describe how you will model the changes to the rock layers.

_____

_____

_____

## Analyze and Interpret Data

**4. SEP Construct Explanations** Swap your model with a partner. How did your partner's event change the rock column he or she modeled?

_____

_____

**Materials**
- clear plastic cup
- safety goggles

**Suggested Materials**
- clay soil
- fine sand
- coarse sand
- fine gravel
- salt
- small paper clip
- crayon piece
- penny
- index card

⚠ Wear safety goggles.

**Science Practice**

Scientists identify evidence to study objects or support points in an explanation.

## Engineering Practice ▸ Toolbox

Scientists work with engineers to improve ways that they remove rock from fossils. Acids can sometimes be used to dissolve the rock surrounding the pollen fossils. Explain why a chemical might be a great choice to clean pollen fossils.

## Fossil Clues on Earth

Fossils can tell scientists about environments on Earth a long time ago. Pollens can form fossils. By counting the different types of pollen fossils in a small sample, scientists can know what plants grew in the area millions of years ago. The types of organisms that are fossilized in a layer give clues about what the land was like. For example, fossils of shells and fins come from a watery environment.

Some areas far from the ocean today are home to marine fossils, such as corals. Living corals grow in shallow water, so scientists can infer that these areas were once shallow seas. When sea levels go down, parts of the ocean become dry land. When sea levels go back up, the land becomes flooded by the ocean again. This is how fossils of land animals can appear between layers of marine fossils. Studying the fossil record helps us understand how Earth has changed.

✓ **READING CHECK** **Sequence** What sequence of events could lead to land fossils being found between fossils of sea animals?

_____

_____

_____

## Index Fossils

Scientists look at the sequence of fossils to help determine the age of rock layers. Many fossils were formed during a certain period in Earth's history. Scientists find these fossils in many places on Earth, but they are always in the same layer of rock. These fossils are called index fossils. Layers of rock that have the same index fossils are about the same age, no matter where they were formed. Some kinds of trilobites, a form of ancient marine invertebrate, are well-known index fossils. Trilobites can be between 521 and 250 million years old, depending on the species. They are good index fossils because they fossilized easily and lived in many places on Earth. This means that their fossils are very common. Scientists can use them to decide the relative age of other fossils in many different places on Earth.

### Crosscutting Concepts ▸ Toolbox

**Patterns** Scientists look for patterns in nature to help answer questions. What kinds of patterns might you look for to determine whether an area has changed from land to water over time?

**Question It!** One of your friends has a fossil rock that he says is over 100 million years old. What are two questions you could ask to find out if this claim is true?

_____

_____

_____

# How can layers of rock change?

Scientists study how rock formations change.
The changes tell a lot about the history of Earth.
Earth's crust is constantly moving and changing.
The movement causes the formation of mountains.

Faults are deep cracks in Earth's crust. Forces deep inside Earth cause Earth's crust to shift or break apart along the fault during earthquakes.

The fault is always younger than the rock that surrounds it. An older rock layer may now lie higher than a younger rock layer.

A

B

**! Apply Concepts** In diagram B, how might a scientist know that two horizontal rock layers are different ages?

_____

_____

_____

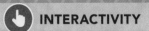
Layers of sedimentary rock change too. A process called folding tilts and bends the rock layers. This can form a mountain.

### Rock layers form.

Sedimentary rocks form in horizontal layers.

### Rock layers fold.

Folding bends the layers upward. A mountain forms.

### Rock layers erode.

Erosion takes place on the mountain. This exposes the rock below.

### New rock layers form over old rock layers.

Sediments are deposited over the eroded rock layers. New layers of rock form. This changes the order of the rock layers in this area.

## Comparing Rock Layers

Scientists can match the rock layers of the same age from different locations. They correlate rocks by studying key beds. A **key bed** is a layer of rock that scientists can clearly identify. They use index fossils or characteristics unique to rock layers to identify the key bed.

Key bed layers form in different ways. Large volcanic eruptions produce a lot of ash. The ash that settles on Earth forms key beds. So does debris from meteorites or asteroids crashing into Earth.

One famous example of a key bed is a thin layer of clay that is called the K-T boundary. The clay layer formed from a meteorite impact at the end of the Mesozoic era. This was about 66 million years ago. At this time, dinosaurs and many other plants and animals became extinct.

**Apply** The diagram shows fossils from two key bed layers. The layers are from different locations. Draw lines to connect the two key bed layers.

## Quest Connection

How did the texture of the rock layers help you connect the key bed layers? How does this relate to the discovery team's core sample?

_____

_____

_____

_____

_____

## Mass Extinctions

When many species go extinct at the same time, it is called a mass extinction. Scientists were puzzled about the mass extinction at the end of the Mesozoic era. They took a small piece, or **sample**, from the key bed layers all over Earth. They discovered that all the samples had a substance called iridium. Iridium is rare on Earth. It is found in objects in space, such as asteroids. Scientists inferred from the iridium that a huge asteroid crashed on Earth. The resulting debris formed a cloud in Earth's atmosphere. It changed the climate. Many plants and animals, including dinosaurs, could no longer survive. They became extinct. From studying the clay key bed, scientists were able to explain an important event in Earth's history.

K-T boundary layer

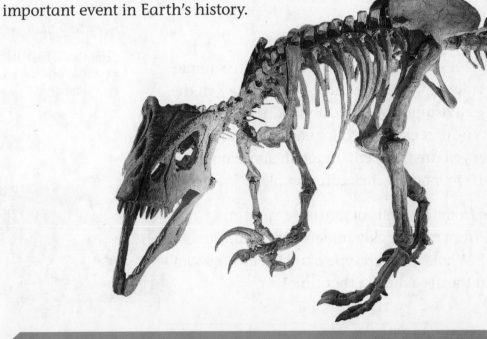

## ☑ Lesson 2 Check

1. **Describe** What can scientists learn about the history of Earth by looking at fossils?

_____

_____

2. **Explain** How do scientists match rock layers from different places on Earth?

_____

_____

# What does a core sample tell us?

You have learned how rock layers can provide clues about changes on Earth over time and about the environments where organisms once lived. Now examine the discovery team's core sample.

**Materials**
- Core Sample sheet
- paper towel tube
- tape
- markers

## Procedure

☐ **1.** The Core Sample sheet shows the layers from the core sample that you need to evaluate. There are three types of rock in the sample: limestone, sandstone, and mudstone. Choose a color to represent each type of rock. Then color each layer in the correct color. When you are finished, attach the handout to the paper towel tube to model a rock core sample.

**Science Practice**

Scientists **construct explanations** based on evidence.

☐ **2.** Limestone is made from the shells of marine organisms. Mudstone is made from mud or clay underwater. Sandstone is made from sand. What can each type of rock tell you about the environment in the area during that time?

_____

_____

_____

_____

_____

_____

_____

_____

3. Write a description of the fossils in the rock layers. Then describe the environment of the island at the time each layer formed. Look for patterns. Did the land change over time?

| Layer | Rock layer description | Environment of island |
|-------|------------------------|-----------------------|
|       |                        |                       |
|       |                        |                       |
|       |                        |                       |
|       |                        |                       |
|       |                        |                       |

# Analyze and Interpret Data

4. **SEP Draw Conclusions** Has the landscape changed over time or stayed mostly the same? Identify evidence to support your claim.

_____

_____

_____

# Dig for the Truth

*How can rocks and fossils describe a location?*

**INTERACTIVITY**

Organize data to support your Quest Findings.

## Evaluate the Evidence

**Phenomenon** Examine the dwarf elephant dig site diagram. Identify the rock formation patterns and fossil types (land or aquatic) in the rock layers. Analyze how the land changed over time. Then compare it to the discovery team's core sample. Look for similarities and differences.

**CCC Patterns** Use the evidence to decide if the two core samples show the same patterns. Evaluate whether the rock layer where dwarf elephants have been found is present in the core sample from the discovery team.

_____

_____

_____

_____

_____

_____

## Construct Explanations

**SEP Use Evidence** Write a report that summarizes your findings. Explain whether or not the core sample from the discovery team provides evidence that the unknown bone is from a dwarf elephant.

QUEST CHECK ✓ OFF

# Museum Fact Checker

A museum fact checker studies the objects that come into a museum. These might include fossils and objects made by humans, such as tools or arrowheads. Museum fact checkers may write labels that go with objects. Or they may provide information to the public about each object.

Museum fact checkers must be sure that information is correct. They need to use reliable sources. A reliable source might be a scientific study about an object, or it might be data gathered from scientific observations. Fact checkers need to be able to tell what sources are trustworthy. That means they need to use good research and critical thinking skills.

**Reflect** In your science notebook, describe the skills that you have that would help you as a fact checker. Why would they be helpful?

## ✓ Assessment

**1. Draw Conclusions** A farmer in the Midwest finds a fossil of a clamshell on his farm. How might the farmer explain the presence of the fossil?

_____

_____

_____

**2. Vocabulary** Which of these describes rock strata?

**A.** scientists who study rock layers

**B.** a crack in Earth's crust where movement occurs

**C.** layers of rock deposited over a long period of time

**D.** minerals that cause rocks to have different colors

**3. Cause and Effect** What might cause a gap in the geologic record between layers of rock?

**A.** erosion

**B.** faulting

**C.** folding

**D.** tilting

**4. Sequence** Place the following events in the sequence in which they happened. Label the first event starting with 1.

_____ Sediments harden into rock layers.

_____ Igneous rocks formed by magma interrupt the layer.

_____ Fish die and are buried in sediment.

_____ Sediments are deposited on the ocean floor.

**5. Interpret Diagrams** Study the diagram. Which layer contains fossils of the most recently living organisms? Explain.

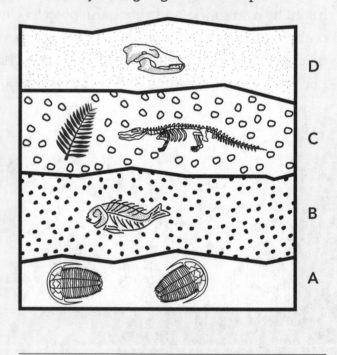

_____

_____

_____

**6. Cause and Effect** Complete the chart. Write an effect for each cause.

| Cause | Effect |
|---|---|
| Earth shifts along a fault in its surface. | |
| A massive asteroid hits Earth at the end of the Mesozoic era. | |
| A large volcanic eruption produces ash. | |

**7. Identify** Which term would describe the fossilized tracks of an organism that lived long ago?

**A.** body fossil

**B.** index fossil

**C.** key fossil

**D.** trace fossil

*What evidence can you find that Earth's surface has changed?*

**Show What You Learned**

Describe three ways that scientists can tell that Earth's surface has changed.

_____

_____

_____

_____

_____

_____

_____

_____

_____

_____

_____

_____

_____

_____

_____

_____

Read this scenario and answer questions 1–6.

A team of students is studying two different rock layers. They uncovered several different kinds of fossils at the dig sites. From their findings, they made two diagrams of the rock layers. They want to compare the fossils to determine the ages of the rock layers. Look at the diagrams and answer questions 1–6

Dig Site 1

Dig Site 2

**1. Construct an Explanation** Which rock layer in Dig Site 1 is the oldest? How do you know?

_____

_____

**2. Patterns** Which layers in Dig Site 1 and Dig Site 2 are about the same age?

  **A.** layers D and I

  **B.** layers A and L

  **C.** layers G and J

  **D.** layers B and I

**3. Use Evidence** Explain your answer to question 2.

_____

_____

**4. Construct an Explanation** If the fossil in layer B is about 400 million years old, how old is the rock in layer J? Explain.

_____

_____

_____

**5. Patterns** Suppose that the leaf fossils in layer K are index fossils that are about 300 million years old. Which layers have fossils that are older than these leaf fossils?

**A.** layers C and B

**B.** layers G and L

**C.** layers E and F

**D.** layers E and L

**6. Construct an Explanation** The students intend to use the evidence they gathered to explain how the environments around the dig sites have changed over time. Use the evidence to explain the changes that happened.

_____

_____

_____

_____

_____

_____

_____

# uDemonstrate Lab

# How can you correlate rock layers?

**Phenomenon** Scientists examine all of the evidence available in order to explain what they observe. How can you use evidence gathered from different places to explain how the places are alike?

## Procedure

☐ **1.** An excavation team examined three dig sites. Your job is to match the rock layers. How can you find the relative ages of the different samples?

_____

☐ **2.** Examine the evidence from the dig sites. Describe what you think is the most important piece of evidence.

_____

_____

**Science Practice**

▶ Scientists **construct explanations** using evidence and observations.

**Location 2**

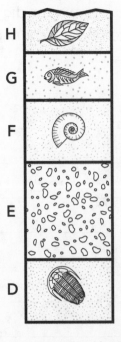

**Location 3**

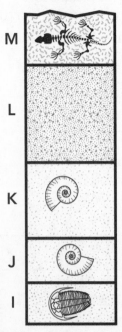

**Location 1**

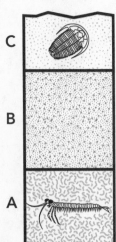

# Analyze and Interpret

**3. Draw Conclusions** Use evidence to identify which rock layers are the same age. Explain your answer.

_____

_____

_____

_____

_____

**4. SEP Construct Explanations** Which fossil layers are older than the index fossil? Explain.

_____

_____

_____

**5. SEP Construct Explanations** Which fossil layers are younger than the index fossil? Explain.

_____

_____

_____

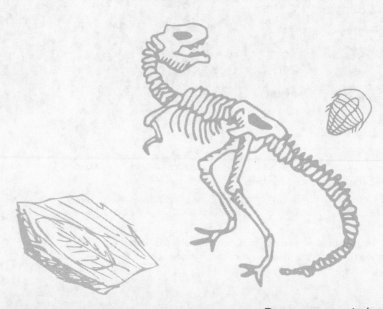

# Structures and Functions

**Next Generation Science Standards**

**4-LS1-1** Construct an argument that plants and animals have internal and external structures that function to support survival, growth, behavior, and reproduction.

**4-LS1-2** Use a model to describe that animals receive different types of information through their senses, process the information in their brain, and respond to the information in different ways.

Go online to access
your digital course.

▶ VIDEO

📖 eTEXT

👆 INTERACTIVITY

⚗ VIRTUAL LAB

🎮 GAME

☑ ASSESSMENT

**The Essential Question** *How do plant and animal structures support growth and survival?*

## Show What You Know

How do the giraffe's long neck, tongue, and legs give it a survival advantage over shorter animals?

_____

_____

_____

### STEM Let Plants and Animals Inspire You!

Which human problem can you help solve using what you learn about plants and animals?

**Phenomenon** Hi! I am Leigh Meredith, and I am a nature photographer. Have you ever noticed the many different shapes, sizes, and colors of both plants and animals? Wouldn't it be fun to see how a plant or animal uses these features? You can do just that! In this problem-based learning activity, you will use what you learn about plant and animal features to solve a human problem of your choosing.

Many products we use every day were inspired by plants and animals. For example, cats have pads on the bottoms of their paws, so when they jump, their fall is cushioned. Similarly, shoes have padding, or soles, on the bottom so our feet do not hurt when we walk on the hard ground.

Follow the path to learn how you will complete the Quest. The Quest activities in the lessons will help you complete the Quest! Check off your progress on the path when you complete an activity with a QUEST CHECK ✓ OFF . Go online for more Quest activities.

## Quest Check-In Lab 1

### Lesson 1
Examine the internal structure of a stem, and apply what you learn to solving a human problem.

**Next Generation Science Standards**
**4-LS1-1 Construct** an argument that plants and animals have internal and external structures that function to support survival, growth, behavior, and reproduction.

## Quest Check-In 4

### Lesson 4
How can lobster claws
inspire a solution to a
human problem?

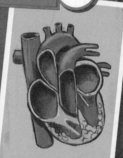

## Quest Check-In 3

### Lesson 3
Think of a product
that could be designed
based on what you
learn about the swim
bladder of a fish.

## Quest Check-In 5

### Lesson 5
Explore how bats
observe their
environment and
how their process
might apply to a
human product.

## Quest Check-In 2

### Lesson 2
Examine the structures
of seeds, and identify
how they might be used to
solve a human problem.

## Quest Findings

Complete the Quest! Choose
a plant or animal structure to
inspire your own design solution
for a human problem. Build a
model to help communicate
your solution.

# How do your eyes respond to differences in lighting?

Scientists analyze how a system changes in response to a variable. How can you investigate how the human eye reacts to light?

**Materials**

- flashlight
- white paper
- tape

⚠ Do not shine the flashlight directly into the eyes.

## Procedure

☐ **1.** Look closely at the eyes of another student. Find the pupil, which is the dark circle in the middle of the eye. Predict what will happen to the pupil when the environment has more and less light.

_____

_____

☐ **2. SEP Plan an Investigation** Make a plan to test your prediction without shining light directly into the eye. Show your plan to your teacher before you begin.

☐ **3.** Conduct your investigation. Record your observations.

**Science Practice**

Scientists **analyze information** from investigations.

## Analyze and Interpret Data

**4. SEP Use Data** Was your prediction right? How do you think the pupil helps humans adapt to different environments?

_____

_____

_____

_____

_____

_____

Observations

# Compare and Contrast

 **GAME**

Practice what you learn with the Mini Games.

Scientists compare and contrast structures of plants. When they compare, they find out what is the same. When they contrast, they find out what is different. Read the text to learn about the trunk of an oak tree and the trunk of a white birch tree.

## Oak Tree

The trunk of an oak tree is sturdy, large, and dark brown. The bark covering its trunk is thick. The trunk supports the tree. Branches grow from the trunk. The internal structures of the trunk take water to all parts of the tree.

## White Birch Tree

The trunk of a white birch tree is narrow and white. The bark covering the trunk is thin. The trunk supports the tree. The trunk has branches growing from it. The internal structures of the trunk take water to all parts of the tree.

☑ READING CHECK **Compare and Contrast** Complete the chart.

| Oak tree trunk | Both trunks | White birch tree trunk |
|---|---|---|
| | | |

# Internal Structures and Functions of Plants

## I can...

Describe some internal structures that help plants survive and reproduce.

**4-LS1-1**

**Literacy Skill**
Compare and Contrast

**Vocabulary**

structure
function
ovary
vascular system

**Academic Vocabulary**

external
internal

▶ **VIDEO**

Watch a video about plant functions and structures.

## CURRICULUM ⟩ Connection

Have you ever made a delicious fruit salad for a picnic? A fruit salad might contain watermelon, oranges, kiwi, papaya, peaches, apricots, nectarines, and bananas. One of the hardest parts about making a fruit salad is avoiding all the seeds that fruits contain.

You may have eaten an orange and a peach. They are both round fruits, but on the inside the orange has small seeds and the peach has one giant pit.

Look at the cross section of an orange and a peach. The peach pit actually contains a seed.

**Infer** Why do you think the peach seed is enclosed in such a hard pit? Explain.

_____

_____

# uInvestigate Lab

# What parts are inside a flower?

Scientists make observations and collect evidence to understand how nature works. How can you dissect a flower to see its parts?

**Materials**
- flower
- forceps
- toothpick
- hand lens

## Procedure

☐ 1. Remove the petals of a flower. Describe what you see at the base of the flower. Predict what you might find inside this part.

_____

_____

 Wash your hands when done.

 Dispose of materials properly.

☐ 2. What do you think is the best way to observe what is inside this part? Write a procedure. Show your plan to your teacher before you begin.

_____

_____

**Science Practice**

Scientists **construct explanations** that are supported by evidence.

☐ 3. Record your observations by drawing what you observe. Include any important notes on your diagram.

## Analyze and Interpret Data

4. **SEP Analyze Information** Do your observations support your prediction? Explain.

_____

_____

_____

_____

_____

Observations

## Literacy ▸ Toolbox

**Compare and Contrast**
You can understand plants better if you know how they are alike and different. Underline the parts of the definitions that describe the difference between external and internal structures in a plant.

# Structures

Each organism is a system. The system is made of different **structures**, or organized parts, that work together to help the organism survive.

Plants have **external**, or outer, structures that are easy to see. The plant system also has structures that are **internal**, or inside the plant. These internal structures can best be seen and understood by cutting, or dissecting the plant. When you cut open an aloe plant, which has a stiff, green exterior, you find a clear gel inside. Internal structures can be surprising like this.

Internal structures in plants take on many shapes. They can be large or so small that you can see them only with a microscope. Each kind can be in just one part of the plant or throughout many parts of the plant. The kinds of internal structures plants have depend on their environment.

**Reflect** What is your favorite plant? What structures does it have that make it different from other kinds of plants?

# Functions

Each structure of a plant has a **function**, or particular job. Some of the most important functions are survival, growth, protection, and reproduction. The internal structures of a plant function to help the plant survive and remain healthy. They may aid in protection or help with growth and reproduction. The functions of each kind of internal structure are more specific. For example, the **ovary** of a flower is the female reproductive part that helps the plant reproduce. Its specific function is to produce eggs and provide a place for seeds to develop. The seeds inside a tomato start out as eggs in the ovary of a tomato flower.

**INTERACTIVITY**

Complete an activity on the structure of flowers.

ovary

☑ **READING CHECK** **Compare and Contrast**
Each plant's system has internal structures that help it survive. How would the functions of a plant system be different between a plant living in a desert and one living in a forest?

_____

_____

_____

_____

_____

**Question It!** Fruits develop when a protective layer grows around a seed. What questions would you ask to determine which fresh produce you eat is a fruit?

_____

_____

_____

# What are some functions of internal leaf structures?

Plants need to make food to survive. Plants use a process called photosynthesis to make food or sugar. Three internal structures of the plant help in this process.

In photosynthesis, the veins of a plant draw water from the soil up into its leaves where, along with carbon dioxide, it is converted into sugar.

**Infer** What do you think would happen to a plant that does not have chloroplasts?

!

_____

_____

**stomata**

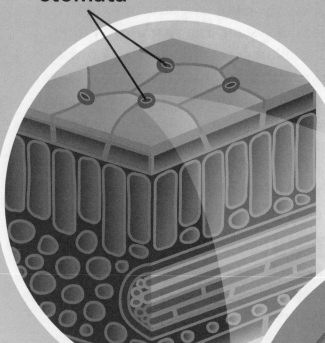

Photosynthesis happens inside chloroplasts, which are found inside leaves. During photosynthesis, energy from the sun is used to convert water and carbon dioxide from the air into sugar and oxygen.

**chloroplasts**

Stomata are tiny openings on a leaf that take in carbon dioxide from air and release other gases from the plant.

**stoma**

## uBe a Scientist

**Make a Plant Collection**

With an adult, go outside and collect three plant parts. Try to pick parts that have already separated from the plant. Safely cut or break the parts open, and use a magnifying lens to search for internal structures. Some suggestions to observe are a twig, a stem of dandelion, or a big leaf. Draw what you see, and try to label the parts.

# Photosynthesis

Plants make their own food using the process of photosynthesis. During photosynthesis, a plant needs sunlight, carbon dioxide, and water. These materials must reach the plant's leaves. In addition, the food that the leaves make must reach the other parts of the plant. Without this food, the plant's cells would not have a source of energy and would die.

Some internal structures of the stem help move these materials throughout the plant. The structures make up the plant's vascular system. The **vascular system** is a collection of small tubes that transports, or carries, materials up, down, and throughout the plant. The two main structures of the vascular system are tubes called xylem and phloem. Xylem moves materials in only one direction—upward from the roots to all the plant parts. It carries water with dissolved nutrients from the roots. Phloem moves in many directions. It transports food from the leaves to all other parts of the plant.

☑ **READING CHECK** **Compare and Contrast** Contrast the movement of materials in xylem and phloem by drawing arrows beside each label on the diagram. Then write one way they are the same.

_____

xylem

phloem

## Quest Connection

▼▼▼▼▼▼▼▼▼▼▼▼▼▼▼▼▼▼▼▼▼▼▼▼▼▼▼▼

Choose a plant. Find a structure of the plant with an interesting shape. What human products have a similar shape with a similar purpose?

_____

_____

_____

## Plant Adaptations to Their Environment

One group of plants that has adapted to its environment is the cactus. The cactus must survive in the desert, where little rain falls. The internal structures of the cactus take in water when it rains and store it for a long time. This process takes place in the cactus stem, which is larger than stems in most kinds of plants. With these internal structures, the cactus can survive in very dry weather.

## ☑ Lesson 1 Check

1. **Define** Fill in the missing spaces in the table to summarize some internal plant structures and their functions.

| Structure | Function |
|---|---|
| xylem | |
| | female flower part used for reproduction |
| | transports sugars throughout the plant |

2. **Explain** Why would the colorful petals of a flower not be an internal structure?

_____

# Quest Check-In — Lab

# How can you **observe** a plant's vascular system in **action**?

Scientists use dyes to highlight certain structures of a plant. The celery that you buy in a grocery store is the stem of the plant. How can you observe how the stem moves materials?

**Materials**
- celery stalk with leaves
- plastic knife
- food coloring
- water
- clear containers
- plastic gloves
- apron

⚠️ Be careful using cutting tools.

⚠️ Do not taste.

⚠️ Wash your hands when finished.

⚠️ Wear plastic gloves and apron.

## Procedure

☐ 1. **CCC Structure and Function** What internal structures do you think are in the stem? Describe their functions.

_____

_____

☐ 2. How can you use the materials to observe the function of the celery stem? Make a plan. Show your plan to your teacher before you begin. Record your observations.

**Science Practice**

Scientists use evidence to construct an argument.

### Observations

# Analyze and Interpret Data

**4. SEP Use Evidence** Make an argument about where the xylem is in the celery stem. What evidence from your investigation supports this argument?

_____

_____

_____

**5. Apply Concepts** Xylem transports water. What human products can you think of that transport water? What human problem do they solve?

_____

_____

_____

_____

_____

# External Structures and Functions of Plants

## I can...

Describe some external structures that help plants survive and reproduce.

**4-LS1-1**

**Literacy Skill**
Compare and Contrast

**Vocabulary**
cuticle
sepal
stamen
pistil

**Academic Vocabulary**
classify

▶ **VIDEO**

Watch a video about external reproductive structures.

## ENGINEERING ⟩ Connection

Have you ever gone apple picking? Most apples that are sold in supermarkets today are picked by hand, and most workers pick thousands of apples a day. Handpicking can be slow and tiring. Engineers tried to make the process faster by developing a machine that shook the apple tree to make the apples fall off. The problem was that when the apples fell, they would bruise.

Engineers designed another machine called the apple vacuum harvester. One part of the machine is a tube with a slippery lining inside it. A worker stands on the edge of the machine, handpicks the apple, and puts it in the tube. The tube carries the apple to a large bin where a fanlike structure gently arranges the apples. The machine eliminates the need for ladders and prevents the workers from having to carry all the apples.

📓 **Write About It** In your science notebook, tell how you think the apple vacuum harvester helps orchard owners and people who buy apples.

# How are leaf coverings different?

Scientists collect evidence to understand plant structures and functions. How do leaf coverings help plants survive in different environments?

**Materials**
- 2 plant leaves
- water
- dropper
- hand lens
- crayons
- gloves

## Procedure

☐ **1.** Observe the leaves. Describe how they are different.

_____

_____

⚠ Wear gloves.

☐ **2. SEP Plan an Investigation** Plan a procedure to investigate what happens to water on each leaf covering. Show your plan to your teacher before you begin. Record your observations.

**Science Practice**

Scientists **gather evidence** to defend conclusions.

### Observations

## Analyze and Interpret Data

**3. SEP Use Evidence** Which type of leaf do you think would function best in a dry climate? Support your conclusion with the evidence you gathered.

_____

_____

**Plant Comparison**
Identify two plants you are familiar with. Develop a diagram that explains how two of their external structures are alike and different. Present your diagram to classmates.

## External Structures of a Plant

The external structures of plants are probably the ones you are most familiar with—the leaf, stem, roots, and flowers. You might also be familiar with two other external features—bark and thorns. Just like internal structures, the external parts of plants help them survive, grow, and reproduce.

Plants lose water through their leaves. The leaves have a **cuticle**, or a waxy outer covering. The cuticle helps limit the amount of water a plant loses. Plants that live in a desert environment often have thick leaves with a smooth, waxy cuticle. The thick, waxy coating gives the plant extra protection against water loss. The thick leaves help the plant store water. The same process also works in reverse. The waxy cuticle prevents unwanted water from entering the plant leaf. While water is good for a plant, it is best taken in through the roots of the plant and not the leaves. The cuticle cannot completely seal the plant leaf. It must work with the stomata to make sure that air can enter the plant.

Plants often attract animals for help with reproduction. When animals eat the red berries on the plant, they help scatter the seeds inside the berries. Plants also need to prevent the animal from eating them. One way to do this is with thorns, which are sharp, pointy structures on plant leaves or stems. Cacti contain a lot of water, and thirsty animals would want to eat them. Thorns like those on this cactus, help keep animals away. Roses have prickles, which are similar to thorns.

☑ READING CHECK **Compare and Contrast**
Even though they look different, how are a leaf cuticle and a thorn the same?

_____

_____

## Stems and Their Coverings

Stems come in many forms. Some stems are green. Other stems are woody. Scientists can **classify**, or group, stems according to their structures and functions. The type of stem a certain kind of plant has depends on the environment in which it must survive.

Tree trunks, for example, are covered in bark. This outside barrier protects the tree from harmful materials or organisms in its environment. The bark of some kinds of trees is thick. Other kinds of trees have thin bark. The bark on this Scots pine tree is very thick. The thick bark protects it from the fires that often happen in its environment. Trees with thin bark are more likely to die when fires happen.

## Model It!

Diagrams are one kind of model. Draw the trunk of a tree that must survive in a windy environment. Next, draw the trunk of a tree that has no wind in its environment. Focus on how the trunk might change because of the wind.

## Quest Connection

Tree bark protects the trunk of a tree. Humans also need protection. What are some kinds of body covering that humans use for protection?

_____

_____

# Which structures do flowering plants use to REPRODUCE?

Flowering plants have external structures that help them reproduce.

The **stamen** is the male part of a flower that makes pollen. Pollen is the male reproductive cell.

Petals have a variety of colors, patterns, shapes, and odors that attract pollinators.

The **pistil** contains a plant's female reproductive parts and receives pollen transferred from a stamen.

The **sepal** protects the budding flower by wrapping around it.

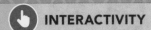
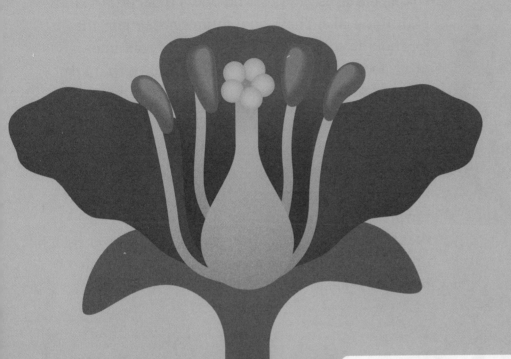

! **Infer** How do you think petals protect the internal structures of a plant?

_____

_____

_____

! **Compare** How do the numbers of male and female reproductive structures of this flower compare?

_____

_____

_____

## Adaptations of Flowers

Why do flowers come in so many different colors? Over time, some kinds of flowers have developed colors, patterns, shapes, and odors that certain kinds of animals like. These adaptations are important for making sure that the right kind of pollinator is attracted to the flower. For example, birds that take nectar from a flower need a flower structure that they can perch on.

A bee is one very important pollinator of flowering plants. Many people think bees are attracted to the bright flower colors we see. However, scientific tests have provided evidence that bees are also attracted to ultraviolet light, which we cannot see. Flower colors and ultraviolet light often make patterns that direct bees to the location of the nectar.

## ☑ Lesson 2 Check

**1. Predict** Suppose a disease caused the cuticle on a plant's leaves to disappear. What would most likely happen to the plant? Why?

_____

_____

**2. Explain** How are the functions of a flower's stamen and pistil related to reproduction?

_____

_____

_____

_____

# Throwing Seeds Around

Plants have developed many different ways to scatter their seeds. If seeds are scattered, they are more likely to survive when they sprout because they do not compete as much for things they need.

The photos show structures that plants have developed to help them disperse their seeds.

> The female pine cone stores the seeds until they are ready to be dispersed.

> The milkweed seed pod explodes, flinging its seeds great distances.

> The coconut can float for long periods because its covering traps air.

> The light fluffy seeds of the dandelion are easily blown by the wind.

**Interpret Photos** Choose one of the seeds and explain how it might be used to solve a human problem.

_____

_____

_____

_____

_____

# Internal Structures and Functions of Animals

## I can...

Describe some internal structures that help animals survive.
**4-LS1-1**

**Literacy Skill**
Compare and Contrast

**Vocabulary**
skeleton
heart
lungs
gills
brain

**Academic Vocabulary**
interpret

▶ **VIDEO**

Watch a video about internal structures of animals.

## STEM ⟩ Connection

Have you heard of catgut? Sounds gross! However, it is not really the guts of a cat. Catgut is made from the intestines of other animals. For a long time, medical sutures were made from catgut. Sutures are the stitches that are used to close up a wound. To make the material of catgut, the animal intestines were twisted into a cord shape. They were sterilized to make them safer to use on wounds. Today, other materials, such as cotton, are commonly used to make sutures. These materials are cheaper to make, and they cause fewer infections.

**Identify** What are two advantages of using newer materials rather than catgut?

_____

_____

Sterile
Surgical Sutures
"THEY ARE HEAT STERILIZED"

(NON-BOILABLE)

KALMERID CATGUT

20-DAY CHROMIC

Size 1    Product 1445

TWELVE TUBES, each contains approximately five feet. Sutures are ready for use as they come from the tubes and require no moistening. Do not boil—to sterilize the exterior of tubes, submerge them in any active alcoholic germicidal solution. Unaffected by age, climate, or light.

# How can you **compare** the stomachs of **cows** and **dogs**?

**Materials**
• Cow and Dog Stomachs sheet
• metric ruler

Scientists compare similar structures in different animals to help them understand how structures are unique to each kind of animal. How can you compare the stomach of a cow and a dog?

**Science Practice**

Scientists use evidence to support an argument.

## Procedure

☐ 1. Observe the diagrams of the cow and dog stomachs. What are three features that you can use to compare and contrast the stomachs?

_____

_____

☐ 2. Make a table to record your observations of the features of the two stomachs.

| Feature | Cow stomach | Dog stomach |
|---|---|---|
| Location in body | | |
| Shape | | |
| Number of pouches | | |

## Analyze and Interpret Data

3. **Compare** A cow is bigger than a dog. How does the size of the animal compare to the size of its stomach?

_____

_____

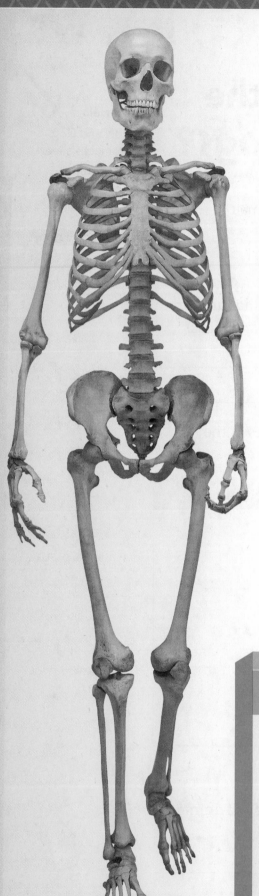

## Animal Structures for Support

Like plant bodies, animal bodies need support. Because most animals move, they need a different kind of support system than plants need. All mammals, including humans and dogs, have a **skeleton**—a rigid support system that includes bones that connect to the soft structures of the body. Without a skeleton, a mammal would have little shape and be unable to move. Animals with an internal bony skeleton are called vertebrates. They include mammals, fish, frogs, snakes, and birds.

☑ **READING CHECK Compare and Contrast** Label the parts of the human skeleton with the same labels shown on the dog skeleton.

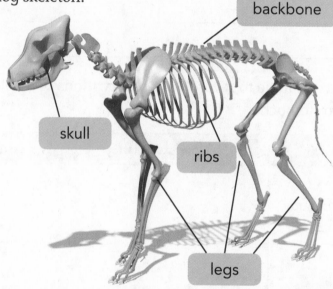

backbone

skull

ribs

legs

## Quest Connection

Identify a situation in which a human might need something strong and sturdy for support. What product would you suggest?

_____

_____

_____

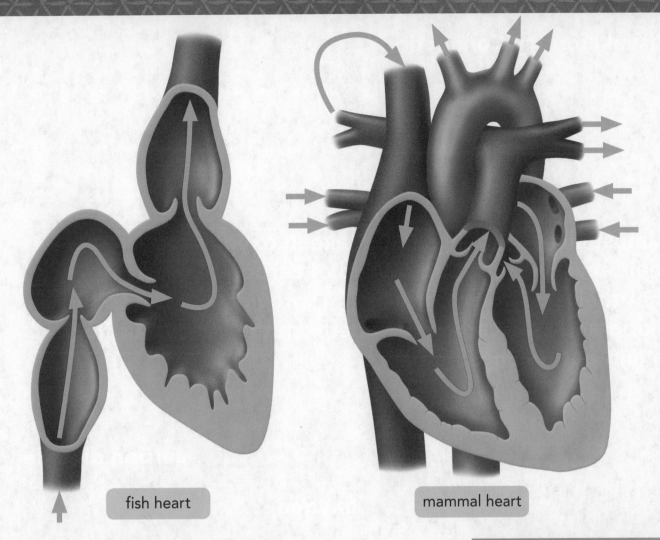

fish heart

mammal heart

## Structure of the Animal Heart

Vertebrates rely on blood to carry many of the materials they need to all parts of the body. For blood to move through the body, something must pump it. In vertebrate animals, the **heart** is the internal organ that pumps blood. It usually is located near the center of the body. The ribs of the skeleton protect it.

Most vertebrates that live in water have hearts that pump blood around the body in one circular motion. Vertebrates that live on land usually have hearts that pump blood in two different circles. One side of the heart pumps blood from the heart to and from the lungs. The other side of the heart pumps blood from the lungs to all parts of the body.

☑ **READING CHECK** **Compare and Contrast** Underline the differences between the hearts of vertebrates that live in water and the hearts of vertebrates that live on land. Circle the similarities.

### Math ▸ Toolbox

**Compare Amounts** An adult heart pumps about 5 L of blood each minute. An athlete's heart can pump as much as 35 L a minute. How much more blood does an athlete's heart pump per minute when compared to an average adult heart?

# How do lungs and gills compare?

Almost all living things must take in oxygen gas from their environments and get rid of carbon dioxide gas that their bodies produce. **Lungs** provide oxygen to the blood and take carbon dioxide from the blood. Air flows in and out of lungs.

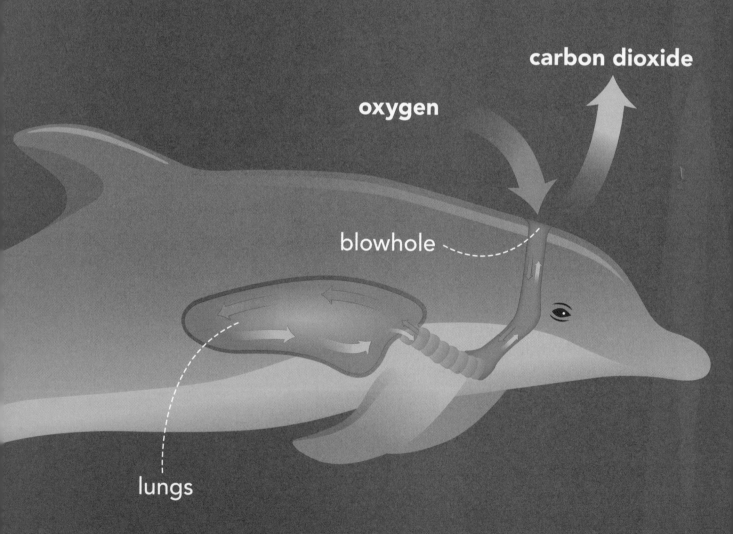

carbon dioxide

oxygen

blowhole

lungs

**INTERACTIVITY**

Complete an activity on the structures and functions of internal animal parts.

In fish, the process happens in its gills. **Gills** are organs found in fish that extract oxygen from the water as water flows around gills.

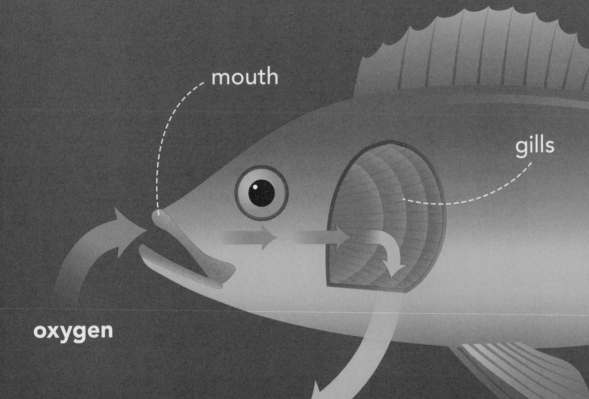

mouth

gills

oxygen

carbon dioxide

! **Infer** Why do you think mammals, such as dolphins, and fish have different structures to perform the same function?

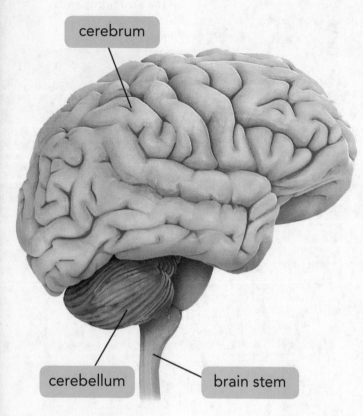

cerebrum

cerebellum

brain stem

## Structure of the Animal Brain

The **brain** is the structure that receives information about an animal's environment. It **interprets**, or figures out the meaning of, the information it receives and tells the body how to respond. In vertebrates, the brain is located inside the protective skull. Different parts of the brain are involved in different functions. For example, the cerebrum is the thinking part of the brain. It gets the information about an animal's environment. The cerebellum coordinates the animal's movement. The brain stem controls how many internal structures function.

**Infer** People sometimes say that serious thinkers are *cerebral*. Why do you think they use that word?

_____

_____

_____

_____

## ☑ Lesson 3 Check

**1. Identify** What is the function of the vertebrate skeleton?

_____

_____

**2. Evaluate** How are lungs and gills adapted for different types of environments?

_____

_____

_____

# Fish Float and Sink

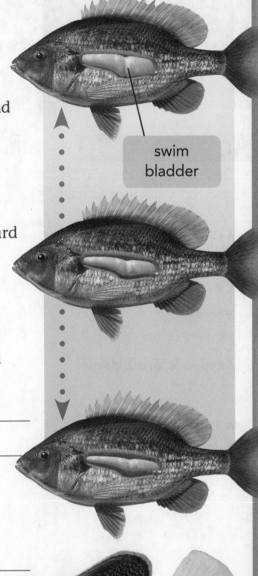

swim bladder

Did you ever wonder why a fish can float day after day? And how does it move upward or downward? The reason is that some fish have a swim bladder. The swim bladder is like a balloon inside the fish. The more gas that is in the swim bladder, the higher the fish will float.

The swim bladder is surrounded by muscles. To move upward in the water, the fish relaxes the muscles around the bladder, and it fills with more air. To move deeper, the fish tightens the muscles, and the air is pushed out. By sinking and floating, the fish can gather food and avoid predators.

**Identify** Which existing human inventions are similar to a fish's swim bladder?

_____

_____

**Brainstorm** Think of an invention based on a fish's swim bladder that could solve a human problem. Identify the problem in your response.

_____

_____

_____

# External Structures and Functions of Animals

## I can...

Describe some external structures that help animals survive and reproduce.

**4-LS1-1**

**Literacy Skill**
Compare and Contrast

**Vocabulary**
exoskeleton

**Academic Vocabulary**
characteristic

▶ **VIDEO**

Watch a video about external structures of animals.

## CURRICULUM ⟩ Connection

A horse's tail is surrounded by long, flowing hair. The long hair has a useful function of swatting away flies that bite the horse. Humans use the hair of the horse's tail in a different way. If you have ever seen someone play the violin, you have seen one way humans use horsehair. It is used in the bow of the string instrument. The horsehair is stretched into a thin ribbon to serve as the bow. When it glides across the violin strings, it makes a sound that we hear as music. People have been using horsehair this way for more than 400 years.

**Infer** Why do you think horsehair is preferred for bows over dog hair ?

_____

_____

_____

_____

# How can you design a protective insect shell?

Scientists design models to find solutions to problems. How can you design a model insect with a protective shell that helps the insect survive?

## Design and Build

☐ **1.** Consider the scenario your teacher has provided. What criteria must the outer shell of your insect meet to protect the insect?

_____

_____

_____

☐ **2. SEP Develop a Model** Draw a design for your insect. Plan how you will test your insect to see whether it meets the criteria. Show your drawing and plan to your teacher. Build your model. Record your observations.

## Evaluate Your Design

**3. SEP Evaluate Models** Compare your design with those of others. Which design met the criteria best? Why do you think that is so?

_____

_____

_____

_____

_____

**Suggested Materials**

- aluminum foil
- paper
- tape
- small foam balls
- toothpicks
- pipe cleaners
- cardboard
- crayons
- pieces of plastic

**Science Practice**

Scientists **develop and use models** to test interactions.

My Insect

# What do exoskeletons do?

Not all animals have support systems similar to those of vertebrates. The support structure for some animals is an **exoskeleton,** a hard external covering that is waterproof. The exoskeleton protects the soft body underneath. Large exoskeletons are called shells.

## Snail

A snail's exoskeleton, or shell, protects the snail from the sun and water loss. The shell also acts as a way for the snail to camouflage into its environment.

**INTERACTIVITY**

Complete an activity
on external structures
of organisms.

## Ladybug

A ladybug's exoskeleton helps to protect
its wings. Ladybugs have two pairs of
wings, a set of wings that are hard like
their exoskeleton, and then a set of
flying wings that are softer for flight.

## Crab

A crab's shell helps protect its
internal structure from the
aquatic environment that it
lives in. Its shell is waterproof,
which helps crabs survive.

## Other External Structures of Animals

For animals that do not have an exoskeleton, other external structures provide protection.

**Skin** Skin protects the animal body and acts as a barrier against harmful materials. Skin can be different colors or textures. Rhinoceroses have thick, rough skin to protect them from the hot African sun and biting insects. Naked mole rats have soft, thin skin because they live underground where the soil is cool and dark.

**Fur, Feathers, and Scales** Some animals have fur, feathers, or scales for protection. The bear's fur is thick to keep it warm in cold weather. Bird feathers protect against temperature changes. Feathers also enable most birds to fly. Birds can fly to avoid predators, to look for food, and to migrate. The scales of reptiles and fish are a rough covering that protects and insulates the body.

**Claws** Claws are sharp, pointy structures on the feet of mammals, reptiles, and birds. They are used for capturing, carrying, and tearing apart prey.

☑ **READING CHECK** **Compare and Contrast** Underline the words that show how the skin of a naked mole rat and the scales of a fish are alike. Circle how they are different.

## Quest Connection

Fur covers some animals and helps them regulate their body temperature in different climates. What is a product for humans that can regulate body temperature? How does it work?

_____

_____

_____

## Animal Characteristics

A **characteristic** is a quality or trait. Some characteristics of animal structures include color, size, and shape. Animals of the same kind share most characteristics, but sometimes the characteristics of the same structures are a bit different. An animal's characteristics enable the animal to survive and reproduce in its environment. For example, when male tree frogs are looking for a mate, they croak loudly by using special folds of skin that they can inflate, or blow up. Female tree frogs are usually attracted to the loudest sound because it often means that this male frog is the healthiest among other males.

📖 **Make Meaning** In your science notebook, identify some characteristics you share with other humans. Which of your characteristics are unique to you?

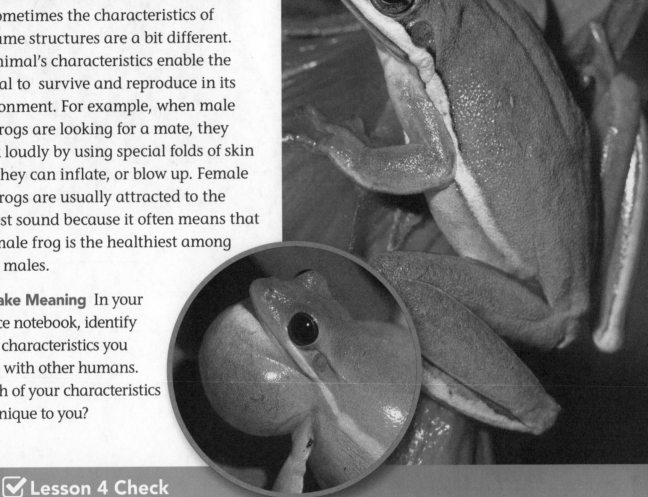

## ✅ Lesson 4 Check

1. **Identify** What are two external structures of the frogs in the picture? How do they help the frogs survive?

_____

_____

_____

2. ✅ **READING CHECK** **Compare and Contrast** How is an exoskeleton similar to the skeleton of vertebrates?

_____

_____

# Lobster **Claws**

One external structure that all lobsters share is their claws. A lobster has two types of claws—crusher claws and pincher claws. The crusher claw is larger and used to crush prey. The pincher claw has small "teeth" that help the lobster capture and open the shells of its prey.

**Brainstorm** Can you think of an invention that would help humans and is inspired by one type of lobster claw? How would the invention help humans?

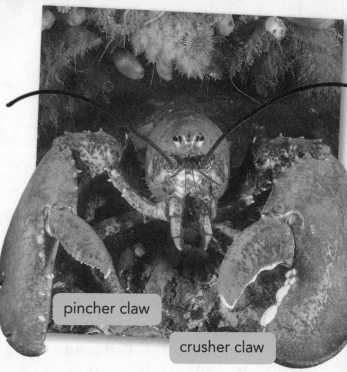

pincher claw

crusher claw

_____

_____

_____

**Design a Model** Draw a design of your invention.

## My Model

# Why do animals shed their exoskeletons?

**Phenomenon** Did you ever need new clothes because you outgrew your old ones? As your body grows, your clothes do not grow with it. In some ways, a rigid exoskeleton is similar to the clothes that humans wear. When an animal sheds its exoskeleton, the exoskeleton separates from its body, and the animal leaves it behind. A new exoskeleton then forms around the animal.

Why does the praying mantis in the photo need to shed its exoskeleton? Use evidence from the text as you consider these questions.

- What are some functions of exoskeletons?
- How does an exoskeleton limit an animal?
- What do you think might happen if the insect did not shed its exoskeleton?

Use what you considered to write a **science-based explanation** to answer the question in the title.

_____

_____

_____

_____

_____

_____

# Plant and Animal Responses to the Environment

## I can...

Explain how animals use sensory information to respond to their environments.
Describe how plants and animals can survive in different environments because of adaptations.
**4-LS1-2**

**Literacy Skill**
Compare and Contrast

**Vocabulary**
extinct

**Academic Vocabulary**
stimulus

 **VIDEO**

Watch a video about animal responses.

## ENGINEERING ⟩ Connection

Dogs have heightened senses and can often hear and smell things that a human cannot. For this reason, dogs are often used to detect particular odors. For example, at airports, dogs are used to sniff for bombs and drugs. The dogs help keep people safe so that nothing harmful gets on a plane. Dogs are also often sent on search parties to find people who are missing. They will smell a shirt that has the scent of a person on it. Then they will search for a similar scent. When they get on the trail of a scent, dogs will follow it with their nose until they find the missing person. Engineers are working to design an artificial, or human-made, nose that can act like a dog's nose. They have analyzed the way a dog detects a scent and have begun to mimic it in their designs.

**Apply** If you had a keen sense of smell like that of a dog, what do you think you would smell that you cannot smell now?

_____

## uInvestigate Lab

# How can YOU locate an object using only sound?

Scientists use models to answer questions about how animals sense the world around them. How can you find an object using only the sound it makes?

**Suggested Materials**
- blindfold
- bucket
- bell
- cooking pot

## Procedure

☐ **1.** Choose any object that makes a sound. Make a plan to model an animal that relies on sound to locate what they need.

☐ **2.** **SEP Develop a Model** Show your plan to your teacher. Build your model. Record your observations.

**Science Practice**

Scientists use models to better understand how something works.

### Observations

## Analyze and Interpret Data

**3.** **SEP Explain** How successful were you in locating the sound? Explain.

_____

_____

_____

_____

_____

# How do elephants respond to stimuli?

When animals receive a **stimulus**, or a nerve signal, the signal is sent to their brain. The brain interprets the signal. It then sends messages telling the body how to respond. Elephants receive information through their sense of sight, hearing, and touch.

See

Most elephants form family groups. The oldest elephant leads other elephants to find water. She uses the direction of her body to signal to other elephants which way they should go.

# Hear

Elephants use their trunks to make loud calls to signal the other elephants of danger in their environments. Usually, the older elephants will form a circle around the younger elephants to protect them.

# Feel

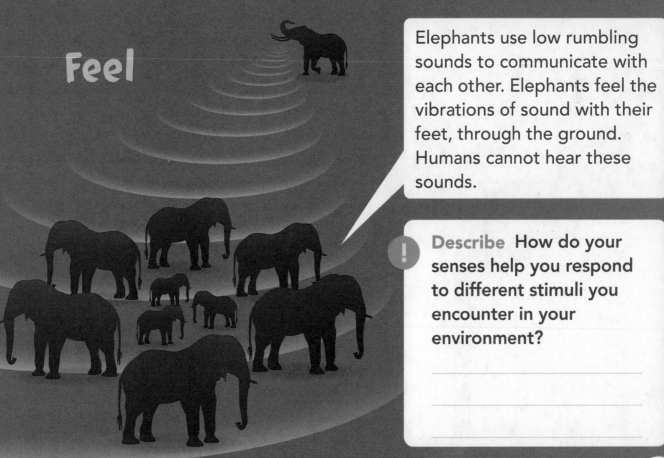

Elephants use low rumbling sounds to communicate with each other. Elephants feel the vibrations of sound with their feet, through the ground. Humans cannot hear these sounds.

**! Describe** How do your senses help you respond to different stimuli you encounter in your environment?

_____

_____

_____

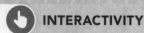

## uBe a Scientist

**Test Your Senses**
Plan an investigation that will test your sense of smell. Write a procedure, and share it with an adult before you begin. Present your results to your classmates.

## Animal Responses to Smell

Some animals have a sense of smell that is much stronger than that of humans. Animals with a keen sense of smell include bears, sharks, dogs, and snakes. These animals use their keen sense to find food or to observe that another animal is nearby. If they identify the approaching animal as an enemy, they can flee or hide. Snakes collect scent through their nostrils, though their tongue is better.

**Apply** How might the sense of smell help a mother protect her offspring?

_____

_____

## Quest Connection

How could you study an animal's senses to design a product for humans who are missing one of their senses?

_____

_____

_____

## Changing Environments and Survival

Environments can change, and plants and animals must be able to survive in those changed environments. Plants and animals that have adaptations to live in the new environment will survive. If an environment changes and a particular kind of plant or animal cannot survive there, that kind of organism may become extinct. When a kind of organism becomes **extinct**, no more of that kind of organism lives on Earth. Once a kind of organism is gone, it is gone forever.

**Analyze** What changes in the environment could cause a plant or animal to become extinct?

_____

_____

_____

**Science Practice**
▸ Toolbox

**Ask Questions** Suppose a kind of animal is in danger of becoming extinct. What questions would you ask to find out how you could help save the animal?

## Behaviors and Survival

Many animal behaviors help animals survive. Some animals, such as deer, form groups for safety. Animals that stick together are often better able to communicate that a predator is near. Bears hibernate in cold weather when food is scarce. While it hibernates, a bear does not need as much energy from food. Penguins do not hibernate, so they form huddles to survive cold winter climates. Some animals that are not adapted to the cold migrate. Many birds fly south for the winter to avoid colder temperatures and fly north again when it is warmer.

📖 **Reflect** In your science notebook, tell how you survive changes in your environment.

## ✓ Lesson 5 Check

1. **Analyze** An animal is not able to see in a dark environment. What other ways could the animal gather information about its surroundings to find food in the dark?

_____

_____

2. ✓ **READING CHECK Compare and Contrast** How are seasonal behaviors of bears and penguins alike and different?

_____

_____

_____

# Sound Off!

Bats are nocturnal, which means they are awake at night and asleep during the day. They live in dark environments, such as caves. Because there is little light when they hunt insect prey, they rely on their sense of hearing. They do this through a process called echolocation.

When a bat emits, or lets out, a sound, the sound bounces off the wall of the cave, an insect, or other objects in its environment. The bounced sounds reach the bat's ears. These bounced sounds give the bat information about the objects in its environment. The information allows the bat to know how close or how large an object is. This helps the bat locate its prey.

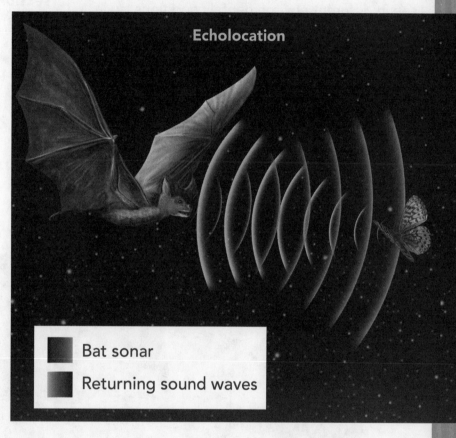

Echolocation

■ Bat sonar
■ Returning sound waves

**Summarize** How does a bat use sound to find an insect?

_____

_____

_____

**Relate** In which situations do you think it could be helpful for humans to locate objects using sound?

_____

_____

_____

_____

# uEngineer It! Model STEM

▶ VIDEO

Watch a video about optical detection technology and how it was modeled after an animal eye.

# Eye See You!

**Phenomenon** Animal eyes are unique and extraordinary. Different kinds of animals can see in different environmental conditions, such as dark and light. Nature photographers use different kinds of cameras that can produce good images in different conditions. Cameras function the same way eyes do—both have a lens that focuses the light that comes into the eye. When animals need to see prey at night, the pupils of their eyes allow more light to come in so that their vision is enhanced.

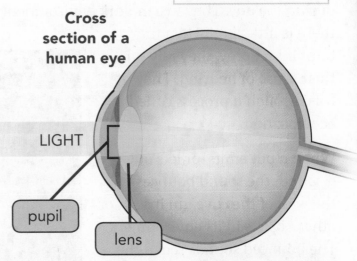

**Cross section of a human eye**

LIGHT

pupil

lens

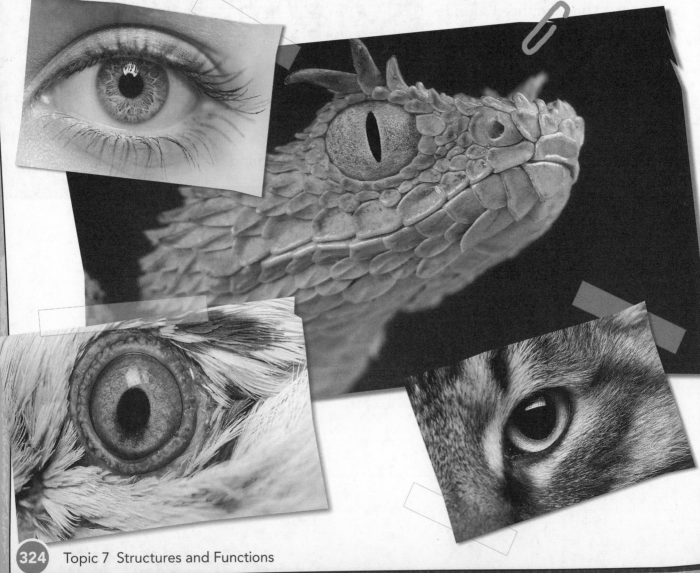

# Model It

Suppose you want to make a model that you could use to teach younger students about animal eyes.

☐ Choose an animal and research how it sees.

☐ In your model, what stimulus will the eye receive? For example, will it see food or a prey animal?

_____

_____

☐ What are the conditions of the environment—dark, light, hot, cold?

_____

_____

☐ Think about how to show all the parts of the eye in your model.

☐ Draw and label your model animal eye. Show how light travels when it enters the eye.

**INTERACTIVITY**

Organize your information to build your model.

STEM › Let Plants and Animals **Inspire** You!

Which human problem can you help solve using what you learn about plants and animals?

**Phenomenon** You explored many plant and animal structures that have useful functions. Now it is time to choose a plant or animal structure to inspire a product that will solve a human problem of your choosing. It can be an internal or an external structure. Be creative!

## Explain

Choose one plant or animal structure. Decide how you will use this structure to create a product that could solve a human problem. What problem will it solve?

_____

_____

_____

_____

_____

_____

## Design and Build Your Model

Draw your design. Present your design idea to the class, and ask for feedback to improve your design. Then build your model!

QUEST CHECK ✓ OFF

# Nature Photographer

A nature photographer takes pictures of scenes and objects in nature. These include flowers, rocks, trees, mountains, grass, and rock formations. A nature photographer also photographs animals in their natural habitats. The animals can be as common as birds, insects, and prairie dogs, or as exotic as cheetahs, pythons, and lions.

The tools nature photographers use are a camera with film or a digital photo card and the photographer's creative mind. They capture different angles of objects. Their photos are used for scientific research about plants and animals. Pictures are also used in textbooks, on Internet Web sites, in travel brochures, and sometimes just for fun!

You can be a nature photographer no matter where you live because nature is everywhere, but you have to like working outdoors! Also, sometimes travel is involved because different nature scenes may be in another state or country.

The job of nature photographers is rewarding because people are often inspired by their photos. Without nature photographers, we would know less about what certain plants and animals look like in places we do not visit.

📓 **Write About It**
Do you think you could be a nature photographer? What are things in nature you would like to photograph?

**1. Identify** Which one of these is an internal structure?

    **A.** eye

    **B.** skull

    **C.** nose

    **D.** ear

**2. Explain** Name three adaptations a tree might have that help it survive in its environment. For each adaptation, tell how it helps the tree survive.

_____

_____

_____

_____

_____

_____

**3. Explain** Name two external structures that help animals survive. Explain how the structures benefit the animal.

_____

_____

_____

_____

_____

Look at the picture to answer questions 4 and 5.

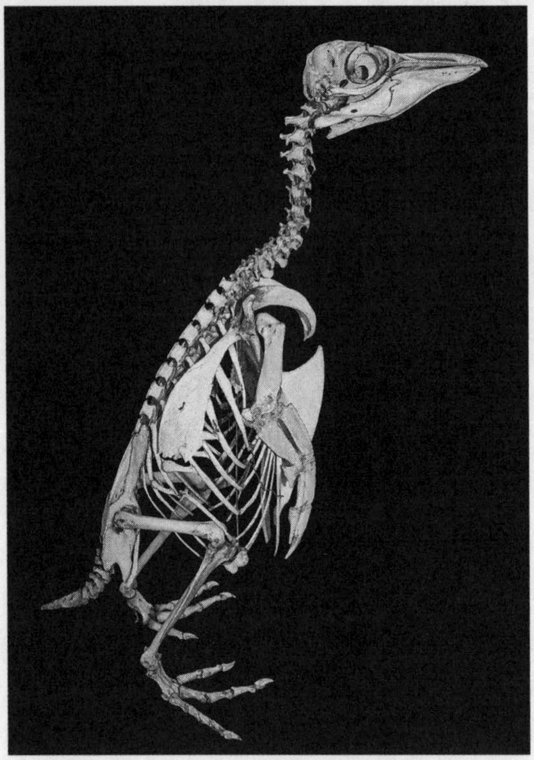

**4. Identify** What is the name of the internal structure shown?

    **A.** skeleton

    **B.** cerebellum

    **C.** exoskeleton

    **D.** brain stem

**5. Describe** What is the most important function of the internal structure shown?

_____

_____

_____

**6. Compare and Contrast** Choose one plant structure and one animal structure. Tell one way they are similar and one way they are different.

_____

_____

_____

_____

_____

_____

**7. Apply** Which sentence describes a behavior that helps an animal survive?

**A.** An animal goes into hibernation during winter.

**B.** The heart pumps blood through an animal's body.

**C.** Animals become tired after running long distances.

**D.** Fur coloration helps an animal blend into its environment.

*How do plant and animal structures support growth and survival?*

## Show What You Learned

How do plant and animal structures help them survive in different environments?

_____

_____

_____

_____

_____

_____

_____

_____

_____

_____

_____

# Evidence-Based Assessment

Read the scenario and answer the questions that follow.

Kyle is a scientist that travels around the world studying different organisms. He recorded some of his observations in the table.

| Organism | Structure | Internal/External | Function |
|---|---|---|---|
| oak tree | trunk | | support |
| beetle | exoskeleton | external | |
| tomato plant | seeds | internal | reproduction |
| cactus | spines | external | protection |
| eagle | claws | | protection |
| Arctic fox | skull | | support |

1. **Interpret Tables** Complete the table using what you know about structures and functions.

2. **Use Data** Which structures from the table have the same function but one is external and the other is internal?

   **A.** claws and spines

   **B.** a trunk and a skull

   **C.** exoskeleton and spines

   **D.** seeds and spines

3. **Compare and Contrast** Choose two organisms that have structures with the same function. Identify the structures and their function.

   _____

   _____

   _____

**4. Explain** Based on his data, Kyle made the claim that all structures for reproduction are internal. Does he have enough evidence to support his argument?

**A.** Yes, an example from one organism is enough to make conclusions about all organisms.

**B.** Yes, all of the reproductive structures he looked at were internal so they must all be internal.

**C.** No, reproductive structures could be very different in different organisms so Kyle needs more evidence to support his argument.

**D.** No, Kyle is not a professional biologist so he cannot make any arguments about structures in organisms.

**5. Construct an Argument** Use the data in the table to come up with a hypothesis about the structures and functions of different organisms. How would you collect data to test your hypothesis?

_____

_____

_____

_____

_____

_____

_____

_____

# uDemonstrate Lab

# How do earthworms respond to stimuli?

**Phenomenon** Scientists observe how animals respond to different situations. How can you investigate how an earthworm responds to a stimulus in its environment?

## Procedure

☐ **1.** Choose a stimulus that you want to test with your earthworm. Predict how an earthworm will react to this stimulus.

_____

_____

_____

_____

☐ **2.** Make a plan to test the stimulus you chose. Remember to control your variables. Show your plan to your teacher before you begin.

_____

_____

_____

_____

_____

_____

_____

☐ **3.** Conduct your investigation and record your results.

**Materials**
- earthworm
- plastic gloves

**Suggested Materials**
- container
- spray bottle with water
- water dropper
- soil
- warm and cold water
- paper towels
- aluminum foil

 Be careful with live animals.

 Wash your hands when done.

 Wear plastic gloves.

### Science Practice

Scientists **analyze information** from investigations.

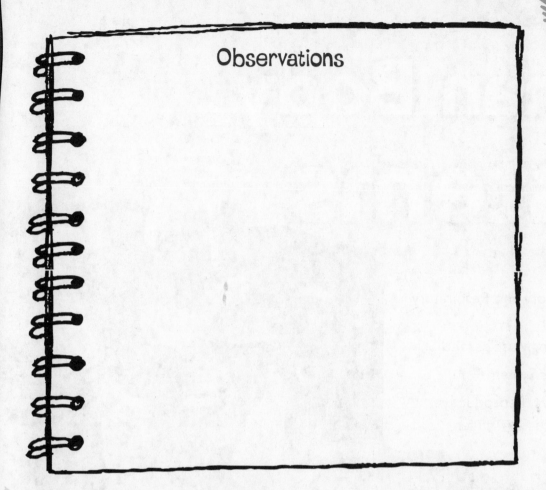

Observations

## Analyze and Interpret Data

**4. Analyze Data** Does your data support your prediction? Explain.

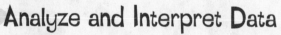

_____

_____

_____

_____

**5. Draw Conclusions** What conclusion can you draw from your observations?

_____

_____

_____

_____

# Topic 8

# Human Body Systems

**Next Generation Science Standards**

**4-LS1-1** Construct an argument that plants and animals have internal and external structures that function to support survival, growth, behavior, and reproduction.

**4-LS1-2** Use a model to describe that animals receive different types of information through their senses, process the information in their brain, and respond to the information in different ways.

Go online to access
your digital course.

▶ VIDEO

📖 eTEXT

👆 INTERACTIVITY

📱 VIRTUAL LAB

🎮 GAME

☑ ASSESSMENT

**The Essential Question**

How can you model the interactions between human body systems?

**Show What You Know**

An athlete races toward the finish line. How do the parts of the athlete's body work together to push ahead to the finish line?

_____

_____

# Make a Human Body Road Map

## How can you help a tiny camera navigate the human body?

**Phenomenon** Hi, I'm Warren Snyder, a medical imaging technician. I would like you to provide guidance for creating a remote-controlled micro-camera to navigate inside the body for a new imaging procedure.

In this problem-based learning activity, you will choose the body part for the procedure and how the camera technology will be used. You will provide instructions for using the camera.

Follow the path to learn how you will complete the Quest. The Quest activities in the lessons will help you complete the Quest! Check off your progress on the path when you complete an activity with a QUEST CHECK ✓ OFF . Go online for more Quest activities.

## Quest Check-In 1

### Lesson 1

Learn about the circulatory system to help you determine how to navigate the remote-controlled camera through the blood vessels of the body.

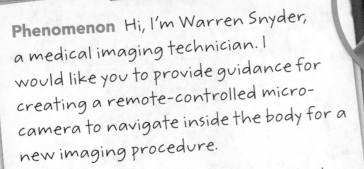

**Next Generation Science Standards**

**4-LS1-1** Construct and argument that plants and animals have internal and external structures that function to support survival, growth, behavior, and reproduction.

**4-LS1-2** Use a model to describe that animals receive different types of information through their senses, process the information in their brain, and respond to the information in different ways.

## Quest Check-In 2

### Lesson 2
Use what you learn about the skeleton, muscles, and skin to find out how your camera can travel to a broken bone.

**VIDEO**
Watch a video about a medical imaging technician.

## Quest Check-In Lab 3

### Lesson 3
Learn how signals travel through the body. Apply what you learn to determine how to guide your camera with messages.

## Quest Check-In 4

### Lesson 4
Find out about the immune system, and then tell how to track the path of germs as they enter the body and affect body parts.

## Quest Findings

You've finished your tour of the human body. Choose one body system and write or draw instructions to complete your Quest.

# Which body parts work together to do a task?

**Suggested Materials**
- books
- stopwatch
- basketball
- 2 rubber balls
- yo-yo

When scientists investigate a question, they base their arguments on their observations. How can you observe your body parts working together as you do a simple task?

**Science Practice**

Scientists use evidence to construct an argument.

## Procedure

1. Choose a simple task you can perform using any of the materials.

2. As you perform the task, observe which body parts are involved. Record your observations.

3. Choose a second task, and repeat step 2.

⚠ Do not perform any physical activities if you have a health problem.

| Task | Body Parts Involved |
| --- | --- |
|  |  |

## Analyze and Interpret Data

4. **Compare and Contrast** Were the body parts you used for both tasks the same? Why do you think that is so?

_____

_____

5. Did your observations provide evidence of body parts working together? How?

_____

_____

# Main Idea and Details

The main idea in a text is the overall message an author is trying to share. The specific details in the text help to support the main idea.

Here are some strategies for identifying the main idea and details:

- Underline any text that supports a similar idea or provides new information about the same subject.
- Use the text you underline to infer what the author wants the reader to take away from this reading.

Read the following information about chimpanzees.

🎮 **GAME**

Practice what you learn with the Mini Games.

## Chimpanzees and Humans

Like humans, chimpanzees are intelligent animals that can communicate with actions. But there are plenty of differences between chimpanzees and humans. Humans walk differently than chimpanzees, and we use language to communicate.

Many people would also include the difference of strength. That is true, but not in the way you might think. While chimpanzee muscles are similar to those of humans, chimpanzees are actually two to three times stronger than humans. Humans have more control as they move muscles, but this also limits the amount of power we can exert. Because chimpanzees do not have the same kind of muscle control, they are much more powerful when they take action.

☑ **READING CHECK** **Main Idea and Details** What did the author want you to take away from this text? Underline the details that helped you come to this conclusion.

_____

_____

# Circulatory and Respiratory Systems

## I can...

Explain how the heart helps move blood through the body. Explain how the circulatory and respiratory systems interact to move oxygen through the body.
**4-LS1-1**

**Literacy Skill**
Main Idea and Details

**Vocabulary**
organ system
organ
tissue
lungs
diaphragm
heart

**Academic Vocabulary**
function

**VIDEO**

Watch a video about the circulatory and respiratory systems.

## CURRICULUM  Connection

Think about how you are breathing right now. You feel the air move in through your nose or mouth. Your rib cage rises and falls as air moves in and out of your body. If you take a deep breath, you might feel your belly rise. But how does the breathing change when you talk or sing? Many professional singers learn and practice useful breathing methods while singing. These methods improve the quality of their voices. Singers practice expanding their rib cage to produce sound. When they breathe out, they control the air to help them hit high and low notes, as well as maintain long, slow phrases.

**Compare and Contrast**  Besides singing and talking, when do you take deeper breaths? Why do you think that is so?

_____

_____

_____

# uInvestigate Lab

# How can you model how you *breathe?*

Scientists often build models to study how something works. What pulls air into your body when you breathe?

**Materials**
- top of plastic bottle with bottom cut off
- 2 balloons
- tape
- safety goggles
- scissors

⚠ Be careful handling scissors and with sharp edges on plastic bottles.

⚠ Wear safety goggles.

## Procedure

☐ 1. **SEP Develop a Model** Sit quietly and observe what happens in your body as you breathe in and out. Use all the materials. Plan a model to show how air gets in and out of your body.

☐ 2. Draw your model. Ask your teacher for permission before you begin to build your model.

**Science Practice**

Scientists use models to construct an argument.

## Analyze and Interpret Data

3. **SEP Use Models** How does your model demonstrate what happens when you breathe?

_____

_____

_____

_____

My Model

4. **SEP Explain** Based on your model, how might you explain how air gets in and out of your lungs?

_____

_____

_____

_____

_____

## Tissues, Organs, and Organ Systems

If you are sitting quietly in a chair, you might think that not much is happening in your body. But a lot goes on in your body all the time. Your heart pumps, and your brain receives and sends messages. Muscles and bones work together so that you can move. All the parts of your body work together as organ systems to do a specific **function**, or job. An **organ system** is made up of a group of organs that do a particular job.

**Organs** are body parts that perform specific functions. Your heart, for example, is an organ that is part of the circulatory system. The function of this system is to move materials throughout the body in the blood. All the body's systems work together to help the cells of your body meet their needs for survival.

Organs are made up of **tissues**, groups of cells of the same kind that have a specific function. Your heart is an organ that contains muscle tissue. The cells that make up heart muscle tissue work together to make the heart pump.

☑ READING CHECK **Main Idea and Details** Underline the sentences that tell how tissues, organs, and organ systems are related. Then match the labels with the parts of the diagram.

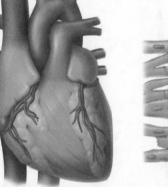
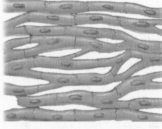

( cell )    ( tissue )    ( organ )    ( organ system )

## Respiratory System

Air in, air out—again and again. A person must breathe in and out for an entire lifetime. Cells in the body need a steady supply of oxygen to function properly. Oxygen is a part of air. The respiratory system takes in oxygen from the air so that it can be delivered to all body cells. It also gets rid of gaseous wastes produced by body cells.

Air enters your body through the nose or the mouth. It flows through the throat into a hard tube called the trachea, or windpipe. The trachea divides into two smaller tubes. Each tube leads to one of the two main parts of the **lungs**, the main organs of the respiratory system. Inside the lungs, these tubes branch out into smaller and smaller tubes until they form tiny sacs. In the sacs, oxygen is added to the blood, and wastes are removed from the blood.

The lungs cannot expand on their own to move air into the body. The **diaphragm**, a muscle located below the lungs, causes air to flow in and out of your lungs.

**Interpret Diagrams** Use what you have learned to label the parts of the respiratory system.

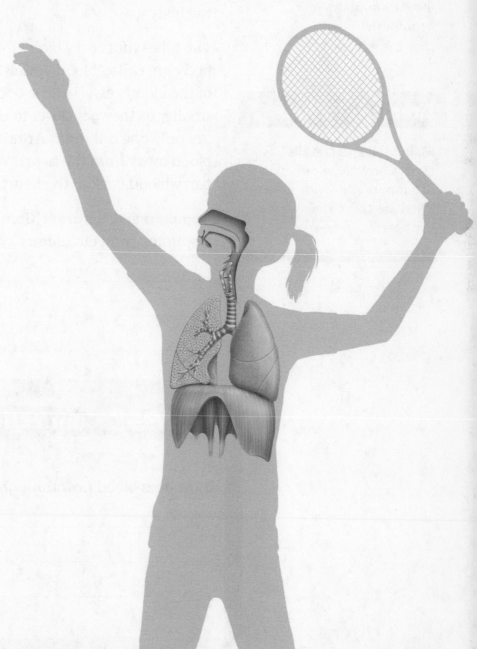

**Investigate Your Heartbeat**
Find your pulse. Place
two fingers under your
jawbone. Count the
number of times your heart
beats in 1 minute. What
will happen to your pulse
when you exercise? Write
a hypothesis. Do jumping
jacks for 30 seconds.
Record your pulse. Does
the data support your
hypothesis?

## Literacy ▸ Toolbox

**Main Idea and Details**
Details provide information
to support a main idea.
What are two details about
the heart?

## Circulatory System

If you place two fingers below your jawline on your neck,
you can feel your pulse. Your pulse is your heart rate, or
how many times a minute your heart beats. The **heart**
is a muscular organ that pumps blood throughout your
body. The heart is part of the circulatory system, a network
made up of the heart, blood, and blood vessels. Follow the
path of blood through the heart in the picture. When the
chambers of the heart relax, they fill up with blood. Then,
the chambers squeeze the blood to force it out. With each
heartbeat, blood is pumped through tubes to all parts of
the body.

The tubes that carry blood throughout every part of the
body are called blood vessels. The diagram shows only a few
of the blood vessels in the body. The vessels get smaller and
smaller as they get closer to the body's cells, until their walls
are only one cell thick. Arteries are blood vessels that carry
blood away from the heart. Veins are blood vessels that
carry blood back to the heart.

**Compare and Contrast** Contrast the functions of the
respiratory and circulatory systems.

_____

_____

_____

## Quest Connection

How does blood flow through the body?

_____

_____

_____

**Identify** On the heart diagram, label where the blood is going and coming from. Draw arrows to show the path of blood through the heart.

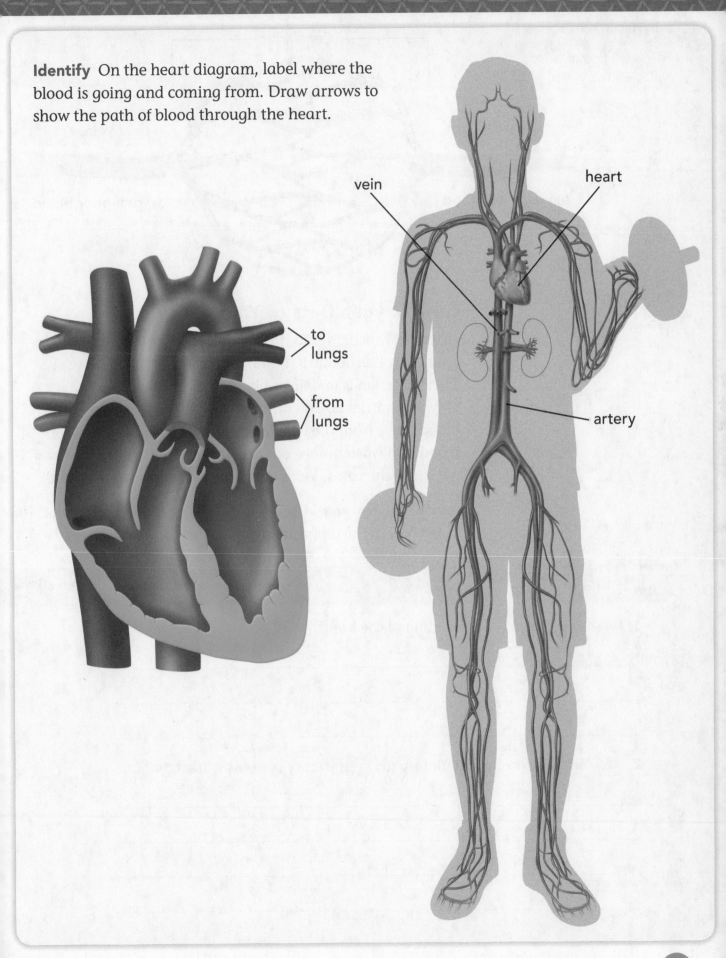

to lungs

from lungs

vein

heart

artery

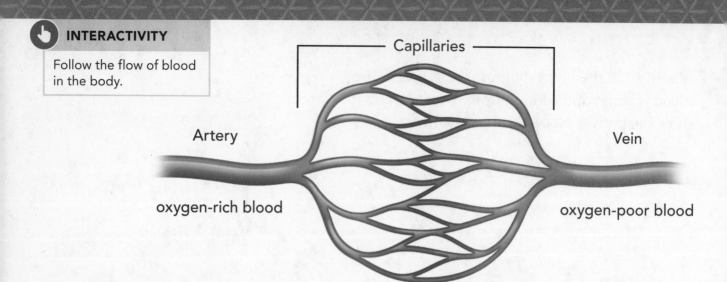

Capillaries

Artery

Vein

oxygen-rich blood

oxygen-poor blood

## How Oxygen Gets to Your Cells

Arteries branch off into tiny blood vessels called capillaries. Your body has about 10 billion of these tiny blood vessels! Their function is to deliver blood to all the body's cells. Oxygen, nutrients, and other materials that are carried by blood move from the capillaries into the cells. Oxygen-poor blood and wastes move out of cells into capillaries, and then back into the veins. Veins carry the blood back to the lungs.

**Interpret Diagrams** Use an arrow to show the direction of bloodflow in the diagram of capillaries.

## ☑ Lesson 1 Check

**1. Describe** What is the function of the lungs?

_____

_____

_____

**2. Explain** How do the circulatory and respiratory systems work together?

_____

_____

_____

_____

_____

# Go with the Flow

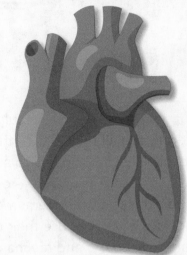

It is time to think about how you can use your remote-controlled camera. Sometimes arteries and veins become blocked. You can use your camera to check whether certain blood vessels are blocked.

One thing you should think about as you plan is that the force with which the blood flows in blood vessels is stronger than the force you will be able to apply to move the camera forward. So the camera must move in the same direction as the blood.

Where will the path of your camera begin? Explain.

_____

_____

_____

Draw a path that shows how the camera will flow through the circulatory system.

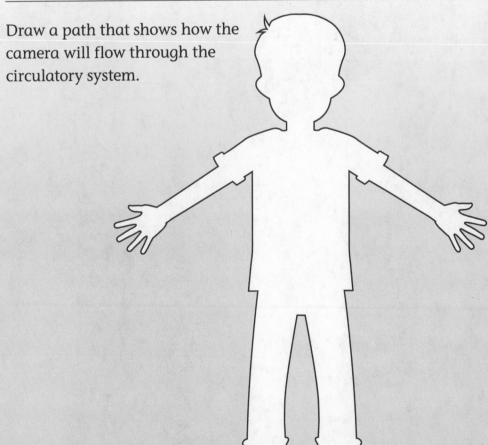

# μEngineer It! Build STEM

**INTERACTIVITY**

Go online to evaluate and suggest improvements for models.

# Pump It Up!

**Phenomenon** How the circulatory system works is not easy to observe. Not only are all the parts of the system inside the body, some parts, such as capillaries, are too tiny to see without a microscope. When something is too small—or too large—to see, engineers and scientists often build models to see how systems work. Scientists can observe the action of their models. They might use their observations to develop technologies such as artificial hearts and mechanical heart valves. They might even use a 3D printer to make a model of a particular person's organ. They can practice on the model before a surgery.

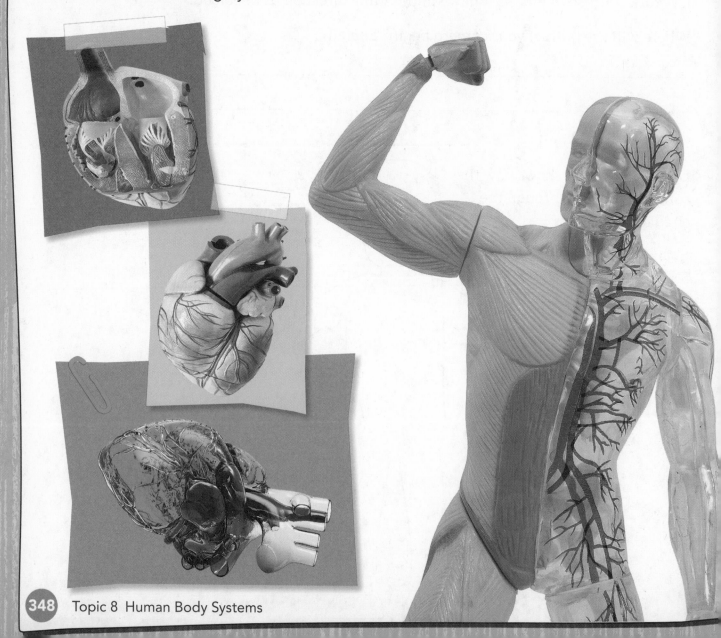

# Build It

You will build a model of the circulatory system. Your model should show how blood flows through the four parts of the heart and how it flows to and from other parts of the body.

☐ Plan your model. Decide which materials you will use for each part. How will the model work? Make a drawing to show your plan.

☐ Show your plan to your teacher before you begin. Then build your model.

☐ Test your model. Identify any problems. Make any necessary changes.

☐ Share your model with others.

# Skeleton, Muscles, and Skin

## I can...

Describe the functions of the skeleton, muscles, and skin. Explain how the skeletal and muscular systems interact to allow movement.

4-LS1-1

**Literacy Skill**
Main Idea and Details

**Vocabulary**
skeletal system
muscle
skin

**Academic Vocabulary**
extend

### ▶ VIDEO

Watch a video about the functions of the skin.

## SPORTS ▷ Connection

Imagine whizzing along on a skateboard or inline skates. Suddenly you find yourself upside down in the air. You land on your head. OUCH! It's a good thing you are wearing a helmet to protect your skull from injury. Each year, more than 3.5 million children under the age of 14 are injured in sports activities. About half of all injuries occur while bicycling, skateboarding, or rollerskating. Injuries to the skull are especially dangerous because the skull protects the brain. Helmets, eye goggles, knee pads, and elbow pads all help to reduce injuries, such as broken bones, cuts, and bruises. Remember to reduce serious injuries by wearing protective gear!

**Communicate** For what other sports should a person wear protective gear?

_____

_____

_____

## uInvestigate Lab

# How can you test the strength of a bone?

People who play many sports need healthy bones to support their body as they play. How can you compare the strength of different bones?

**Suggested Materials**
- construction paper
- cardboard
- hole puncher
- scissors
- books
- tape

 Be careful using scissors.

## Procedure

☐ 1. Make a plan to make and use models to answer the question. Tell how you will test your model bones. Show your plan to your teacher before you begin.

☐ 2. **SEP Develop a Model** Build your models.

☐ 3. Test your models. Record your observations.

**Science Practice**

Scientists **construct arguments** that are supported by evidence.

## Analyze and Interpret Data

4. **SEP Use Evidence** How does the structure of a bone affect its strength? Cite evidence from the data you collected.

_____

_____

_____

_____

_____

_____

_____

_____

_____

Observations

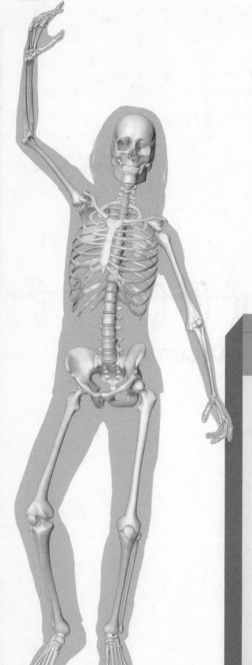

**Test a Weak Bone**
Place a chicken bone in a glass of vinegar. Allow the bone to soak for several days. Remove the bone. Bend it. How does the vinegar affect the bone?

## Skeletal System

What do you think would happen if your bones suddenly disappeared? You would fall onto the floor in a blob! Your body has 206 bones that make up the **skeletal system.** The skeletal system supports your body and gives it shape. Your bones also protect your internal organs.

**Identify** Mark an X on the bones you think protect your internal organs. Circle the bones that help your body stand upright.

Bones are made up of living tissues. They also contain nonliving materials called minerals. Calcium is a mineral that is important for strong, healthy bones. Bones contain a bendable material called cartilage. Feel your nose and ears. They can bend. That is because parts of your nose and ears are made of cartilage. Cartilage also acts as a cushion between bones that meet, such as where your leg bones meet at the knee.

**Main Idea and Details** Underline the sentences that tell the main idea about the skeletal system.

## Quest Connection

How could a remote-controlled camera be used to identify an injury inside the human body?

_____

_____

_____

_____

_____

_____

## Muscular System

The bones in your body would not be able to move without muscles. **Muscles** are organs that contract, or shorten, and relax, or lengthen, to move bones. Three kinds of muscles make up the muscular system: smooth muscle, cardiac muscle, and skeletal muscle. Body organs, such as the stomach, are made up of smooth muscle. Cardiac muscle makes up the heart. Muscles need oxygen to perform their tasks.

Skeletal muscles are attached to your bones by tough rope-like tissues called tendons. Skeletal muscles can only pull on bones. They cannot push bones. So they work in pairs to move bones. For example, bend your arm at the elbow. You can feel the muscle on the top of your upper arm contract, or shorten. This action causes bones to move so that your arm bends at the elbow. Now **extend**, or straighten, your arm. Feel the muscle underneath your arm. When this opposite muscle contracts, your arm straightens.

**Structure and Function** The structure of skeletal muscles allows them to contract. How is this structure related to the the function of muscles?

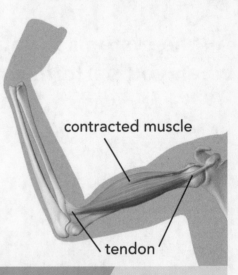

contracted muscle

tendon

**Design It!** Draw a design that you could use to make a model that shows how muscle pairs work together to move a bone.

# How do we SKATE ON ICE?

All the systems in your body work together when you perform a task or activity.

lungs

heart

Muscles contract and relax, helping the skater move across the ice.

The skater uses a lot of energy. The heart pumps faster to get oxygen to the parts of the body. The lungs work harder to move oxygen in and out of the body.

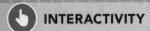
The skater begins to sweat as he reaches the end of the performance.

The bones of the skater support the body as the skater jumps in the air and lands.

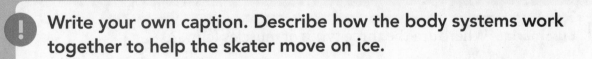

**❗ Write your own caption. Describe how the body systems work together to help the skater move on ice.**

_____

_____

_____

_____

_____

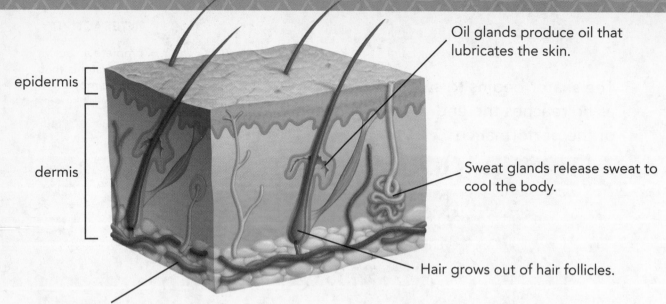

epidermis

dermis

Oil glands produce oil that lubricates the skin.

Sweat glands release sweat to cool the body.

Hair grows out of hair follicles.

Blood vessels carry nutrients and oxygen to skin cells.

## Skin

Your **skin** is your largest organ. It covers and protects your internal organs. It also protects your body from disease-causing germs and helps keep you cool by sweating. The skin has two layers. When you look at your skin, you see the thin outer layer, the epidermis. Pinch some skin on your arm. You can feel the dermis beneath the epidermis. The dermis layer is thick with structures that have different functions. Below the dermis are layers of fat, blood vessels, and muscles.

📓 **Make Meaning** In your science notebook, write about why taking care of the skin is important. List ways you take care of your skin.

## ☑ Lesson 2 Check

**1. Summarize** Where are the three types of muscles found?

_____

_____

_____

**2. Explain** How do muscles and bones work together to move the body?

_____

_____

# Injury Search

Suppose someone just had a cast placed on her leg. The cast must stay on for several weeks while a broken bone below the knee mends. During that time, the person will not be able use her lower leg muscles.

What might happen to the muscles attached to the leg bones? You can use the remote-controlled camera to find out! The camera can be injected through a short needle. What path must the camera follow to check on the health of the muscle? Draw the path of the camera.

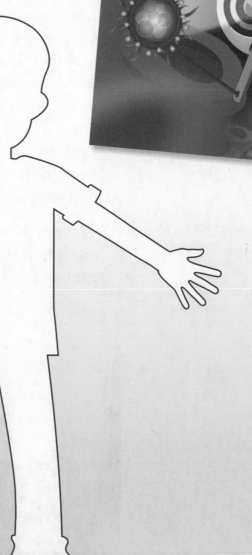

What might your camera discover about the health of the muscle?

_____

_____

# Nervous System

**I can...**

Describe the functions
of the brain and
sensory organs.
**4-LS1-1, 4-LS1-2**

**Literacy Skill**
Main Idea and Details

**Vocabulary**
sensory organ
brain

**Academic Vocabulary**
respond

**VIDEO**

Watch a video about
the sensory organs.

## ENGINEERING Connection

Do you think about how you move your arm? Or do you just move it without giving it much thought? How does the brain send signals to cause parts to move? That is something that scientists and engineers have been learning more about. They have used what they know to develop a "bionic" arm. A bionic arm is an artificial arm that people can control with their thoughts. People who have lost an arm due to injury use bionic arms to do many different tasks. When a person thinks about doing a task, such as picking up an object, messages move from the brain through the nervous system to the bionic arm. The bionic arm then interprets the message and completes the task.

**Write About It** In your science notebook, write about how you think signals from the brain can reach the bionic arm.

## uInvestigate Lab

# Which parts of the body are more sensitive?

**Materials**
- metric ruler
- erasers
- tape

A medical imaging technician might make images that show nerves in your body. How can you find out whether the nerves in different body parts are more sensitive to touch?

**Science Practice**

Scientists develop and use models to predict phenomena.

## Procedure

☐ **1.** Is your fingertip, arm, or ankle the most sensitive to touch? Write your prediction.

_____

☐ **2.** Plan a procedure to test your prediction. Show your plan to your teacher before you begin. Record your observations.

## Analyze and Interpret Data

**3. SEP Develop a Model** Draw a picture to show how you think the numbers of nerves in the three areas you tested are different.

| Observations | How Number of Nerves Compare |
| --- | --- |
| | |

# What are sensory organs?

Your body connects to the world through the **sensory organs.** Each sensory organ gathers specific kinds of information. The information is sent to your **brain**, which is the control center of the body. The brain interprets the information and then tells the body how to react to the information.

## Eye

The eye allows us to see. Light enters the eye through a small opening called the pupil. A lens behind the pupil focuses the light onto the back of the eye. From there a nerve sends signals to the brain. The brain interprets the signals to form a visual image.

## Ear

You can hear because of your ears. Sound waves enter the ear and cause the eardrum to vibrate. The ear changes the vibrations into nerve signals. A nerve carries the signals to the brain. The brain interprets the signals as words, music, or other sounds.

## Tongue

The sense of **taste** comes from the tongue. It has small structures called taste buds. They send signals to your brain. The brain interprets the signals as taste—sweet, salty, bitter, or sour.

## Nose

The nose detects **smell**. Small structures in the tongue pick up chemicals in the air. They change the chemicals into nerve signals that are sent to the brain. The brain identifies these signals as various smells. Your sense of smell also helps you taste things.

## Skin

The sense of **touch** comes from nerve endings in the skin. They help you feel pressure, pain, hot, and cold. Some parts of the body, such as the fingertips, have more nerve endings than other parts of the body.

**Choose one of the senses. Draw something you detect with that sense.**

**INTERACTIVITY**

Do an activity about the nervous system.

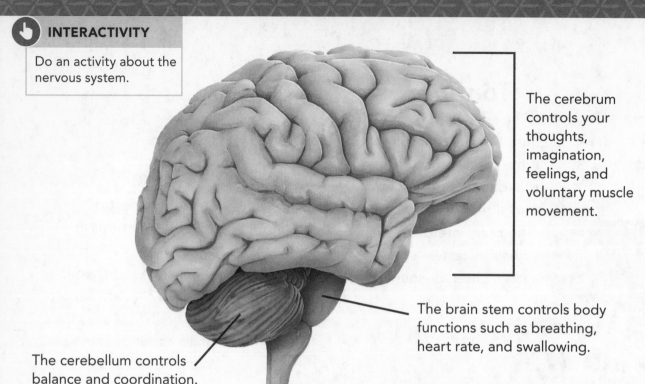

The cerebrum controls your thoughts, imagination, feelings, and voluntary muscle movement.

The brain stem controls body functions such as breathing, heart rate, and swallowing.

The cerebellum controls balance and coordination.

The spinal cord carries messages to and from the brain.

## uBe a Scientist

**Reaction Time**

The time it takes you to react to something is called reaction time. With a partner, design a way to test your reaction time. Make a prediction. Does your reaction time improve with practice?

## Brain

The nervous system sends messages throughout your body. Your brain is your body's most complex organ. It does more than just think! It interprets the information it receives about conditions inside and outside the body. Then it sends messages telling the body how to **respond**, or react. The brain is made up of nerve cells. Nerve cells also carry messages through the spinal cord to and from all parts of the body.

## Quest Connection

To what kinds of messages might the brain respond to keep you balanced on one foot?

_____

_____

_____

## Nerves

The brain and the spinal cord make up the central nervous system. The spinal cord is made up of a thick bundle of nerves. Messages to and from your brain travel through the nerves of your spinal cord. These nerves branch out to other parts of the body. Some of these nerves are motor nerves that carry messages from the brain to other parts of the body. Other nerves are sensory nerves that carry messages from sense organs and other body parts to the spinal cord.

**Identify** Draw an arrow to show the direction a message would travel through the body from the fingertip. Label where the message starts and where it ends.

brain

spinal cord

nerves

### Crosscutting Concepts ▸ Toolbox

**Structure and Function** The way a structure is shaped is closely related to its function. How does the shape of the nervous system enable the brain to get messages from all parts of the body?

## ☑ Lesson 3 Check

**1. Explain** How does your nervous system work to help you hear sounds?

_____

_____

_____

**2.** ☑ **READING CHECK Main Idea** Write a main idea statement about the nervous system.

_____

_____

_____

Lesson 3 Nervous System **363**

# How can you test signals to and from your brain?

The brain must interpret messages to tell other parts of the body what to do. How do signals from your brain help you walk in a straight line?

**Materials**
• masking tape

Engineering Practice

Engineers **construct explanations** using models.

## Design a Solution

☐ **1.** Think of what information your brain receives to help you walk in a straight line. Predict what would happen if your brain did not receive the information.

_____

_____

_____

_____

_____

☐ **2.** Use the materials to help you test your prediction. Show your plan to you teacher before you start. Record your observations.

_____

_____

_____

_____

☐ **3.** **CCC Systems** Think of how your signals travel in your body. How is that similar to the remote-controlled micro-camera? Draw a model that shows the path a signal must travel from the technician to the camera and back.

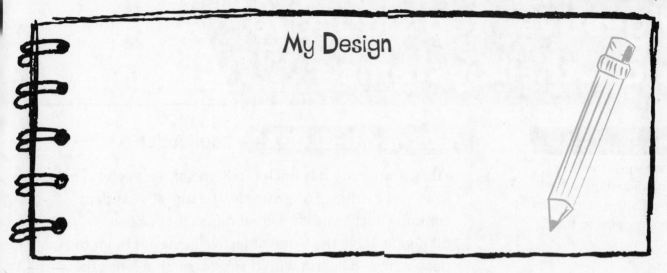

## My Design

## Communicate Your Solution

4. **SEP Explain** Does your model show how the model remote-controlled camera will stay on the correct path through the body? Explain.

_____

_____

_____

_____

_____

5. **SEP Analyze** Show your model to another pair of students. Compare the path that you made with that of other students. Discuss any differences.

_____

_____

_____

_____

_____

_____

# Digestive, Reproductive, and Other Systems

## I can...

Relate the structures in the digestive, reproductive, and other systems to their functions.

4-LS1-1

**Literacy Skill**
Main Idea and Details

**Vocabulary**
small intestine
large intestine
pancreas
liver
stomach
excretory system
kidneys
bladder

**Academic Vocabulary**
connect

▶ **VIDEO**

Watch a video about the digestive system.

## LOCAL-TO-GLOBAL ⟩ Connection

Yikes! Your body has bacteria! Some of the bacteria helps keep you healthy. For example, the digestive system contains bacteria that help to digest food. However, not all people have the same digestive bacteria. In Japan, people have bacteria with a substance that helps them digest seaweed. These bacteria are not found in people from North America. Scientists think the bacteria got into Japanese intestines over many generations as a result of eating the seaweed in many Japanese meals. The bacteria live on the seaweed that people eat.

**Explain** Why are these bacteria found only in Japanese people?

_____

_____

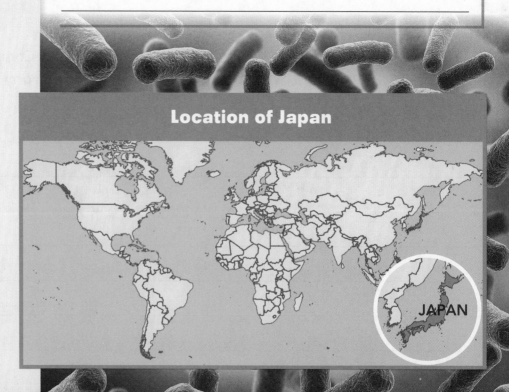

**Location of Japan**

JAPAN

# uInvestigate Lab

# How are intestines arranged inside your body?

Scientific data shows that the small intestine is very long. How can something so long fit inside your body?

## Procedure

☐ 1. Trace the outline of another student's body on the large sheet of paper.

☐ 2. Your small intestine is about 3.5 times your height. Calculate in meters the length of the small intestine of the student you outlined. Record your data.

_____

_____

☐ 3. Choose a material to represent the small intestine. Use the material to model how the intestine might be arranged in the outlined body. Draw how your model looks.

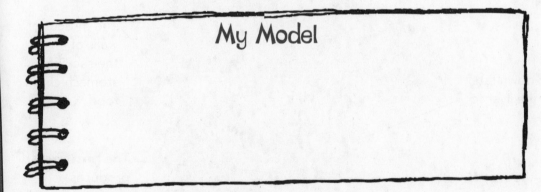
My Model

## Analyze and Interpret Data

**4. SEP Use Evidence** How do you think the small intestine is arranged to fit into a small space? Provide evidence from your observations.

_____

_____

_____

**Materials**
• large sheet of paper
• tape measure

**Suggested Materials**
• string
• rope
• yarn
• glue
• scissors

⚠ Be careful using scissors.

**Science Practice**

Scientists use evidence to construct an argument.

**Structure and Function**
Look in a mirror to see how
your teeth are shaped.
Contrast the front teeth and
the back teeth. How are they
different? How are these
two kinds of teeth used
differently?

## Digestive System

What did you eat for breakfast today? Once you swallowed
the food, where did it go? It entered the digestive system.
The digestive system breaks down food into nutrients and
other substances that the body can use. Cells use these
substances for energy, growth, and repair. Food undergoes
many changes as it passes through the digestive system.

Digestion begins in the mouth, where your teeth tear and
crush food. Saliva, the liquid in your mouth, begins to
chemically break down some food. Study the diagram to see
how food is broken down and absorbed as it passes through
the rest of the digestive system.

**Identify** Label the missing part of the diagram.

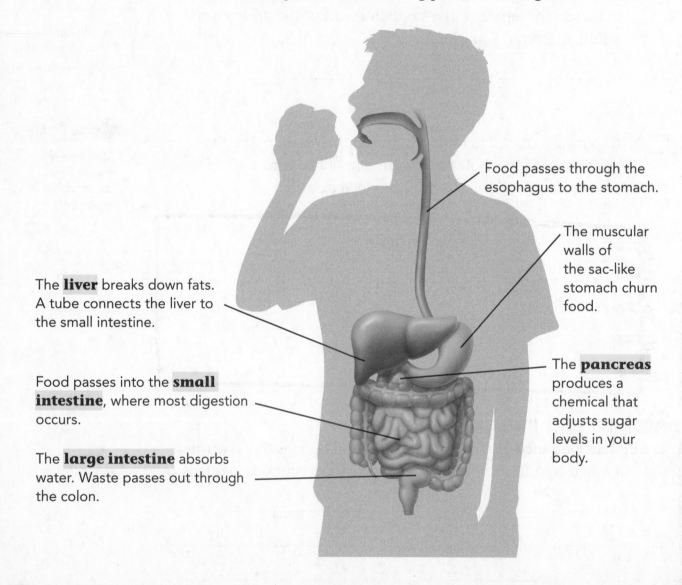

Food passes through the
esophagus to the stomach.

The muscular
walls of
the sac-like
stomach churn
food.

The **liver** breaks down fats.
A tube connects the liver to
the small intestine.

The **pancreas**
produces a
chemical that
adjusts sugar
levels in your
body.

Food passes into the **small
intestine**, where most digestion
occurs.

The **large intestine** absorbs
water. Waste passes out through
the colon.

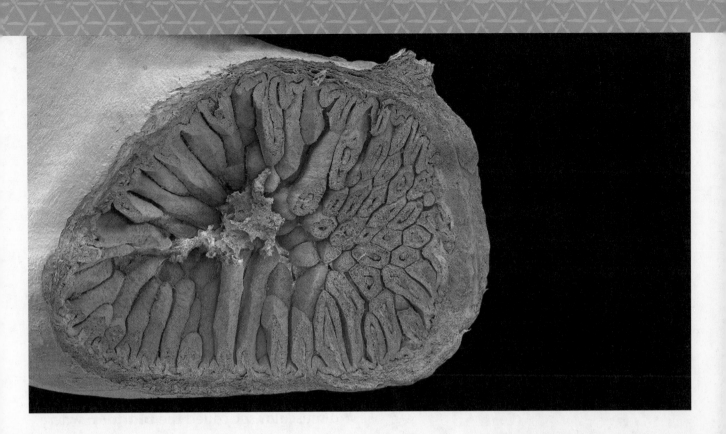

## How Nutrients Get to Parts of the Body

We often think of the stomach as the organ that digests our food. But the **stomach** is involved in the digestion of only certain kinds of food. Most digestion takes place in the small intestine. In addition to the digestive juices produced by the intestine, the liver and the pancreas send chemicals to the small intestine to break down food.

Find the small fingerlike structures in the cross-section photo of the small intestine. They are the villi on the inside of the small intestine. Capillaries line the walls of villi. Food that is completely digested is absorbed through the walls of the villi into the capillaries. The capillaries **connect**, or attach, with larger blood vessels that carry nutrients to all parts of the body.

**Relate** Why is it important for the villi to absorb digested food into the blood?

_____

_____

_____

............*u*Be a Scientist............

**Digestion in the Mouth**
Put a saltine in your mouth and observe how it tastes. Then chew the saltine for about a minute. What change do you notice in its taste? Why do you think the taste changed?

## Excretory System

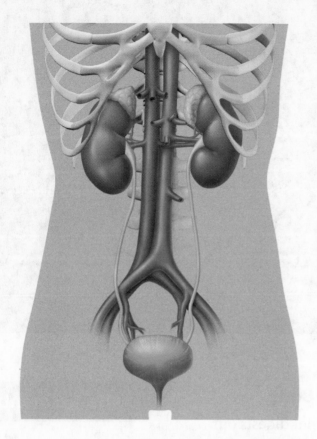

Cells absorb nutrients from the blood, but in return they produce wastes. These wastes are removed from the body by the **excretory system**. Several organs help with this process. They include the lungs, the liver, and the skin, but mostly the kidneys, the bladder, and the urethra.

The **kidneys** are a pair of bean-shaped organs that filter wastes from the blood. As blood passes through the kidneys, capillaries remove these wastes. The wastes combine with water to form urine. The urine travels through tubes called ureters to a muscular sac called the **bladder**, where it is stored until it is released from the body.

**Identify** Label the kidneys, the bladder, and the ureters.

## Quest Connection

How could a remote-controlled camera be used to find an unhealthy kidney?

_____

_____

_____

_____

_____

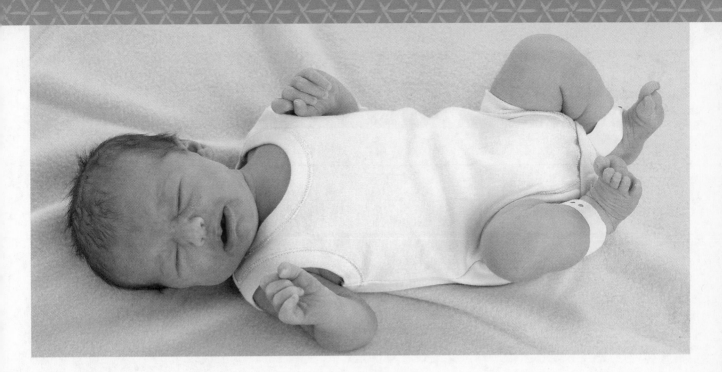

## Reproductive System

Living things can make other living things similar to themselves. This process is called reproduction.

The baby in the picture is very young. Its body will go through many stages. The first stage is infancy and lasts from birth to approximately 2 years old. Early childhood lasts from approximately 3 to 8 years old. Then, middle childhood follows from approximately 9 to 11 years old. Then the child reaches a stage called adolescence. This stage occurs between 12 to 18 years of age. At this stage the body becomes able to reproduce, or produce offspring. The reproductive system is made up of organs that allow people to reproduce.

☑ READING CHECK **Main Idea and Details** Underline the main idea about what happens during adolescence.

_____

_____

_____

_____

_____

_____

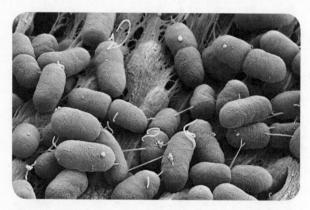

Some bacteria can cause illness, but most bacteria are harmless. Helpful bacteria in your intestines aid in digesting food.

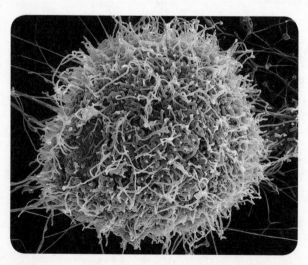

Viruses are germs that cause colds and flu.

## Immune System

Have you ever missed school with a cold or flu? If so, your body was invaded by germs. Germs, such as some bacteria, cause diseases that prevent the body from staying healthy. Your immune system protects your body against diseases. It has an army of defenses that can destroy germs or prevent them from entering the body.

One of the first lines of defense, or protection, in the body's army is the tiny hairs and mucus in the nose and windpipe. The hairs and mucus trap germs you may breathe in. Saliva, another defense, kills germs that enter the mouth.

**Main Idea and Details** Circle two ways the immune system protects the body.

Fever is another defense. Sometimes when you are ill, you get a fever. The rise in body temperature kills the invading germs. If germs get into the stomach, digestive juices destroy the germs.

The skin is another line of defense. It acts like a wall to stop germs from getting inside the body. If you cut yourself, germs can enter the body through the cut and get into your blood. The picture shows one kind of blood cell that fights germs. These white blood cells surround and engulf the germs.

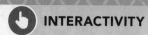
**INTERACTIVITY**

Do an activity about the human body.

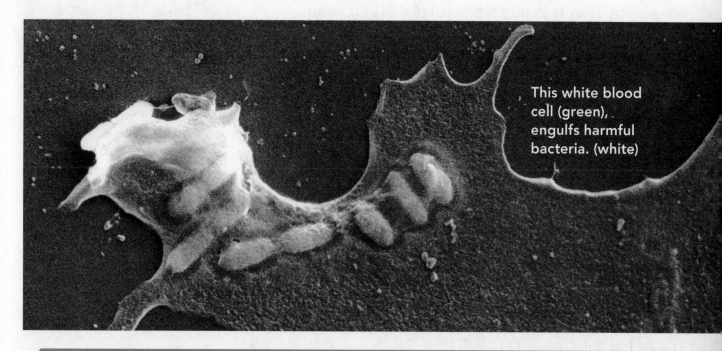

This white blood cell (green), engulfs harmful bacteria. (white)

## ☑ Lesson 4 Check

**1. Explain** How does a white blood cell help the body survive?

_____

_____

**2. Relate** How does the circulatory system work with the digestive system?

_____

_____

_____

**3. Explain** What must happen for digestion to begin?

_____

_____

# Tracking Germs

When germs enter the body, they can attack more than one place. They may attack several places at the same time. Or they may move from one place to another. How can you use your remote-controlled camera to follow germs that invade your body?

Identify where the germs enter the body.

_____

_____

What parts of the body are the germs affecting?

_____

_____

Draw the path the camera will follow. Label the organs it will travel through.

# Lines of Symmetry

If you fold the figures in half along the black line, both sides of each figure will be the same. The two halves of each figure will have the same size and shape. The figures have symmetry. Each fold represents a line of symmetry that separates the two identical parts.

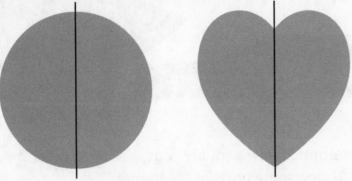

The human body has symmetry. Draw a picture of your face. Then draw a line of symmetry. Do the parts match?

Identify a body system that has a line of symmetry. Explain.

_____

_____

_____

# Quest Findings

## Make a Human Body Road Map

*How can you make a tiny camera navigate the human body?*

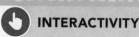
**INTERACTIVITY**

Organize data to support your Quest Findings.

### Make a Plan

**Phenomenon** You have determined how to guide your remote-controlled camera to view some parts of the human body. Now it is time to provide guidance for a way the camera can be used for a specific part of the body during a medical checkup.

Choose a body organ or system that you have studied. Think about the parts of that organ or system and how they function together.

What specifically will be checked using the camera?

How will the camera be used during the checkup procedure?

Decide whether you will write instructions or provide a map to explain how to use the camera. Then make your instructions.

How will you show a path on a map through the body system you have chosen? Write your ideas.

_____

_____

_____

Draw your map. You may wish to include "road signs" to direct the camera. Include diagrams and directions. Draw your map on a poster.

Present your map to the class.

# Medical Imaging Technician

A medical imaging technician works with challenging cases and specialized medical equipment. A medical imaging technician helps to capture images through a variety of tests, including MRIs, X-rays, and ultrasounds. These tests help diagnose, treat, or track patients with a variety of symptoms.

For instance, when a medical imaging technician does a CT scan, the technician can capture the right details. The computer technology the technician uses combines several X-ray images to provide more detail and information about the condition of a patient that may not have been easy to see in a regular X-ray or other testing.

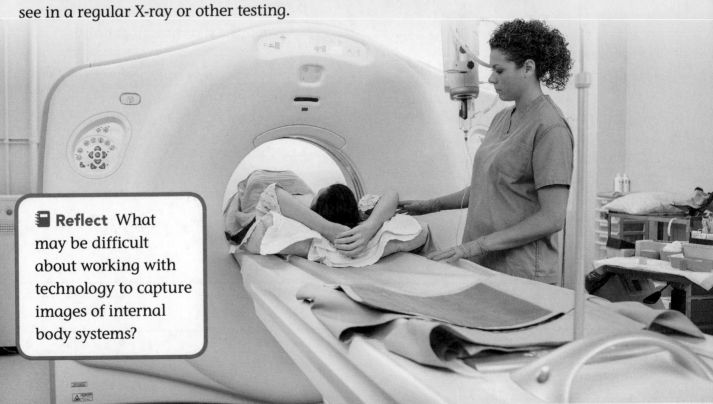

**Reflect** What may be difficult about working with technology to capture images of internal body systems?

1. **Vocabulary** Which organ breaks down fats?

   A. bladder

   B. diaphragm

   C. liver

   D. pancreas

2. **Use a Diagram** Match the labels to the correct area of the digestive system.

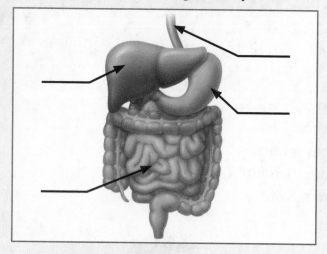

   A. esophagus

   B. liver

   C. small intestine

   D. stomach

3. **Summarize** What are two main functions of the skeletal system?

   _____

   _____

   _____

   _____

   _____

4. **Identify** Which of the following attaches muscles to the bones of the skeleton?

   A. cartilage

   B. ligaments

   C. joints

   D. tendons

5. **Explain** Which statement describes how the body absorbs nutrients?

   A. Nutrients travel along neurons to cells of the body.

   B. Nutrients pass into the capillaries of the villi.

   C. Nutrients travel along the spinal cord to the organs of the body.

   D. Nutrients are pulled into the body when the diaphragm expands.

6. **Summarize** How are the circulatory system and the respiratory system related?

   _____

   _____

   _____

   _____

   _____

   _____

   _____

**7. Use Tables** The table shows organs of the body and their functions. Complete the table.

| Organ | Function |
|---|---|
| bones | |
| brain | |
| skin | |
| kidneys | |
| esophagus | |

**8. Interpret a Diagram** Which structures would most likely respond to a person who is running a 5-kilometer race?

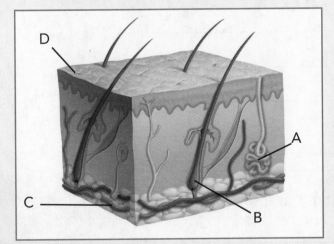

**A.** A and C

**B.** B and C

**C.** A and B

**D.** B and D

**9. Describe** Which statement **best** describes the blood that enters the heart from the lungs?

**A.** Blood is oxygen-rich.

**B.** Blood contains carbon dioxide.

**C.** Blood comes from the lungs.

**D.** Blood flows through a vein.

**The Essential Question** *How can you model the interactions among human body systems?*

## Show What You Learned

Choose two organ systems that you studied. Describe how you would make a model to show how the two systems interact with each other.

_____

_____

_____

_____

_____

_____

_____

_____

_____

_____

_____

# ☑ Evidence-Based Assessment

Read this scenario and answer questions 1–5.

A group of students conducted an investigation to see how heart and breathing rates change with exercise. Students measured and recorded their pulse and breathing while resting. Then they performed various physical activities for 2 minutes and repeated the measuring of pulse and breathing rates. They recorded their data in the following table.

| Activity | Heart rate before exercise | Heart rate after exercise | Breathing rate before exercise | Breathing rate after exercise |
|---|---|---|---|---|
| Running in place | 78 | 102 | 17 | 23 |
| Push ups | 72 | 95 | 15 | 22 |
| Balancing an egg on a spoon | 75 | 75 | 14 | 14 |

**1. Make Inferences** Suppose that the students first ran in place and then did push ups. What evidence do you see that they rested between these activities? Explain.

_____

_____

_____

_____

_____

_____

**2. Use Tables** What evidence did the students find that showed that body systems work together?

**A.** Heart and breathing rates increased after running in place.

**B.** Breathing rates increased after doing push ups.

**C.** Heart and breathing rates did not change after balancing an egg on a spoon.

**D.** Heart rate increased after running in place.

**3. Use Evidence** Given the results of pulse rates, how can you explain the changes that occurred?

_____

_____

_____

_____

_____

**4. Use Evidence** Given the results of breathing rates, how can you explain the changes that occurred?

_____

_____

_____

_____

**5.** How can you explain the difference in the heart and breathing rates before and after balancing an egg compared to the results for the other two tasks?

_____

_____

_____

_____

# How do your sensory organs gather information?

**Phenomenon** Scientists study how different parts of a system work together to explain how the system functions. What evidence can you use to explain how your sensory organs work as a system?

**Suggested Materials**
- blindfold
- scented candle
- feather
- paper tube
- soap

## Procedure

☐ **1.** Choose two sensory organs to learn more about how they work. Think of a way to test how your eyes, ears, nose, or skin gather information.

☐ **2. CCC Systems and System Models** Make a plan. Show your plan to your teacher before you begin. Conduct your investigation.

☐ **3.** Record your observations.

 Be aware of physical safety!

 Do not taste anything in lab.

**Science Practice**

Scientists *use evidence* to construct arguments.

## Observations

# Analyze and Interpret Data

**4. Explain** What did the tests you conducted show about how sensory organs work as a system? Use your observations to support your explanation.

_____

_____

_____

_____

_____

_____

_____

_____

**5. Present an Argument** Use evidence to explain how having more than one sensory organ helps humans. What would happen if one did not work?

_____

_____

_____

_____

_____

_____

_____

_____

_____

_____

# Science Practices

## Ask Questions

Science is the study of the natural world using scientific tools and methods. The natural world includes things such as matter, energy, the planets, and living things. It does not include things such as opinions about art or music.

A scientist asks questions and then tries to answer them. For example, a scientist might wonder how a large whale finds its food deep in the ocean. The scientist could first study what others have already learned. Then the scientist could investigate questions that have not been answered. Questions could include "How can a whale hold its breath underwater when it makes a deep dive?" Or, "How does a whale find food in the darkness of the deep ocean?"

**Ask Questions** What question would you ask about the animal in the photograph?

_____

_____

_____

_____

_____

_____

_____

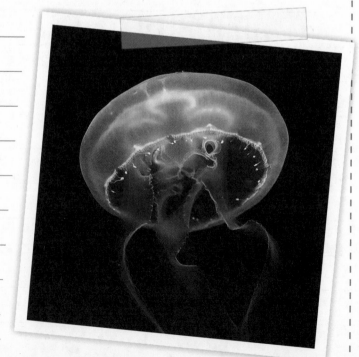

**SEP.1** Asking questions and defining problems
**SEP.3** Planning and carrying out investigations
**SEP.4** Analyzing and interpreting data

# Carry Out Investigations

Scientists use investigations and experiments to do their work. Part of an investigation is to observe the natural world to learn about how it works. When scientists make observations, they do not change anything. Scientists collect data from their observations. Quantitative data are expressed as numbers. Qualitative data describe something, such as how it smells or what color it is.

Scientists also investigate the world using experiments. In an experiment, scientists make a change to the object or process they are observing. For example, the amount of salt dissolved in ocean water is not the same everywhere. To find out how quickly salt dissolves in water at different temperatures, a scientist might put identical amounts of salt and water in several containers at different temperatures. The scientist changes the temperature of the containers and measures the time the salt takes to dissolve in each. The part of the experiment that the scientist changes is called the independent variable. The part that changes as a result is called the dependent variable. In this case, the independent variable is temperature, and the dependent variable is the time the salt takes to dissolve. All scientific investigations include collecting data.

**Plan an Investigation** A scientist is investigating how the amount of salt in water affects the growth of young fish. What are some quantitative data that the scientist can record?

_____

_____

# Science Practices

## Science Tools

Scientists use tools to take measurements when they collect data. They also use tools to help make observations about the natural world. Scientific tools expand the type of observations that can be made.

Tools for measuring include rulers to measure length, certain glassware to measure volume, thermometers to measure temperature, and balances to measure mass. Different types of tools are needed for taking very small or very large measurements. It is important to use the right tool for the measurement that is to be taken.

Tools that expand what we can detect and measure include microscopes and telescopes. These tools allow people to observe things that are too small or too far away to see.

**Cause and Effect** Red tides occur when the population of tiny algae grows. The organisms can make toxic substances that harm wildlife and make the water unsafe for people. How would scientists use a microscope when they study a red tide?

_____

_____

# Digital Tools

Many modern tools operate using microprocessors or computers. These objects are digital tools. Digital tools include measuring tools such as digital balances and thermometers. They also include tools that scientists use to record and analyze data. Many scientific instruments have a computer that guides data collection and records results. Digital cameras are often a key part of telescopes, microscopes, and other tools used to make observations.

A solar panel provides power for the digital instruments and computer on this buoy. The instruments can measure changes in the ocean.

Computers and other digital devices make data collection faster. Processors can respond to changes and record data much faster than a human observer can. Computers are also important for keeping records and analyzing large numbers of data. Computers and other digital devices are an important part of communication networks that allow scientists to share data and results.

**Communicate** Scientists communicate in different ways. How could a scientist use a computer to communicate with another scientist?

_____

_____

# Science Practices

## Analyzing and Interpreting Data

Scientists use empirical evidence when they study nature. Empirical evidence is information that can be observed and measured. Scientific conclusions are always based on evidence that can be tested. These observations and measurements are data that can be used to explain the natural world.

Measurements and observations provide scientists with evidence of changes. For example, when a natural system changes, the change can affect organisms in the system. Scientists can observe and record the changes, such as how many organisms are living in an area at one time compared to another time. Then the scientists can analyze those data to make predictions about the effects of other changes.

Scientists analyze measurements and observations to answer scientific questions. Analyzing measurements of changes in an ecosystem can provide information about how different parts of the natural system work together.

**Measure** The temperature of water affects ocean currents and marine habitats. How could scientists get empirical evidence about the temperature of the water? Why is this empirical evidence?

_____

_____

_____

_____

_____

## Using Math

Careful measurements are necessary for collecting reliable data. Scientists make measurements several times to be sure that the results can be repeated. In general, scientists use digital instruments to collect quantitative data.

Scientists use mathematics to analyze quantitative data. They record measurements and compare them to find out what changes and what stays the same. A number of measurements can be compared to show if something changes over time. Mathematical analysis can also show how fast a change occurs.

When a scientist makes a claim based on evidence, other scientists can check the claim. When other scientists check the claim and find similar results, the claim or findings are supported by similar evidence.

**Evaluate** How do numerical data from measurements make it easier to compare results in an investigation?

_____

_____

Research ships carry many instruments that gather data.

# Science Practices

## Constructing Explanations

After scientists analyze data, they use their results to construct explanations of natural phenomena. A scientific explanation often uses the change in variables to relate one change to another. For example, as conditions in marine ecosystems change, organisms living in the water might change in response. Scientists observe changes in ecosystems and study populations of organisms to learn about effects of changes. Then they construct explanations about the organisms.

## Developing and Using Models

Scientists often use models to help them understand something. Models are objects or ideas that represent other things. A model only shows part of the thing that it represents.

Scientists also use computers to make models. You can watch on a computer screen how ocean conditions change over time. The model can show you how plant and animal populations are affected. You can even make a model using words. When you describe something, you are making a verbal model of the object. Other people can learn about the object from your spoken model.

**Evaluate** How could you make a model to explain how a lobster survives on the ocean floor?

_____

_____

_____

**SEP.2** Developing and using models
**SEP.6** Constructing explanations and designing solutions
**SEP.7** Engaging in argument from evidence

# Engaging in Arguments from Evidence

Scientific observations are different from opinions. An opinion is a personal belief and is not always based on facts. An example of an opinion is that tuna tastes better than salmon. No facts support this opinion. An example of a fact is that salmon lay their eggs in fresh water. This statement can be supported by observation.

Scientists use evidence to support their conclusions. For example, the conclusion that whales migrate is based on evidence. Whales can be seen in some areas but not in others, depending on the season. Scientists can also track individual whales to see where they go.

When a scientist makes a claim or argument, other scientists can check the evidence that the claim is based on. Different people making the same observation will find the same evidence. Scientific explanations are always based on empirical evidence.

Explain No one has seen a giant squid with a length of 20 meters. How could scientists use evidence to decide whether these animals exist?

_____

_____

_____

_____

_____

_____

_____

# Science Practices

## Habits of Mind

Scientists must be creative when they design experiments. Science is focused on answering new questions. That often means that scientists must come up with new ways to answer questions. Designing a good experiment requires them to think of new ways to solve problems. They need to think about what could go wrong and how to fix it. For example, a scientist who studies tiny organisms in the ocean might try to count them using a medical machine that counts blood cells.

When scientists develop new methods, they evaluate them to be certain they are collecting the right data to answer the question. After they have analyzed data and reached a conclusion, scientists share the results. Other scientists then review and evaluate the methods and conclusions. This peer review process helps confirm that investigations were correctly designed. Other scientists may also repeat the investigation to confirm that they obtain the same results.

**Plan an Investigation** Sea urchins eat a lot of kelp, an underwater organism. A scientist concludes that increasing populations of sea otters would help restore kelp forests because otters eat sea urchins. How could other scientists confirm this conclusion?

_____

_____

_____

_____

## Communicate Information

Scientists communicate with other scientists to share what they learned. The words that scientists use sometimes have meanings different from the same word used in everyday communication. *Current, heat,* and *record* are examples of words that have a specific meaning in science. In science, for example, *heat*

Scientists around the world communicate and evaluate results.

refers to the flow of thermal energy. In everyday use, heat may refer to the temperature on a warm day.

Scientists do not perform a single observation or experiment and then come to a conclusion. They repeat experiments and gather the same kind of information. If the results cannot be repeated, then some of the observations may include errors. It is also important that scientific observations can be repeated by other researchers. Sometimes, other researchers cannot get the same result. Then the scientists compare their methods to find out what is different. An error could have happened in one of the methods.

Being able to repeat results makes a conclusion more reliable, so communication among scientists is important. Scientists communicate their methods and results, so other scientists can repeat them and then compare.

Evaluate  A scientist repeats an experiment and gets a different result. What should the scientist do next?

_____

_____

_____

# Engineering Practices

## Defining Problems

Scientists study the natural world. Engineers apply scientific knowledge to solve problems. The first step of the engineering process is stating a well-defined problem. The engineering problem states exactly what the solution to the problem should accomplish. Engineers ask questions to define problems that need to be solved. For example, an engineer might want to build a probe to take samples very deep in the ocean. The engineer might start by asking "What kinds of tools can do that specific job?" Engineers use scientific knowledge and principles to solve the problem.

Before designing a solution, engineers identify criteria and constraints of the problem. The criteria are what the solution must accomplish. For example, one criterion when building a research submarine is that it must work well under the great pressure of the deep ocean. Constraints are limits on the solution. A constraint could be that a solution not go over a certain cost.

**Evaluate** A classmate says that the cost of an environmental project should not be considered a constraint. Do you agree? Why or why not?

_____

_____

_____

_____

**SEP.1** Asking questions (for science) and defining problems (for engineering)
**SEP.6** Constructing explanations (for science) and designing solutions (for engineering)
**SEP.8** Obtaining, evaluating, and communicating information

## Designing Solutions

Before designing a solution, engineers identify criteria and constraints of the problem. For example, one criterion of a solution to rebuild a harbor could be that it restores a habitat for certain animals. A constraint of the harbor restoration could be that it not cost too much money.

Engineers use the criteria and constraints to develop a solution to the problem. They may think of different ways to solve the engineering problem, then decide which way fits the criteria and constraints best.

After they decide on a solution, engineers build the solution and test it. They may use several different design ideas and evaluate each one. They often can combine the best features of each to come to a final design solution.

`Design Solutions` When ships release water from distant places, they can introduce invasive species. What kind of engineering solution would help prevent the spread of invasive species?

_____

_____

_____

_____

_____

_____

_____

# Engineering Practices

## Using Models and Prototypes

Similar to scientists, engineers frequently use models as they design solutions. Engineering models can be actual working devices of a proposed solution. Sometimes these devices represent the final solution, but perhaps on

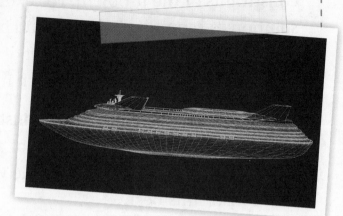

a smaller scale. They may only model one part of the solution. Other models are an actual device at full scale and perform all parts of the solution. This kind of model is called a prototype. Engineers use a prototype to collect data that can help them evaluate the design.

Engineers may use other kinds of models, such as drawings or computer models. A computer model can compare parts of a very complex solution. It allows engineers to make changes and observe what happens without investing a large amount of time or resources to actually build the solution. For example, an engineer investigating ways to restore a damaged ecosystem could use a computer to model changes to the system. The computer could model the effects of changes before the engineer decides which changes to make in a large area.

Infer Why would a computer model of a new ship design save time or money during the construction of the ship?

_____

_____

_____

**SEP.2** Developing and using models
**SEP.3** Planning and carrying out investigations
**SEP.5** Using mathematics and computational thinking
**SEP.7** Engaging in argument from evidence

## Optimizing Solutions

Engineering is focused on solving problems. A successful solution must meet all of the criteria and constraints. Even if a solution is successful, a better solution may still be possible. When the design is tested, engineers may think of new ideas that might work. The criteria or constraints may also change during the process.

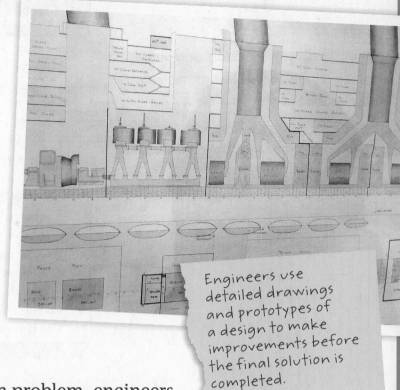

Engineers use detailed drawings and prototypes of a design to make improvements before the final solution is completed.

Even after solving the design problem, engineers continue to work on the solution to optimize it, or make it better. They evaluate the results and consider ways to improve on them. Then they may make a new prototype to determine whether it is a better solution. Like scientists, engineers make a change and then observe or measure the results of the change. After analyzing and evaluating their data, engineers may change the solution or develop a new engineering problem.

Optimize Solutions An engineer designs a project to restore a forest after a mining project. After the design is complete, more funding becomes available. How could the engineer optimize the design solution?

_____

_____

_____

_____

# Glossary

The glossary uses letters and symbols to show how words are pronounced. The mark " is placed after a syllable with a primary or heavy accent. The mark ' is placed after a syllable with a secondary or light accent.

## Pronunciation Key

| | | | | | | |
|---|---|---|---|---|---|---|
| a | in hat, cap | k | in kind, seek | th | in thin, both |
| ā | in age, face | l | in land, coal | TH | in then, smooth |
| â | in care, fair | m | in me, am | u | in cup, butter |
| ä | in father, far | n | in no, in | u̇ | in full, put |
| b | in bad, rob | ng | in long, bring | ü | in rule, move |
| ch | in child, much | o | in hot, rock | v | in very, save |
| d | in did, red | ō | in open, go | w | in will, woman |
| e | in let, best | ȯ | all, caught | y | in young, yet |
| ē | in equal, be | ô | in order | z | in zero, breeze |
| ėr | in term, learn | oi | in oil, voice | zh | in measure, seizure |
| f | in fat, if | ou | in house, out | ə a | in about |
| g | in go, bag | p | in paper, cup | e | in taken |
| h | in he, how | r | in run, try | i | in pencil |
| i | in it, pin | s | in say, yes | o | in lemon |
| ī | in ice, five | sh | in she, rush | u | in circus |
| j | in jam, enjoy | t | in tell, it | | |

**absorb** (ab zôrb") to take in something steadily

**amplitude** (am" plə tüd′) the greatest height of a wave in its resting position

**analog** (an" l ȯg) a continuous signal that sends information

**antenna** (an ten" ə) the part of a device that receives radio-wave signals

**appear** (ə pir") to be seen or show up

**available** (ə vā" lə bəl) can be used

**avalanche** (av" ə lanch) a massive amount of snow, ice, and rocks suddenly sliding down a slope

**battery** (bat" ər ē) device that stores chemical energy that can change into electrical energy

**bladder** (blad" ər) an organ that stores urine until it is released from the body

**brain** (brān) an organ that receives information from sense organs about the environment and then tells the body how to react

**butte** (byüt) a steep hill with a small, flat top

**canyon** (kan" yən) a deep, narrow area surrounded by mountains

**characteristic** (kâr′ ik tə ris″ tik) a trait, feature, or quality

**circular wave** (sėr″ kyə lər wāv) a disturbance at a single point that moves outward in all directions

**classify** (klas′ ə fī) to sort objects or living things into groups based on shared traits

**coal** (kōl) a solid fossil fuel that is burned to transfer energy

**collision** (kə lizh″ ən ) the action of one object bumping into another

**combustion** (kəm bəs″ chən) the burning of a fuel to produce heat and light

**compass rose** (kum″ pəs rōz) a four-pointed symbol that shows which directions are north, east, south, and west on a map

**conductor** (kən duk″ tər) a material that energy can easily flow through

**connect** (kə nekt″) to attach or put together

**crest** (krest) the top point of a transverse wave

**cuticle** (kyü″ tə kəl) a waxy outer coating on a leaf that helps a plant control the amount of water that leaves the plant.

**device** (di vis″) objects made for a specific purpose

**diaphragm** (di″ ə fram) a muscle below the lungs that causes the flow of air into and out of the lungs

**digital** (dij″ ə təl) signals that use clear-cut numbers to represent data

**drought** (drout) a long, dry period of weather

**earthquake** (ėrth″ kwäk′) a shift that releases pressure on Earth's crust and causes the crust to shake

**electric charge** (i lek″ trik chārj ) a property that causes matter to have a force when it is placed near other charged matter

**electric current** (i lek″ trik kėr″ ənt) the flow of charged particles in the same direction

**emission** (i mish″ ən) the release of something into the environment

**energy** (en″ ər jē) the ability to do work or cause change

**erosion** (i rō″ zhən) the process where particles are removed from land by wind, ice, or water

**eruption** (i rup″ shən) the release of material from a volcano

**evidence** (ev″ ə dəns) something easily observed that can be used to confirm or deny an idea

# Glossary

**excretory system** (ek" skrə tôr′ ē sis" təm) the organs that remove waste from the human body

**exoskeleton** (ek′ sō skel" ə tən) a hard external covering on many invertebrates that maintains their shape and protects their organs

**extend** (ek stend") to stretch or strengthen

**external** (ek stėr" nl) something that is on the outside of an organism or object

**extinct** (ek stingkt") the death of all organisms in a species

**fault** (fȯlt) an area in Earth's crust where tectonic plates meet

**feature** (fē" chər) a characteristic or part of something

**flood** (flud) an overflow of water that spreads over land that is not normally covered in water

**fossil** (fos" əl) remains or evidence of plants and animals preserved in minerals

**fossil fuel** (fos" əl fyü" əl) a substance produced by pressure and decaying organisms that is used for energy

**frequency** (frē" kwən sē) the number of times a wave repeats itself in a certain amount of time

**fuel** (fyü" əl) a substance that releases energy when it burns

**function** (fungk" shən) the job that something is made to do

**generate** (jen" ə rāt′) to make or produce

**generator** (jen" ə rā′ tər) a device that changes the energy of motion into electrical energy

**geothermal energy** (jē ō thėr" məl en" ər jē) energy created by pressure and heat underneath Earth's crust

**gills** (gils) the organ in fish and young amphibians that takes in oxygen from water

**greenhouse gas** (grēn" hous′ gas) a gas that makes the atmosphere able to hold more heat, such as carbon dioxide and water vapor

**hazard** (haz" ərd) a danger caused by an event

**heart** (härt) an organ that pumps blood

**heat** (hēt) the transfer of thermal energy

**horizontal** (hôr′ ə zon" tl) parallel to Earth's surface

**hydropower** (hī" drō pou′ ər) energy from the movement of water

**igneous** (ig" nē əs) a type of rock made from molten lava

**impact** (im" pakt) an effect

**insulator** (in" sə lā′ tər) a material that stops the flow of electric current

**internal** (in tėr" nl) something that is on the inside of an organism or object

**interpret** (in tėr" prit) to figure out the meaning of something

**key bed** (kē bed) a layer of rock that scientists can clearly identify the time in Earth's period in which it formed

**kidney** (kid" nē) bean-shaped organ that filters wastes from the blood

**kinetic energy** (ki net" ik en" ər jē) the energy of a moving object

**landslide** (land" slīd′) a large amount of rock or soil sliding down a slope

**large intestine** (lärj in tes" tən) the organ that absorbs water from digested food and helps get rid of waste

**legend** (lej" ənd) an explanation on a map for the meaning of the symbols on the map

**light** (līt) a form of energy we can see

**liver** (liv" ər) an organ that breaks down fats and helps with digestion

**longitudinal** (lon′ jə tüd" nəl) a wave that moves in the same direction as the particles it travels through

**lungs** (lung) the main respiratory organ that takes in and releases air

**metamorphic** (met′ ə môr" fik) a type of rock formed when particles of other rocks are combined by great pressure and very high temperatures

**muscle** (mus" əl) an organ that contracts and relaxes to make bones move

**natural gas** (nach" ər əl gas) a fossil fuel gas that is burned for energy

**nuclear fuel** (nü" klē ər fyü" əl) an energy source made from unstable elements, such as uranium

**organ** (ôr" gən) a group of tissues that has a specific function

# Glossary

**organ system** (ôr" gən sis" təm) a group of organs that work together to fill a specific need of the body

**outcome** (out" kum′) the result of an event

**ovary** (ō" vər ē) the female reproductive part of a flower that holds the eggs

**pancreas** (pan" krē əs) the organ that manages sugar levels in the body

**pattern** (pat" ərn) something that appears or happens in the same way again and again

**petroleum** (pə trō" lē əm) a liquid fossil fuel that can be burned to transfer energy

**pistil** (pis" tl) the part of a flower that receives pollen and contains the ovary

**plane wave** (plān wāv) a wave that is made when a line of matter is disturbed

**pollutant** (pə lüt" nt) a harmful substance released into the environment

**potential** (pə ten" shəl) possible

**potential energy** (pə ten" shəl en" ər jē) stored energy in an object

**primary** (pri" mer′ ē) first or most important

**radiation** (ra′ dē ā" shən) energy that travels as a wave

**range** (rānj") all possibilities between two end points

**ray** (ra") a line of energy that moves in one direction until it hits an object

**receiver** (ri sē" vər) the part of a device that changes radio waves into a useable message

**reflect** (ri flekt") to bounce off of an object

**refract** (ri frakt") to bend when passing through an object

**resistor** (ri zis" tər) a device used to control the flow of electricity

**respond** (ri spond") to react

**sample** (sam" pəl) small amount of a material that is used for observation

**scrubber** (skrub" ər) a device in a power plant that reduces the amount of released pollutants sent into the air

**sedimentary** (sed′ ə men" tər ē) a type of rock that formed when particles, such as dirt, sand, and fossils, settled into layers and became compressed

**sensory organ** (sen" sər ē ôr" gən) an organ that collects specific information about the body's surroundings

**sepal** (sē" pəl) the green, leaf-like part of a plant that protects a budding flower until it is ready to bloom

**signal** (sig" nəl) a message

**simulate** ( sim" yə lāt) to demonstrate or copy something to make it easier to understand

**skeletal system** (skel" ə təl sis" təm) the bones in the human body that interact to move, protect the body, and give it shape

**skeleton** (skel" ə tən) an rigid inner support in vertebrates made of bones

**skin** (skin) the organ that surrounds and protects the body

**small intestine** (smȯl in tes" tən) the organ where most digestion occurs

**sound** (sound) energy that can be heard

**source** (sôrs) the point that something comes from

**speed** (spēd) the distance an object moves in a specific amount of time

**stamen** (stā" mən) the male part of the flower that makes pollen

**stimulus** (stim" yə ləs) an action or change that causes a certain reaction in an animal

**stomach** (stum" ək) the organ that breaks down certain kinds of food in the process of digestion

**strata** (strā" tə) layers of rock

**structure** (struk" chər) an arrangement of particles for a specific purpose

**superposition** (sü' pər pə zish" ən) waves meeting and combining amplitudes as they move

**symbol** (sim" bəl) pictures, colors, and lines on a map that have a specific meaning

**system** (sis" təm) a group of parts that work together to complete a task

**tissue** (tish" ü) group of the same kind of cells with a particular function

**transfer** (tran sfėr" or tran" sfėr) to move from one object to another

**transform** (tran sfôrm") to change from one type of energy to another

**transmitter** (tran smit" ər or tranz mit" ər) the part of a device that sends radio signals

**transverse** (trans vėrs" or tranz vėrs") a wave that moves and carries energy perpendicular to the particles it travels through

**trench** (trench) a long, narrow, sunken area of the ocean floor

# Glossary

**trough** (tro̊f") the bottom point of a transverse wave

**tsunami** (su̇ nä" mē or tsu̇ nä" mē) a massive wave created by an earthquake

**turbine** (tėr" bən or tėr" bin) a device that contains a wheel with blades that rotate by the pressure of moving water, steam, or air.

**uranium** (yu̇ rā" nē əm) an unstable element used by humans as an energy source

**vascular system** (vas" kyə lər sis" təm) the tube-like parts of a plant that transport materials throughout the plant

**volcano** (väl kā" no) an opening in Earth's crust that allows superheated rock and other materials below the crust to reach the surface

**wave** (wāv) a disturbance that travels in a pattern and carries energy

**wavelength** (wāv length or wāv lengkth) the distance between similar points on a wave

**wave period** (wāv pir" ē əd) the time it takes a wave to move one wavelength

**weathering** (weTH" ər ing) the process that wears away or breaks down rock

**wildfire** (wīld" fir') an out of control, destructive fire

# Index

* Page numbers for charts, graphs, maps, and pictures are printed in italics.

**D**

**E**

# Credits

## Illustrations

Aaron Ashley Illustration; Peter Bull Art Studio; Sara Lynn Cramb/ Astound US; Dan Crisp/The Bright Agency; Patrick Gnan/ IllustrationOnline.com; Stuart Holmes/Illustration Inc.; Mapping Specialists, Ltd.; Bojan Orešković; Pronk Media Inc.; Rob Schuster; Geoffrey P. Smith; Jim Steck/Steck Figures; Symmetry Creative Productions; Sam Valentino/Bumblecat Design & Illustration, LLC; Ralph Voltz/IllustrationOnline.com

## Photographs

Photo locators denoted as follows: Top (T), Center (C), Bottom (B), Left (L), Right (R), Background (Bkgd)

## Covers

Front Cover: Scanrail/iStock/Getty Images;
Back Cover: Marinello/DigitalVision Vectors/Getty Images;

## Front Matter

iv: Clari Massimiliano/Shutterstock; vi: Hongqi Zhang/Alamy Stock Photo; vii: Michaeljung/Fotolia; viii: StockLite/Shutterstock; ix: Isuaneye/Fotolia; x: Szefei/123RF; xi: Matthew Ennis/Shutterstock; xii: Racorn/Shutterstock; xiii: Medioimages/Photodisc/ Getty Images; xiv B: Lakov Kalinin/Fotolia; xiv TR: Barry Tuck/ Shutterstock; xv B: Pearson Education; xv T: Pearson Education

## Topic 1

000: ImageBROKER/Alamy Stock Photo; 002: Hongqi Zhang/Alamy Stock Photo; 005 C: Adil Yusifov/Fotolia; 005 R: Adil Yusifov/Fotolia; 006: Dpa picture alliance/Alamy Stock Photo; 008 BR: Hongqi Zhang/ Alamy Stock Photo; 008 T: Ryhor Bruyeu/Alamy Stock Photo; 009: Africa Studio/Fotolia; 012: Sergey Nivens/Alamy Stock Photo; 013 BL: Matúš Lošonský/Alamy Stock Photo; 013 BR: irishphoto.com/ Alamy Stock Photo; 013 CR: IStockphoto_RAW/Getty Images; 013 TL: Hongqi Zhang/Alamy Stock Photo; 014 BL: Andrew Twort/ Alamy Stock Photo; 014 CL: Krasyuk/Fotolia; 014 CR: Photolife2016/ Fotolia; 016 BL: JulieRob/Getty Images; 016 BR: Margoe Edwards/ Shutterstock; 020 BR: Hongqi Zhang/Alamy Stock Photo; 020 TL: Andresr/Shutterstock; 021: ErickN/Shutterstock; 022: Hongqi Zhang/ Alamy Stock Photo; 024: Joseph Giacomin/Science Source; 029: Zastolskiy Victor/Shutterstock; 030 BR: Hongqi Zhang/Alamy Stock Photo; 030 CL: JGade/Shutterstock; 030 T: Janecat/Shutterstock; 032: Hongqi Zhang/Alamy Stock Photo; 033: Blend Images/Alamy Stock Photo; 034: 3drenderings/Shutterstock; 035: Hchjjl/Shutterstock; 036 C: 5/Shutterstock; 036 CL: Einar Muoni/Shutterstock; 037 BC: Hongqi Zhang/Alamy Stock Photo; 037 R: Maksimka37/Fotolia; 039: Marius Graf/Alamy Stock Photo; 040: Hongqi Zhang/Alamy Stock Photo; 041: Robert Crum/Shutterstock; 042 Bkgrd: JTB MEDIA CREATION, Inc./Alamy Stock Photo; 042 TR: Hongqi Zhang/Alamy Stock Photo; 043 B: Mark Scheuern/Alamy Stock Photo; 043 TR: Monty Rakusen/ Getty Images; 046: Tetra Images/Alamy Stock Photo

## Topic 2

050: Cultura Creative (RF)/Alamy Stock Photo; 052: Michaeljung/ Fotolia; 054: Hchjjl/Shutterstock; 055: David Brimm/Shutterstock;

056: Idealink Photography/Alamy Stock Photo; 057: Lineartestpilot/ Shutterstock; 058: Shutterlk/Shutterstock; 059: Africa Studio/ Fotolia; 062 CL: Scanrail/Fotolia; 062 CR: Michaeljung/Fotolia; 063: Michaeljung/Fotolia; 064 BL: Eric Isselee/Shutterstock; 064 BR: TomasSereda/Getty Images; 065: DesignPie.cc/Shutterstock; 066: Kustov/Shutterstock; 067 Bkgrd: Huyangshu/Shutterstock; 067 TC: Michaeljung/Fotolia; 070: Unlisted Images, Inc./Alamy Stock Photo; 071: blickwinkel/Alamy Stock Photo; 072: Michaeljung/ Fotolia; 073 BL: msk.nina/Fotolia; 073 BR: Alexander Potapov/ Fotolia; 074: Nd700/Fotolia; 075: 1973kla/Shutterstock; 078: Elbud/ Shutterstock; 080: Michaeljung/Fotolia; 082 B: Maicasaa/Fotolia; 082 C: Scyther5/Shutterstock; 082 CR: Elbud/Shutterstock; 083: Tidarat Tiemjai/Shutterstock; 084: Vaclav Volrab/Shutterstock; 086: Martin33/Shutterstock; 087 BC: Michaeljung/Fotolia; 087 CR: Gudellaphoto/Fotolia; 090: Tigergallery/Shutterstock; 091 Bkgrd: buranasak wongsiriphakdee/Shutterstock; 091 TL: Michaeljung/ Fotolia; 092 Bkgrd: Chukov/Shutterstock; 092 CR: Michaeljung/ Fotolia; 093 B: Jens Brüggemann/123RF; 093 TR: Kadmy/Fotolia

## Topic 3

100: PsyComa/Shutterstock; 102: StockLite/Shutterstock; 105 CR: Bedecs_HU/Shutterstock; 105 R: Scanrail1/Shutterstock; 106: Trubavin/Shutterstock; 108: StockLite/Shutterstock; 112: Dudarev Mikhail/Shutterstock; 113 B: Natalia_Maroz/Shutterstock; 113 TL: StockLite/Shutterstock; 114 BL: cristi180884/Shutterstock; 114 BR: Alsu/Shutterstock; 114 C: Pyty/Shutterstock; 115: EW CHEE GUAN/Shutterstock; 116: Aubord Dulac/Shutterstock; 118 BR: StockLite/Shutterstock; 118 T: Inked Pixels/Shutterstock; 119 B: Dave and Les Jacobs/Getty Images; 119 CR: AMCImages/Getty Images; 123 BR: Tan Wei Ming/Shutterstock; 123 CR: Photo Melon/ Shutterstock; 123 TC: StockLite/Shutterstock; 124: Tsuneo/123RF; 125: GIPhotostock/Science Source; 126 B: Matthias Kulka/Radius Images/Getty Images; 126 CR: StockLite/Shutterstock; 130: Tiffany Bjellmus/EyeEm/Getty Images; 131: Itsmejust/Shutterstock; 132 BR: Coprid/Shutterstock; 132 TR: StockLite/Shutterstock; 134: World History Archive/Alamy Stock Photo; 136 BL: Kathathep/ Shutterstock; 136 CL: Itsmejust/Shutterstock; 138: StockLite/ Shutterstock; 139: Studiovin/Shutterstock; 140 TL: StockLite/ Shutterstock; 140 TR: Universal Images Group North America LLC/Alamy Stock Photo; 141 BR: Baipooh/Shutterstock; 141 TR: Vladimir Nenezic/Shutterstock; 142 Bkgrd: BESTBACKGROUNDS/ Shutterstock; 142 TCR: StockLite/Shutterstock; 143 B: Pressmaster/ Shutterstock; 143 TR: Andrey_Popov/Shutterstock; 146: Tewan Banditrukkanka/Shutterstock

## Topic 4

150: Michael Dorrington/Shutterstock; 152: Isuaneye/Fotolia; 155 Bkgrd: Bruce Roberts/Science Source; 155 CR: Bruce Roberts/ Science Source; 156: Dudarev Mikhail/Shutterstock; 157: Hchjjl/ Shutterstock; 158: Isuaneye/Fotolia; 160: Iryna Bezianova/ Shutterstock; 163: Isuaneye/Fotolia; 164: Bjul/Shutterstock; 165 CR: Padma Sanjaya/Shutterstock; 165 TR: Jon Manjeot/Shutterstock; 166: Brisbane/Shutterstock; 168: 123rf.com; 169: Isuaneye/Fotolia; 173 B: stocker1970/Shutterstock; 173 TL: Isuaneye/Fotolia; 174: Poravute Siriphiroon/123RF; 175: LHF Graphics/Shutterstock; 176 BC: Sonsam/Shutterstock; 176 BL: Vvoe/Shutterstock; 176 BR: Vvoe/Fotolia; 176 CL: Sumikophoto/Shutterstock; 176 TCL:

Siim Sepp/Shutterstock; 176 TL: George Burba/123RF; 177 BC: Isuaneye/Fotolia; 177 Bkgrd: Niti_Photo/Shutterstock; 177 CR: Sakdinon kadchiangsaen/123RF; 180 BL: Mark A. Schneider/Science Source; 180 BR: Albert Russ/Shutterstock; 180 CL: Stefan Malloch/Shutterstock; 182 C: PurpleImages/Getty Images; 182 CL: Nikolay Se/Shutterstock; 182 CR: stocker1970/Shutterstock; 182 TC: Isuaneye/Fotolia; 184: Sherry V Smith/Shutterstock; 186: Photo Passion/Fotolia; 187 B: NNerto/Fotolia; 187 C: Isuaneye/Fotolia; 188: pisaphotography/Shutterstock; 189 BR: blickwinkel/Alamy Stock Photo; 189 T: Patrick Rambaldo/Shutterstock; 190: Josef Hanus/Shutterstock; 191: Atm2003/Shutterstock; 192: Isuaneye/Fotolia; 193 CR: Aleksej Orel/123RF; 193 TR: Gorov/Fotolia; 194 Bkgrd: Alexander Demyanenko/Fotolia; 194 CR: Isuaneye/Fotolia; 195 Bkgrd: Jeremy Bishop/Science Source; 195 TR: William J. Wysession/Courtesy of Michael Wysession; 197: Bildagentur Zoonar GmbH/Shutterstock; 201: Doodleboards/Shutterstock.

## Topic 5

202: Henri Leduc/Getty Images; 204: Szefei/123RF; 207: Tribune Content Agency LLC/Alamy Stock Photo; 208: Science History Images/Alamy Stock Photo; 209: Christos Georghiou/Shutterstock; 210: Aurora Photos/Alamy Stock Photo; 211 BC: Szefei/123RF; 211 T: Naypong/Shutterstock; 214: Dpa picture alliance/Alamy Stock Photo; 215 Bkgrd: Larigan Patricia Hamilton/Moment/Getty Images; 215 TL: Szefei/123RF; 216 BC: Lloyd Cluff/Corbis/Getty Images; 216 C: Chase Smith/Corbis/Getty Images; 218: StockShot/Alamy Stock Photo; 222 B: Robert Timoney/Alamy Stock Photo; 222 BR: Szefei/123RF; 222 CL: Willoughby Owen/Moment/Getty Images; 222 TL: Michael Doolittle/Alamy Stock Photo; 224 B: BanksPhotos/E+/Getty Images; 224 TL: Szefei/123RF; 225: Raphotos/E+/Getty Images; 226: W K Fletcher/Getty Images; 227: Kulyk/123RF; 228: DaveArnoldPhoto.com/Moment Open/Getty Images; 229 C: Kum Son Leem/EyeEm/Getty Images; 229 T: Science History Images/Alamy Stock Photo; 230: Szefei/123RF; 231: Fstop123/E+/Getty Images; 232 BR: Roman Bykyhalov/123RF; 232 T: Szefei/123RF; 234 Bkgrd: Siim Sepp/123RF; 234 TR: Szefei/123RF; 235 Bkgrd: RGB Ventures/SuperStock/Alamy Stock Photo; 235 TR: Tanguy de Saint Cyr/Alamy Stock Photo; 241: Wang Wen Chia/123RF.

## Topic 6

242: Sumikophoto/Shutterstock; 244: Matthew Ennis/Shutterstock; 247 C: Vvoennyy/123RF; 247 R: LiuSol/Shutterstock; 248: Reuters/Alamy Stock Photo; 249: LemonadePixel/Shutterstock; 250 BR: Matthew Ennis/Shutterstock; 250 L: Blickwinkel/Alamy Stock Photo; 251: Antonio Ribeiro/rf123.com; 252 CL: Adam Platt/Alamy Stock Photo; 252 CR: Ste Lane/Shutterstock; 253: 123RF; 254: Matthew Ennis/Shutterstock; 256 BR: MarcelClemens/Shutterstock; 256 C: Rene Martin/Shutterstock; 256 CL: APaterson/Shutterstock; 257: Jiri Vaclavek/Shutterstock; 258: Rafael BenAri/Alamy Stock Photo; 259: ArtAllAnd/Shutterstock; 260: Tom Grundy/Shutterstock; 261 CL: Scigelova/Shutterstock; 261 CR: 3drenderings/Shutterstock; 264 B: Sumikophoto/Shutterstock; 264 CR: Matthew Ennis/Shutterstock; 265 C: Lefteris Papaulakis/Shutterstock; 265 TR: Francois Gohier/Science Source; 266 BC: Tonobalaguer/123RF; 266 BR: Alicephoto/Shutterstock; 266 CR: Shi Yali/Shutterstock; 266 TR: Matthew Ennis/Shutterstock; 268 Bkgrd: Henry Georgi/All Canada Photos/Getty Images; 268 TR: Matthew Ennis/Shutterstock; 269 B: Monkey Business Images/Shutterstock; 269 TR: logosland/Shutterstock.

## Topic 7

276: Scotty/Fotolia; 278: Racorn/Shutterstock; 281 CR: JG Photography/Alamy Stock Photo; 281 R: Alvis Upitis/Photographer's Choice RF/Getty Images; 281 TR: Chris Baynham/Alamy Stock Photo; 282 BL: RuslanHoroshko/iStock/Getty Images Plus/Getty Images; 282 BR: Adriana Marteva/EyeEm/Getty Images; 284 B : Lubilub/E+/Getty Images; 284 CL: Sabine Scheckel/Photodisc/Getty Images; 285: Patrick Walchshofer/EyeEm/Getty Images; 288: Racorn/Shutterstock; 289: Jerry Horbert/Shutterstock; 290 BR: Elina Li/Shutterstock; 290 TC: Racorn/Shutterstock; 291: Syaber/iStock/Getty Images Plus/Getty Images; 292 B: Westend61/Getty Images; 292 BL: David Palos/EyeEm/Getty Images; 293: Elina Li/Shutterstock; 294 BL: Akshit Ughade/EyeEm/Getty Images; 294 CL: Chris Hiscoke/Alamy Stock Photo; 295 BC: Racorn/Shutterstock; 295 R: Judith320/iStock/Getty Images Plus/Getty Images; 298 Bkgrd: Jasmina81/iStock/Getty Images Plus/Getty Images; 298 TL: Jgareri/iStock/Getty Images Plus/Getty Images; 299 BL: Brian A Jackson/Shutterstock; 299 BR: 123RF; 299 CL: Mike Truchon/Alamy Stock Photo; 299 CR: Thomas & Pat Leeson/Science Source; 299 TL: Racorn/Shutterstock; 300 BL : Mihail Syarov/Hemera/Getty Images; 300 BR: Hemera Technologies/PhotoObjects/Getty Images; 301: Bukhavets Mikhail/Shutterstock; 302 BR: Racorn/Shutterstock; 302 L: Potapov Alexander/Shutterstock; 307 B: 123RF; 307 TL: Racorn/Shutterstock; 308 B: Karen Patterson/Alamy Stock Photo; 308 BR: Phekthong Lee/Hemera/Getty Images; 312 bear: Sergey Uryadnikov/Shutterstock; 312 bird: Boonchuay Promjim/Shutterstock; 312 BR: Racorn/Shutterstock; 312 iguana: Stayer/Shutterstock; 312 mole: Dorling Kindersley ltd/Alamy Stock Photo; 312 paw: Pongsathon; 312 rhino: Eric Nathan Alamy Stock Photo; 312 talons: Studybos/Fotolia; 313 C: Gary Retherford/Science Source; 313 TR: Millard H. Sharp/Science Source; 314 TL: Racorn/Shutterstock; 314 TR: Andrew J. Martinez/Science Source; 315: Scott Camazine/Science Source; 316: Ttempus fugit1980/Fotolia; 320 Bkgrd: VisionDive/Shutterstock; 320 BR: Racorn/Shutterstock; 320 CR: Gnagel/Fotolia; 321: Johner Images/Alamy Stock Photo; 322 Bkgrd : Malcolm Schuyl/ lamy Stock Photo; 322 TL: 123RF; 323: Racorn/Shutterstock; 324 BL: Preobrajenskiy/Shutterstock; 324 BR: DC Studio/Fotolia; 324 C : Mgkuijpers/Fotolia; 324 CL: Piotr Krzeslak/Shutterstock; 326 Bkgrd: Dariush M./Shutterstock; 326 TR: Racorn/Shutterstock; 327 Bkgrd: Ueuaphoto/Shutterstock; 327 TR: Rafael BenAri/Alamy Stock Photo; 328: Sabena Jane Blackbird/Alamy Stock Photo; 332: Mhatzapa/Shutterstock.

## Topic 8

334: Sportpoint/Shutterstock; 336: Medioimages/Photodisc/Getty Images; 339 C: Penny Tweedie/Alamy Stock Photo; 339 R: Praweena style/Shutterstock; 340: Highwaystarz/Fotolia; 344: Medioimages/Photodisc/Getty Images; 347: Medioimages/Photodisc/Getty Images; 348 BL: Medical_IllustrationCorner/Alamy Stock Photo; 348 BR: Lady_in_red13/Shutterstock; 348 CL: Komsan Loonprom/Shutterstock; 350: Angela Hampton Picture Library/Alamy Stock Photo; 352: Medioimages/Photodisc/Getty Images;

357: Medioimages/Photodisc/Getty Images; 358: Erik Tham/Alamy Stock Photo; 362: Medioimages/Photodisc/Getty Images; 364: Medioimages/Photodisc/Getty Images; 366: Jezperklauzen/iStock/Getty Images; 369: Steve Gschmeissner/Science Source; 370: Medioimages/Photodisc/Getty Images; 371: Roddy Paine/Pearson Education Ltd; 372 BL: Callista Images/Cultura/Getty Images; 372 CL: Eye of Science/Science Source; 373: Biophoto Associates/Science Source; 374: Medioimages/Photodisc/Getty Images; 376 Bkgrd: Science Photo Library/Brand X Pictures/Getty Images; 376 CR: Medioimages/Photodisc/Getty Images; 377 Bkgrd: Tyler Olson/Shutterstock; 377 TR: Echo/Cultura/Getty Images

## End Matter

EM0: Aleksey Stemmer/Shutterstock; EM1: SergeUWPhoto/Shutterstock; EM2 Bkgrd: Don Paulson/Purestock/Alamy Stock Photo; EM2 BR: Rattiya Thongdumhyu/Shutterstock; EM3: Suzanne Long/Alamy Stock Photo; EM5: National Oceanic and Atmospheric Administration (NOAA), U.S. Department of Commerce.; EM6: Fotosearch/Getty Images; EM7: M. Timothy O'Keefe/Alamy Stock Photo; EM9: Hero Images Inc./Alamy Stock Photo; EM11: CANARAN/Shutterstock; EM12: Vandrage Artist/Shutterstock; EM13: Stephen Barnes/Alamy Stock Photo

# My Notes and Designs

Draw, Write, Create

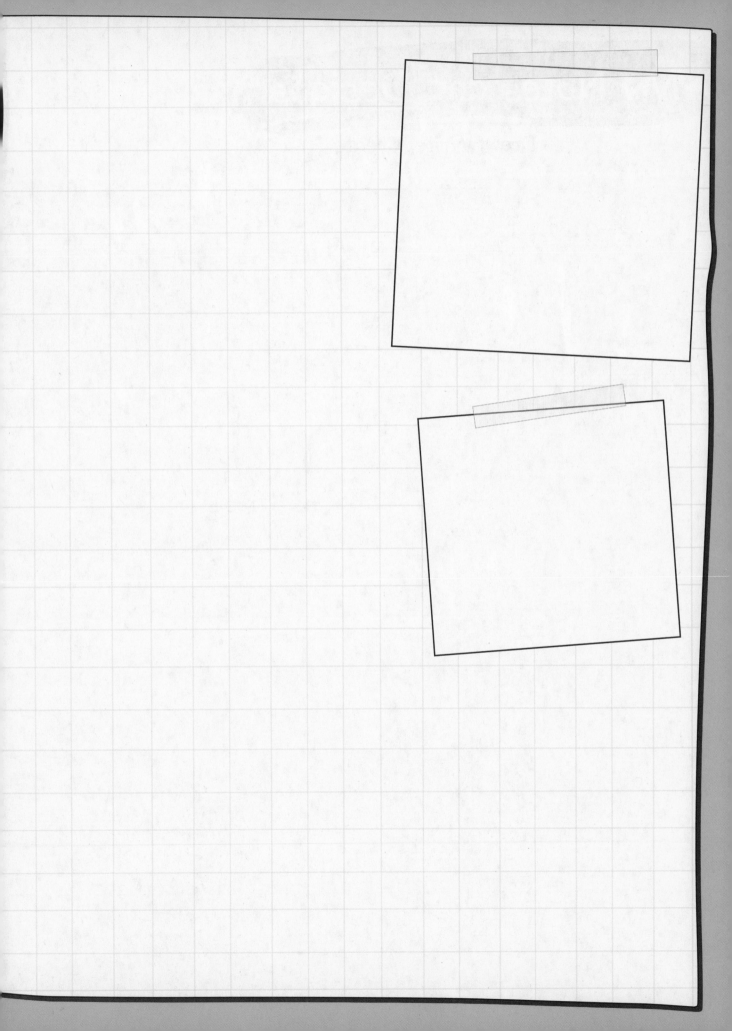

# My Notes and Designs

Draw, Write, Create

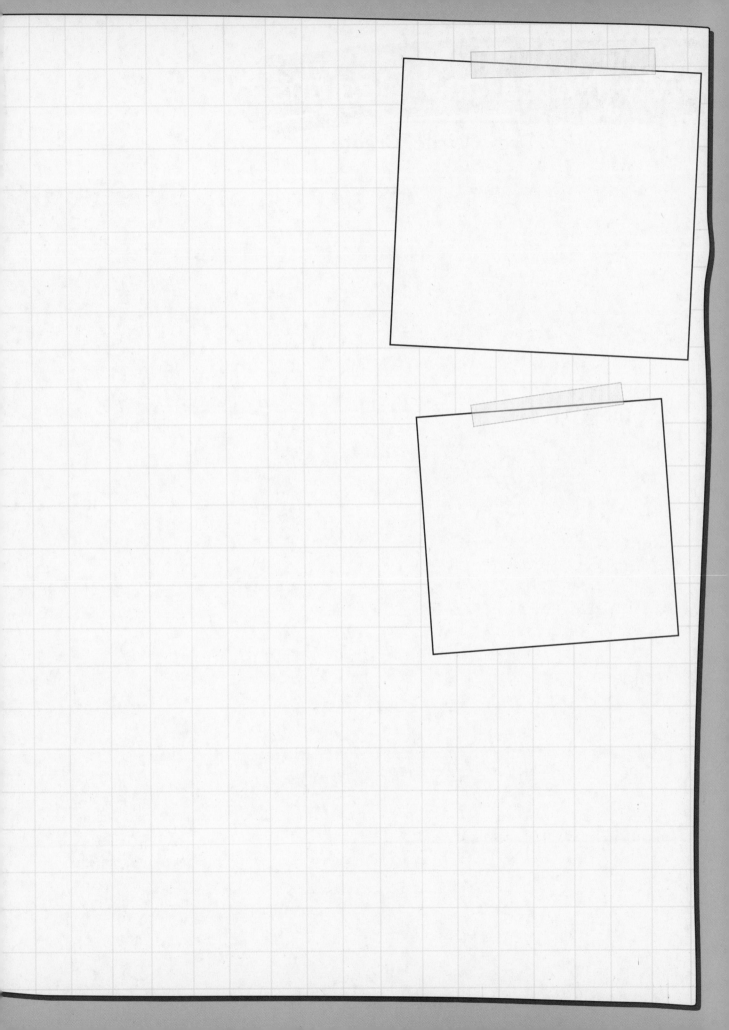

# My Notes and Designs

Draw, Write, Create

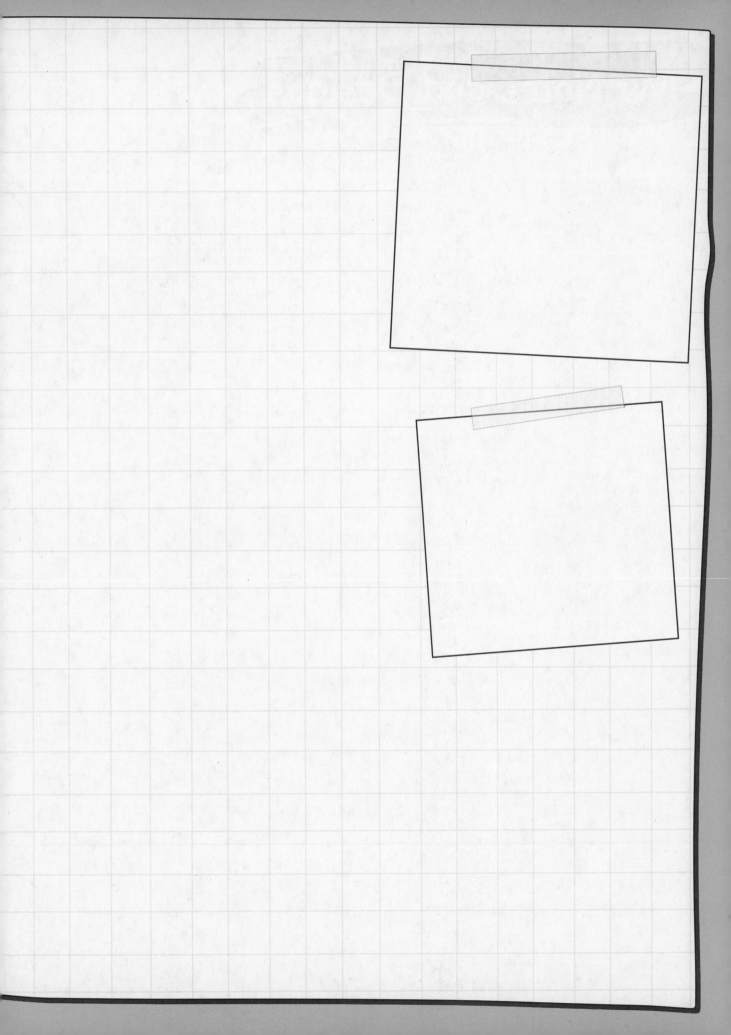

# My Notes and Designs

Draw, Write, Create

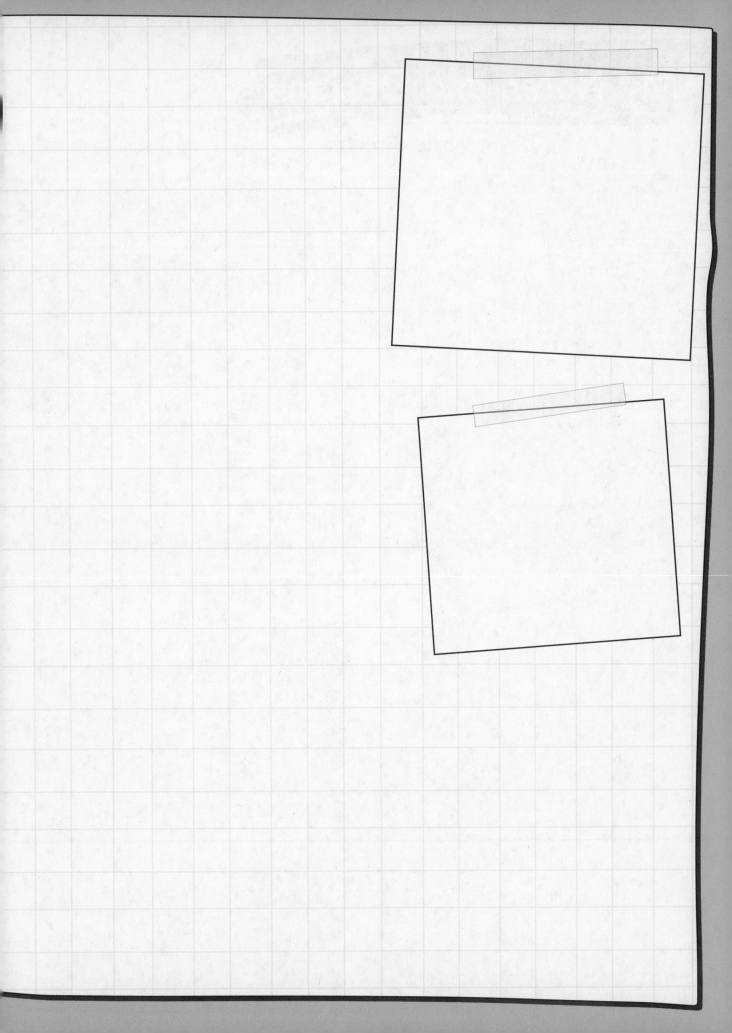

# My Notes and Designs

Draw, Write, Create

# My Notes and Designs

Draw, Write, Create